I0816426

Originale

Recipes and Essentials of Italian Cooking

gestalten

Remo Viani

ANTIPASTI & CONTORNI

PIZZA E PANINI

PRIMI

SECONDI

DOLCI

BASICS

The Art of Authentic Italian Cooking

Italian cuisine is beloved worldwide, with many of us preparing classics like pasta, pizza, risotto, and tiramisu at home. Some more adventurous cooks might even have tackled gnocchi, focaccia, or *Saltimbocca alla Romana.* Yet, those who have visited Italy often notice a stark difference between authentic Italian dishes and what is served in restaurants abroad or cooked at home, and there are two main reasons behind this.

The first is that many of the dishes we cook at home or are served in many restaurants are adapted to our local tastes, often using low-quality, mass-produced ingredients for convenience. For instance, *Carbonara* sauce is frequently made with cream, while *Spaghetti Bolognese* uses ground meat—both far from their authentic counterparts. This book aims to rectify that, offering genuine regional Italian recipes collected by Remo Viani during his travels across Italy, from the alpine meadows of South Tyrol to the salty beaches of Pantelleria. These authentic recipes come directly from local producers, who know best how to use their olives, tomatoes, and capers, and from wonderful *agriturismi*—agrotourism

Cucina povera is masterfully making the best out of very little, with no frills, but with great dedication and carefully selected ingredients.

establishments that blend farming with hospitality.

The second reason for why things taste better in Italy is equally important: No other cuisine is so obsessed with the quality of ingredients and dependent on knowing how to properly prepare them. While regional and seasonal cooking has influenced chefs and restaurateurs worldwide, its roots lie in humble Italian farmhouse cooking, which has always used what is fresh, tasty, and locally available. Italian shops, markets, and pots brim with delicacies often overlooked elsewhere: dandelions, chestnuts, pork fat, tiny fish, and especially a variety of beans, all contributing to a colorful and rich culinary palette. Nothing edible goes to waste. Italians have great respect for simple food, exemplified by the country's renowned *cucina povera*, literally "the cuisine of the poor"—masterfully making the best out of very little, with no frills, but with great dedication and carefully selected ingredients. And that is precisely why it is so revered throughout Italy. Nowhere else is good food and drink discussed with such passion, sometimes even approaching religious fervor.

A satisfying meal requires good company, an elegant setting, and a pleasant ambience. The Italian way celebrates communal eating—gatherings where food is always shared, accompanied by lively conversation.

One taste of premium San Marzano tomatoes, Amalfi lemons, or Piedmont hazelnuts instantly reveals their superiority over mass-produced alternatives. Many regional Italian recipes feature just two or three ingredients, yet when prepared at the right time with the right ingredients, they rival dishes from Michelin-starred restaurants.

As the ingredients are paramount, this book includes practical and detailed sections on authentic Italian ingredients like pasta, tomatoes, vegetables, olive oil, vinegar, cheese, and salami. These tell us everything we need to know about these ingredients, covering their origins, uses, varieties, processing methods, seasonality, availability, and quality indicators. Choosing ingredients is not necessarily a question of price, but rather of timing—knowing the best time to prepare them. DOP and IGP labels serve as important guides here, along with your own taste, of course. The DOP seal stands for *Denominazione d'Origine Protetta*, protected designation of origin, and is awarded to genuine specialties where every stage of production takes place in the original region, from production to processing and refining, while the less strict IGP, *Indicazione Geografica Protetta*, is a designation of origin for products requiring that only one step be region-specific. As these authentic ingredients are

sometimes hard to come by, we provide readily available alternatives found in well-stocked grocery stores.

For genuine Italian cuisine, source your ingredients from farmer's markets or Italian grocery stores, avoiding pre-packaged discount store options. Embrace the philosophy of "less, but better." This approach not only supports small-scale local producers; it also benefits your personal health.

This book's recipe structure loosely follows the traditional Italian menu sequence: *antipasti*, *primi*, *secondi*, and *dolci*. We have also included *contorni* (side dishes) and *panini* (sandwiches for between-meal snacks), as well as recipes for pizza and pasta dough and flavorful sauces. To round off the recipes, we offer regional insights and origin stories of various dishes, along with information on where the ingredients can be found in Italy and wine pairing suggestions.

Eating meals transcends mere sustenance, and not just in Italy. A satisfying meal requires good company, an elegant setting, and a pleasant ambience. The Italian way celebrates communal eating—gatherings where food is always shared, accompanied by lively conversation and entertaining stories. After all, this is how food tastes best. Eating better and more mindfully makes life fulfilling.

Finocchio arrostito con Arancia rossa e Peperoncino

Roasted Fennel with Blood Oranges and Peperoncino

Serves 4

PREP TIME
30 minutes

INGREDIENTS

2 medium fennel bulbs

2 blood oranges

4 tbsp. medium extra virgin olive oil

Fine sea salt

½ cup (120 ml) fresh orange juice

¼ cup (60 ml) white wine

¼ cup (60 ml) vegetable stock (see p. 267)

1 pinch peperoncino flakes

Freshly ground pepper

1 pinch fennel pollen

In Italy, salad is commonly ordered as a side dish to be eaten with the main course, and it is located on the menu among the contorni, *the side dishes you can choose from to complete your meal. With its roasted nuances and refreshing vinaigrette of citrus juice and blood orange fillets, this salad boasts complex flavors as companion for your main dish. However, it is also ideal as a simple summertime midday snack along with white bread. Fennel is a very popular vegetable in Italy, whether it is the freshly harvested version or in the form of fennel seeds. Fresh fennel can be used as a vegetable bed for baked fish, it is delicious with Parmesan cheese baked on top, or enjoyable as a tasty risotto ingredient. Fennel seeds are a popular seasoning for pork, whether you are making the Tuscan roast pork dish known as* Arista di Maiale, *pancetta,* salsiccia, *or* finocchiona *fennel salami. Fennel is even served as a refreshing sorbet as part of a particularly lavish menu.*

Remove the stalks and greens from the fennel bulbs. Cut each fennel bulb into 8 thick slices. Set the fennel greens aside and cut the stalks into thin slices.

Heat the olive oil in a frying pan and place the fennel wedges side by side. Brown for about 3 minutes on each side, salt the fennel and add the finely chopped stalks. Brown for another 2 minutes.

Add the orange juice, wine, and stock. Simmer until the fennel is well cooked and begins to soften. Season with peperoncino flakes and black pepper.

Then arrange the fennel and broth on a plate and garnish with the fennel greens and orange fillets. Sprinkle with fennel pollen.

OUR TIP This salad is a dish in its own right, for enjoying as a starter or as a *contorno* for the main course. It also makes an excellent side dish for grilled fish and meat at barbecues.

Insalata di Finocchio con Aringa, Arance siciliane e Olive nere al forno

Fennel Salad with Herring, Sicilian Oranges, and Oven-Baked Black Olives

Serves 4

PREP TIME
30 minutes

INGREDIENTS

1 small white shallot or spring onion

Trapani sea salt

2 fennel bulbs

2 untreated Sicilian oranges

4 herring fillets in brine

3 tbsp. extra virgin olive oil

4 large romaine lettuce leaves

½ tsp. oregano

Pepper

15 pitted black olives, oven-baked

This salad is an old traditional recipe from Palermo that remains very popular today and is often served on holidays during the winter. It was originally considered a food for those of modest means, as smoked herring was cheap, and, just like salted sardines, it was considered a simple staple. Herring was brought to Sicily by the Normans, who had wrested the island from Arab rule around 1100, leading it to prosperity over their 100-year reign. This salad is made at the start of the orange season in the winter when the oranges are sweet and flavorful. Its surprising harmony of sweet and salty flavors, combined with the fresh taste of fennel and the earthy touch of ripe black olives makes for a delicious treat. In this recipe, we use pickled herring instead of smoked herring, as it has a milder taste and is easier to find.

Remove the skin from the shallot and slice into thin rings. Fill a small bowl with water and add salt. Place the shallot rings in the bowl for at least 10 minutes; this helps remove their smell and makes them milder.

Remove the hard outer leaves from the fennel bulbs. Cut them into quarters, then into fine, long strips. Peel the oranges, cut into slices, and then cut the slices into quarters. Cut the herring fillets into slices 1½ inches (4 cm) long.

Remove the shallot rings from the water, squeeze out any excess water, and pat dry. In a bowl, combine the shallot with the fennel strips, orange wedges, and herring. Tear the romaine lettuce into bite-sized pieces, place in a serving bowl, and combine with the olive oil. Season with oregano, sea salt, and pepper. Place the fennel and herring mixture on the bed of lettuce and top with the olives.

OUR TIP It is important to make sure that the individual ingredients are equally proportioned to avoid any one component dominating the salad, resulting in a harmonious taste and pleasing mouthfeel overall.

Vitello Tonnato con Foglie di capperi

Veal with Tuna Sauce and Caper Leaves

Serves 3 to 4

PREP TIME
20 minutes

COOK TIME
Approximately 1 hour

INGREDIENTS

15 ¾ oz. (450 g) saddle of veal

Fine sea salt

A generous ¾ cup (190 ml) mild extra virgin olive oil

1 organic egg yolk

1 tsp. Dijon mustard

1 tbsp. Condimento Bianco (white balsamic vinegar)

Freshly ground pepper

1 tbsp. capers in salt, rinsed

6 anchovy fillets in oil

4 ¼ oz. (120 g) tuna in oil

A scant 3 ½ tbsp. (50 ml) vegetable stock (see p. 267)

Juice of ½ lemon

2 tbsp. caper leaves

Vitello Tonnato *is a widely popular starter in Italy and beyond. In the summer, this cold, slightly salty dish can also serve as a wonderful main course. The recipe originally comes from the Piedmont region. As always, the success of a simple dish hinges entirely on the quality of its ingredients. This starts with the meat, which can also come from the eye round. It doesn't necessarily have to be veal; the meat of a young cow or bull has an even more intense taste. When it comes to the tuna, you can use an elegant Bonito del Norte white albacore or a yellowfin tuna, both from the Cantabrian Sea off the Spanish coast, or* ventresca, *the fatty belly meat of the tuna. There are also huge differences in the quality of anchovies. We recommend using fillets from anchovies caught in the cool waters of the Cantabrian Sea and processed by Ligurian companies, as they are the experts here.*

Preheat the oven to 210 °F (100 °C) using top and bottom heat. Remove the tendons and fat from the veal and season with salt. In a very hot skillet, heat 2 tablespoons of the olive oil and sear the veal on all sides, then season with pepper. Cook in the preheated oven for about an hour until it reaches a core temperature of 133 °F (56 °C).

In the meantime, place the egg yolk, mustard, vinegar, some salt and pepper, the capers, anchovy fillets, tuna, vegetable stock, and the remaining olive oil in a tall, narrow container. Using an immersion blender, blend everything starting at the bottom and moving up and down with light mashing motions to form a creamy tuna mayonnaise. Add lemon juice to taste. Depending on your preferences, you can make the mayonnaise thinner by adding more stock or thicker by adding more oil. As both capers and anchovies are salty, you should use salt cautiously when seasoning.

Cut the cooled veal into thin slices, preferably using an electric food slicer. Spread a layer of tuna mayonnaise on a large platter or, if you prefer, a circle topped with salad greens such as arugula. Drape the veal slices on top, then decorate the veal with the caper leaves.

OUR TIP Caper leaves have a delicate caper flavor that is more subtle than that of capers themselves. They are also perfect as an elegant finishing touch for tuna or salmon tartare.

Brandacujun

Ligurian Creamed Stockfish

Serves 4

PREP TIME
2 days

COOK TIME
Approximately 1½ hours

INGREDIENTS

1 generous 1½-lb. (700 g) stockfish

14 oz. (400 g) potatoes, floury

2 cloves garlic

1 handful flat-leaf parsley

A scant ½ cup (100 ml) mild extra virgin olive oil

Freshly ground pepper

Fine sea salt

Lemon to taste

Stockfish, or stoccafisso *in Italian, is very popular in Liguria, Veneto, and the Piedmont region. The fish, usually cod, is caught off of Norway's Lofoten Islands and hung on wooden racks to air dry. For centuries, Norwegians have shipped fish preserved like this to numerous European regions, especially those that are landlocked. Sailors also valued this fish meal, as merchant ships did not fish for food on the way; wanting instead to get from port to port as quickly as possible. This dish's name also evokes its historical context: "Branda" comes from the French "brandir," which means "to shake violently," and "cujun" refers to the strength of the sailors who could shake the pot with the fish in such a way that the individual ingredients combined to form a mass. It is rumored that only someone who has, let's say, "balls," or in colloquial terms, cujun, has the ability to do this.*

Soak the dried stockfish in cold water for two days, changing the water from time to time. When it has softened, cut it into three pieces. Place the unpeeled potatoes with the fish in a large pot, fill with cold water until everything is covered, and simmer for approximately an hour. Drain the water, take out the stockfish, remove the skin and bones, and shred the fish into small pieces. Peel and dice the potatoes.

Finely chop the garlic and parsley and add to the pot along with the fish and potatoes. Add the olive oil and return the pot to the stove. Evenly combine the ingredients for approximately five minutes, stirring constantly. Then lower the temperature and cover with a lid.

For the next step, it is advisable to put on oven mitts. Firmly hold the lid down while vigorously shaking the pot in an up-and-down motion until the fish and potato mixture achieves a relatively coarse yet uniform consistency. Add some olive oil if needed. Season with black pepper and sea salt. Add a few squeezes of lemon to taste.

OUR TIP This coarse cream is often spread on toasted bread and eaten with Taggiasca olives.

Sformato di Porri

Leek Flan

Serves 4

PREP TIME
10 minutes

COOK TIME
45 minutes

INGREDIENTS

7 oz. (200 g) leeks

1 tbsp. butter

A generous 6 ¼ oz. (180 g) ricotta cheese

1 ¾ oz. (50 g) Parmigiano Reggiano DOP cheese

1 ¾ oz. (50 g) pecorino cheese

3 eggs

1 clove garlic

1 sprig herbs, such as thyme or marjoram, crushed

1 teaspoon organic lemon zest

Fine sea salt

Freshly ground pepper

Nutmeg

Flans are a popular antipasto in the Piedmont region. As the cuisine of the region was influenced by French cooking during its time under the House of Savoy's rule, this type of flan can only be found in Italy. The French have a recipe for vegetable flan, Flan aux Légumes. *Our recipe can be used with different vegetables as well, such as spinach, asparagus, zucchini, peas, pumpkin, or squash, according to what is in season. Flans are served with salad or a zesty sauce, depending on the vegetables used to make them. One popular example is fonduta, a light cheese sauce made from fontina cheese, egg yolk, milk, and butter. The earthy leek and the cheese pair well with the freshness and acidity of a salad with vinaigrette dressing. Flans are a pleasant way to start a big meal, as they are warm, light, and mild. This way, the seasoning of the subsequent dishes can slowly intensify.*

Clean and trim the leek, cut in half lengthwise, then cut further into pieces ¾ inch (2 cm) wide. Cook the leek for 1 to 2 minutes in salted boiling water. Drain the water and allow the leek to cool. Grease eight metal molds, also called timbale molds, with butter. Preheat the oven to 320 °F (160 °C) using convection.

Using an immersion blender, finely puree the leek together with the ricotta, Parmigiano, pecorino, eggs, garlic, herbs, and lemon zest. Season to taste with salt, pepper, and nutmeg. Fill each mold with the mixture until three quarters full and place in an ovenproof dish, such as a casserole dish. Pour water into the dish halfway up the molds.

Place the dish in the oven on the second-lowest rack position and bake the flans for approximately 45 minutes. After removing the molds from the oven, let them briefly rest, then carefully turn them out onto preheated plates.

OUR TIP This flan goes well with a salad of wild greens with vinaigrette dressing and a glass of Gavi di Gavi DOCG.

Peperonata in Bagna cauda

Grilled Peppers in Anchovy Sauce

Serves 4

PREP TIME
15 minutes

COOK TIME
1 hour

INGREDIENTS

18 cloves garlic

24 anchovy fillets in oil

⅝ cup (150 ml) mild extra virgin olive oil

2 cups (480 ml) whole milk

3 ½ tbsp. (50 g) butter

2 red bell peppers

1 yellow bell pepper

Fine sea salt

Bagna cauda *is a typical rustic fall dish from the Piedmont region. It is usually eaten warm, and the name even means "warm sauce." Little ceramic teapot warmers, called* fojòts, *are placed on the table in front of each person to keep the food warm, transforming the meal into a social occasion, much like fondue. Traditionally, raw vegetables such as celery, carrots, artichokes, and fennel are dipped in the sauce. The intensity of the flavor is exhilarating, but surprising to the untrained palate. In this version of the recipe, the intensity is tempered by adding milk and butter, rounding off the bold flavors somewhat. The use of grilled peppers with this recipe is very popular in the Piedmont region's eateries, and it is often served as a starter, both hot and cold.*

Peel the garlic cloves, halve them, and remove the germ, or core. Dab the anchovy fillets with a paper towel. Place the garlic cloves in a small saucepan, add enough water to cover them, and simmer for about 15 minutes until they are soft, then drain and dry them.

In a medium-sized pot, heat ¼ cup (60 ml) of the olive oil over low heat, add the garlic and sardines, and use a wooden spoon to combine thoroughly and form a paste. Gradually pour in the milk and simmer for a total of 1 hour. Towards the end, add the butter in flakes and stir in another ¼ cup (60 ml) of olive oil.

Wash the peppers and remove the core and white membranes. Cut into slices the width of a finger and season with salt. Coat the peppers in the remaining olive oil, then sauté them in a hot grill pan, allowing the skins to burn slightly. Remove the peppers from the pan and place them with the inside facing down and the skins facing up. Place a cold, wet tea towel on top of them for a few minutes, then peel the skins off the pepper strips.

Place the peppers on a plate and spread the warm *bagna cauda* on top.

OUR TIP This intensely flavored antipasto goes well with a strong red wine from the Piedmont region, such as a young Barbera or a Nebbiolo.

Caponata di verdure

Sweet and Sour Vegetables

Serves 4

PREP TIME
20 minutes

COOK TIME
45 minutes

INGREDIENTS

2 tbsp. pine nuts

2 red onions

1 stalk celery

1 grilled red bell pepper (see p. 24)

3 eggplants

4 ½ cups (1 L) vegetable oil for deep-frying

2 tbsp. extra virgin olive oil

4 anchovy fillets

2 cloves garlic

1 tsp. peperoncino flakes

A scant ½ cup (100 ml) vegetable stock (see p. 267)

1¾ oz. (50 g) golden raisins

1¾ oz. (50 g) Taggiasca olives

¼ cup (60 ml) San Marzano tomato passata (pureed, strained tomatoes)

2 tsp. Crema di Balsamico

2 tbsp. red wine vinegar

Fine sea salt

Freshly ground pepper

Fresh basil

Caponata is an ideal summer dish; although it is a simple vegetable dish, the olive oil makes it a filling meal. Caponata tastes delicious when eaten with bread or as a side dish with fish and meat. Like many foods on the island of Sicily, it is eaten lukewarm, a result of the high summer temperatures. Eating lukewarm dishes is a surprisingly pleasant experience, and you will definitely want to give it a try. Agrodolce, *the combination of sweet and sour, is also enjoyable; it is created here using vinegar and raisins, but sometimes a little sugar is used, too.* Agrodolce *owes its existence to the Arab rule over Sicily from the 9th to the 11th centuries. The recipe varies depending on the region—sometimes pine nuts or almonds are sprinkled on top before serving, sometimes it is made with tomatoes, sometimes without.*

Toast the pine nuts in a pan without oil and set aside. Peel and dice the red onions. Finely dice the celery, peppers, and eggplants.

In a pot, heat the vegetable oil and deep-fry the diced eggplant in it. Once the eggplant is soft, remove and dab with a paper towel.

In a pan, sauté the red onion in 2 tablespoons of olive oil, then add the finely chopped anchovy fillets, celery, and peppers. Chop the garlic and add it to the pan along with the peperoncino. Pour in the vegetable stock and simmer for 10–15 minutes.

Then add the raisins, pine nuts, and Taggiasca olives, pour in the *passata*, add the Crema di Balsamico, and simmer for ten minutes. Add some stock if needed.

Once the celery is soft, add the fried eggplant cubes and pour in the red wine vinegar. Season to taste with salt and pepper and simmer for another five minutes.

Garnish with the pine nuts and basil and eat lukewarm.

OUR TIP Caponata tastes delicious on toasted bread with burrata. In addition to the basil, you can also add chopped flat-leaf parsley and mint to the caponata. We recommend a dry, fruity red wine that does not contain a lot of tannins and has a pleasant red berry flavor, such as a Nero d'Avola from Sicily.

Carciofi bolliti

Artichokes with Oil and Vinegar

Serves 4

PREP TIME
10 minutes

COOK TIME
Approximately 15 minutes

INGREDIENTS

8 small artichokes

3 ½ tablespoons (50 ml) balsamic vinegar

A scant ½ cup (100 ml) medium extra virgin olive oil

Fine sea salt

Freshly ground black pepper

Boiled artichokes are a classic side dish in Italian cuisine and a popular antipasto as well. They are light and tasty and can be prepared in a variety of ways. Their subtle bitterness also stimulates the appetite. Simply boiling this Mediterranean flower vegetable gives it a pure, natural taste, perfect to serve as a starter. It is essential to use fresh artichokes of good quality here. For what may be the world's easiest recipe, we use the small, spiny Albenga variety (carciofo violetta spionoso di Albenga), which is particularly tender and flavorful in winter and is grown on the western coast of Liguria. The inner petals of this artichoke variety are so tender they can also be eaten uncooked as a salad. This cooked version is combined with a simple vinaigrette of extra virgin olive oil and balsamic vinegar.

Peel off all the petals and thorny petal tips from the stems of the artichokes or remove them with a knife. Remove the woody ends of the artichoke stems and shorten them to ensure the artichokes fit into a large pot. In the pot, bring water to a boil, add the artichokes, and boil them for 15 minutes.

After cooking, drain the artichokes well and place them in a bowl on the dinner table, along with a fork, a dinner knife, a sharp knife, and a rimmed or deep plate for each person. To make the vinaigrette, place the dinner knife across the plate to ensure it will collect on one side, then use the fork to whisk the olive oil and balsamic vinegar directly on the plate. Season with salt and pepper.

Next, carefully place a hot artichoke on each plate and remove the outer petals. Depending on the size and freshness of the artichoke, the second or third layer of petals may already be so tender that you can bite off the lower parts of the leaves after pulling them off and dipping them in the vinaigrette. The petals become more tender with each layer and can be eaten whole, except for their thorny tips. When you reach the artichoke heart, use the sharp knife to remove the fuzzy center or "choke," separate it from the stem, and cut it into small pieces. Cut the artichoke stem into small pieces and combine everything with the remaining vinaigrette on the plate. Serve with fresh white bread, ciabatta bread, or baguette slices.

OUR TIP It is a well-known phenomenon that no wine pairs well with the bitterness of artichokes. We suggest you enjoy a good white wine or rosé beforehand instead.

Verdure di primavera

Spring Vegetables

After the endless, often gray days of winter, thoughts turn happily to luxuriant greenery—in our pots and pans. Many types of vegetables are still young and tender and incredibly fresh at this time of year, making them perfect for authentic Italian cuisine. Although the dishes are not necessarily vegetarian, vegetables play a leading role in Italian cooking and are an indispensable part of every meal. One reason for this is undoubtedly the abundance of produce available at markets throughout the country, along with the Italians' uncanny ability to find fresh, high-quality products—and to make the most of them. Combining a few, selected ingredients in ways that bring out their natural flavors is a skill that is practiced to perfection. In the spring, in particular, a healthy dose of vitamins and fresh energy is more than welcome.

These wonderful vegetables can be used to concoct delicious dishes in the spring:

Piselli For over 10,000 years, green peas have been a dietary staple, but their brief freshness window often relegates them to preserved or frozen forms. Unfortunately, this has diminished their standing somewhat. Yet as recently as the 17th century, highly prized and expensive varieties of peas graced the tables of King Louis XIV's court. Peas are now experiencing a bit of a comeback, and rightfully so. They taste wonderful as additions to soups like minestrone, in *sughi*, ragouts, salads, pureed, and, of course, as the star of the Venetian dish *Risi e Bisi*. Their versatility and subtle sweetness make them a favorite ingredient in many contemporary dishes.

Fagiolini Children often have a long face when they see these long green beans, perhaps because they were once a most important staple they had to endure. But those days are long gone, and it is time to welcome green beans back onto our plates. They make a great addition to just about everything—with their pods snapped open as a crunchy treat, as a savory side dish topped with a zesty gremolata, or in a spicy dish with anchovies.

Asparagi Italians overwhelmingly favor green asparagus over the white variety. And we agree with their choice. Not only is it healthier with its higher vitamin content—a fact the ancient Egyptians recognized and used it medicinally for coughs and bladder issues—it also packs more flavor. Green asparagus truly shines when paired with Parmigiano, whether in a creamy risotto, tossed with pasta, or roasted to perfection in the oven.

Lattuga Lettuce plays a prominent role in Italian cuisine, whether as a starter, a snack, or a side dish complementing a robust *secondo.* Rather than drowning it in elaborate dressings, Italians prefer to pair lettuce with hearty ingredients like Parmigiano. The dressing itself is quite straightforward; a drizzle of Aceto Balsamico and some quality olive oil are sufficient to highlight the lettuce's subtle flavor.

Puntarelle With its name translating as "little tips," this quintessential Italian chicory is also aptly called chicory asparagus. It is a staple of traditional cuisine, particularly in the Lazio region. Its distinctive bitterness makes it so popular—and so healthy, as it is high in vitamins and minerals, while also offering a cleansing effect. Puntarelle chicory is usually enjoyed lightly steamed, sautéed, or simply raw in salads with an anchovy-based pesto, creating a wonderful combination of bitter and succulent flavors.

Radicchio Italians appreciate both bitterness and beauty, and the stunning white-pink radicchio perfectly embodies these qualities. This leafy vegetable, originally from Treviso and Trento, has now captivated palates worldwide. The finest varieties, Radicchio di Treviso IGP and Radicchio di Verona IGP, also originate from these regions. As a general rule, darker leaves indicate a more bitter flavor profile. Lighter green varieties taste milder and sweeter, while the elongated, deep purple Radicchio di Treviso tastes quite bitter and spicy. The crisp leaves lend themselves well to baking or grilling, making radicchio a popular side dish for meat, pasta, and risotto.

Cipolle Cooking without onions, while feasible, is pointless in authentic Italian cuisine. Inseparably tied to classics such as agrodolce and soffritto, few other vegetables find such extensive use across a wide array of recipes. Onions are a remarkable exception among plant bulbs, as most others are toxic or, at the very least, difficult for humans to digest. The onion ranks among the world's oldest cultivated plants, having served as both a vegetable and a medicinal plant for over 5,000 years. Today, there are spicy brown, mild white, and sweet red varieties, ensuring there is a fitting onion for every dish. Italians are particularly fond of mild red onions such as Cipolla di Tropea; these are often enjoyed raw in salads or to add a sweet zest to focaccia and *farinata.*

Bietole Swiss chard's popularity in Italy extends beyond its vibrant red-green hues; it is also prized for its abundance of valuable nutrients. Ancient Greeks and Romans appreciated not only its taste but also its healing powers, using it to treat various ailments such as gastrointestinal issues and anemia. Today, Swiss chard is served steamed, sautéed, boiled, or occasionally raw in salads. The use of Swiss chard is particularly widespread in Liguria, most famously used in *Torta Pasqualina*, a traditional savory Easter pie incorporating whole eggs and ricotta. For everyday consumption, there is *Torta verde.* The earthy notes of the leaves add a distinctive flavor to *Minestrone alla Genovese* and Ligurian frittatas.

Cipolline all'Aceto Balsamico di Modena IGP Small *Borettane* onions are used whole in this popular antipasto. The Reggio Emilia variety, known for its mild taste, pleasantly complements prosciutto crudo, hearty salami, and *porchetta,* an herb-infused rolled pork roast. Classic regional cuisine involves combining these onions with Aceto Balsamico IGP, also from Emilia. Here, the onions are gently roasted, allowing their caramelized flavors to harmonize beautifully with the natural sweetness of the onions and the sweetness and tang of the balsamic vinegar.

Verdure d'estate

Summer Vegetables

The scorching sun beats down; the land sizzles with heat. The only respite lies in plunging into the cool sea, then indulging in the refreshing delights of authentic Italian cuisine. Perfectly suited for light summer meals and snacks, Italian fare always incorporates an abundance of fresh vegetables. While tomatoes are a staple, a variety of other unique produce also takes center stage. These invigorating dishes are ideal after a rejuvenating dip in the sea.

"Good food is very often, even most often, simple food."—Anthony Bourdain

Besides tomatoes, beans, salads, and capers, the following vegetables in particular ensure that every plate contains freshness:

Melanzane The eggplant, whether round, oval, or elongated, is a fundamental ingredient in Italian cuisine, despite its somewhat unfavorable beginnings, at least in terms of its Italian name: "*Melanzane*" is derived from "*mela insana*," which roughly translates to "unhealthy or crazy fruit." This association stems from the historical belief that eggplants possessed aphrodisiac properties and induced madness. In reality, while eggplant is inedible when raw and generally lacks a strong flavor profile on its own, it truly comes into its own when combined with other ingredients. Eggplant harmonizes particularly well with tomatoes and cheese, and when cooked, it develops a soft, creamy texture. This makes it the perfect addition to classic dishes like caponata and *Pasta alla Norma*, as well as in risotto or deep-fried. On the Amalfi Coast, eggplant is even enjoyed with chocolate. In short, the eggplant embodies the essence of Mediterranean cuisine with its voluptuous form and rich flavor profile, blending sweetness with complex nightshade notes. However, mastering its preparation is crucial to fully appreciate this versatile vegetable.

Zucchine Zucchini, dubbed "the pumpkin of Italy" by the French, lives up to its moniker as a variation of the pumpkin (Italian: *zucca*) that made its way from America to Europe in the 16th century. It quickly gained a devoted following in Italy, perhaps in part because of its relaxing properties that soothe both body and mind. The zucchini's popularity also stems from its incredible versatility in the kitchen. It can be roasted with potatoes, enjoyed in a flan with ricotta, or served as a crispy, deep-fried side dish to a secondo. A particularly popular treat is deep-fried zucchini blossoms, an absolute must on any summer table. Zucchini's versatile nature allows it to adopt various flavors and its texture makes it a good choice for side dishes or fillings.

Peperoni Bell peppers made their way to Europe from the New World along with tomatoes where, like tomatoes, they were initially only used as ornamental plants. The Hungarians first dared to sample them, soon incorporating them as a primary ingredient in their cuisine. In Italy, they are an indispensable part of summer cuisine, with a higher vitamin C content than oranges. The color of the pepper is determined by the stage of ripeness: Green peppers are unripe and bitter, yellow peppers are medium ripe and mild, while red peppers are fully ripe and almost sweet. Among the notable varieties are the elongated, vivid red, yet delicately mild Peperoni di Carmangola IGP from Piedmont and the elongated, green, spicy Peperoni di Senise IGP from Basilicata. Regardless of the variety, bell peppers are widely popular for baking, deep-frying, sauteing, or braising.

Cetrioli Crunchy, cool, and refreshing, cucumbers are a great pick-me-up thanks to their high water content of more than 95 percent. The Romans, too, held cucumbers in high regard, especially one notable figure: Emperor Tiberius is said to have favored cucumbers above all other vegetables, and cucumbers destined for his consumption were even sheltered behind glass walls during inclement weather. To this day, cucumbers remain a beloved staple in Italian cuisine, particularly when paired with cheese, eggs, and fish. Their summery freshness is particularly appealing in salads, such as Tuscan Panzanella, or Sicilian-style with melon.

Sedano Celery is delightfully crunchy, wonderfully flavorful, and extremely healthy, as it contains an abundance of antioxidants and supports healthy blood pressure. The ancient Egyptians recognized its medicinal properties as far back as 3,000 years ago, and when its healing powers were exhausted, they used it as a burial offering. The Romans, on the other hand, preferred to incorporate celery into their cooking, and it now lends its distinctive crunch to stews, ragus, and salads. And of course, celery is also an indispensable component of *Lasagne alla Bolognese*. Celery is the vegetable that forms the backbone of *soffritto* and numerous recipes that call for a flavorful base. It is suitable for both braising and as a crisp addition to salads or *Tramezzini* sandwiches.

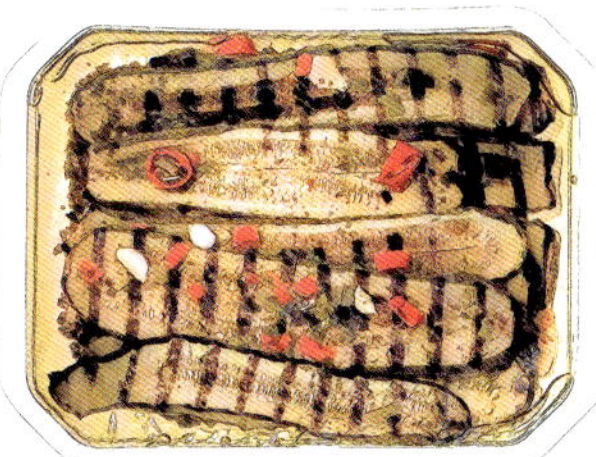

Zucchine grigliate Grilling is one of the best ways to prepare zucchini, transforming this modest vegetable into a flavorful delight. Marinated in oil, the slices develop a pleasant texture between al dente and slightly crumbly. Garlic, herbs, and spices add additional complexity to their flavor. In Italy, grilled zucchini is often enjoyed as part of an antipasto platter, paired with roasted peppers, olives, and cured meats.

Peperoni farciti Piedmont's reputation for refined vegetable antipasti is well-deserved. A prime example is this revived heirloom cherry pepper variety, often served stuffed. The filling features tuna, typical of the Piedmont region, where fish is traditionally obtained from neighboring Liguria.

Caponata Caponata, a vibrant Sicilian summer dish, combines eggplant, tomatoes, celery, and bell peppers. Regional variations may incorporate olives, raisins, pine nuts, capers, or basil. The unifying element is its distinctive sweet-sour taste, achieved by balancing vinegar and sugar. Caponata can be served as an antipasto with buffalo mozzarella or as a warm side dish with grilled fish.

Insalata di Tonno, Fagioli e Patate

Tuna Potato Salad with Beans

Serves 4

PREP TIME
30 minutes, plus: 1 day soak time, approximately 3 hours standing time

INGREDIENTS

2 lbs. 3 oz. (1 kg) waxy potatoes

1 tbsp. capers in salt

1 14-oz. (400 g) jar of beans, cannellini or borlotti (cranberry beans)

11 ¼ oz. (320 g) highest-quality tuna, in oil

2 red onions

Fine sea salt

Freshly ground pepper

A generous ⅓ cup (80 ml) red wine vinegar

½ cup plus 2 tbsp. (150 ml) robust extra virgin olive oil

3 ½ oz. (100 g) arugula

This recipe is a delightful choice for summer, perfect as the main dish for a small gathering or as a side dish at a barbecue party. Beans and tuna come together to form a dream team. Using pre-cooked beans from a jar saves the time otherwise needed to soak them overnight. For recipes like salads or sauces, tuna preserved in olive oil or sunflower oil lends a more robust flavor and juicier quality. The duo of capers and onions is a classic, in salads, in pasta sauces with tuna, or on pizza. Flavor combinations like this have played a part in the global popularity enjoyed by Italian cuisine. It's sure to be a favorite for your next barbecue party!

Boil the potatoes in their peels a day ahead, rinse and set aside.

The next day, place the capers in cold water and soak for at least an hour, changing the water frequently. Drain the beans and place in a large bowl. Pull the tuna apart and add it to the bowl. Peel and slice the potatoes and slice the onions into thin rings. Add the potatoes, onions, and capers to the bowl and combine thoroughly. Season with salt, pepper, red wine vinegar, and olive oil to taste.

Let the salad stand for approximately 3 hours to allow the flavors to infuse. Stir in the arugula just before serving.

OUR TIP When making recipes that call for tuna, it is truly worth it to shop for high-quality tuna. The Cantabrian Sea in the Bay of Biscay off the northern coast of Spain is a source of excellent quality fish like yellowfin tuna and Bonito del Norte (white albacore). The processing of tuna, whether it is done locally on the northern Spanish coast or the fish are imported to Liguria, is part of a long-standing division of labor at companies on the Spanish coast founded by Italians from Liguria.

Insalata Russa

Russian Salad

Serves 4

PREP TIME
60 minutes plus standing time

INGREDIENTS

8 ¾ oz. (250 g) carrots

A generous 1 ½ lbs. (750 g) waxy potatoes

8 ¾ oz. (250 g) beets

8 ¾ oz. (250 g) peas

3 ½ oz. (100 g) cornichons

3 ½ oz. (100 g) pitted Taggiasca olives

3 ½ oz. (100 g) capers

A generous 1 oz. (30 g) anchovy paste

2 tbsp. white wine vinegar

4 tbsp. Taggiasca extra virgin olive oil, mild

Fine sea salt

Freshly ground black pepper

5 oz. (140 g) anchovies

1 large jar mayonnaise

3 hardboiled eggs

11 whole pitted Taggiasca olives, plus a few for garnish

This salad is also known as salade piémontaise, *or Piemontaise Potato Salad. There, in the Piedmont region at the French-speaking court, is where the recipe is said to have been invented in the late 19th century on the occasion of a visit by Czar Nicholas II, offering an apt explanation for the two different names the salad goes by. Ingredients like potatoes and carrots were chosen based on the czar's familiarity with them, and the light color of the sauce was meant to symbolize the snows of Russia. Beets are not only popular in Russia; they are enjoyed in the Piedmont region as well. The dish is now part of Italian tradition, and is often prepared on holidays, for instance, as part of the Easter Monday picnic. It is also a popular summer dish, enjoyed as a cold starter. The process of making it is somewhat time-consuming, especially if you make the mayonnaise from scratch. But the fresh vegetables and light mayonnaise make for a delicious combination. Finishing the salad with a lovingly created garnish makes it the heart of any family meal.*

Wash and trim the carrots, potatoes, beets, and peas, and dice or cut into bite-sized pieces. Cut a few of the potatoes, carrots, and beets into strips or cubes as desired to garnish later. Cook each vegetable variety separately in salted water until al dente, then rinse them in cold water. Set the vegetables for decoration aside.

Cut the cornichons into ⅛-inch slices (3 mm). Put the vegetables in a bowl. Finely chop the olives and capers and add them to the vegetables.

Dissolve the anchovy paste in a little water and season it with vinegar, oil, salt, and freshly ground pepper. Finely chop half of the anchovies and add them to the vegetables together with the anchovy paste, combine well. Fold half of the mayonnaise into the vegetable mixture, then refrigerate overnight or for at least 2 hours to allow the flavors to infuse.

When it is ready, spread the vegetable-mayonnaise mixture in a shallow dish and press it down slightly, then spread the remaining mayonnaise evenly on top. Quarter and slice the hard-boiled eggs, and garnish the salad with the eggs, the vegetables set aside for decoration, a few olives, and the remaining anchovies as desired.

OUR TIP Along with toasted white bread, we recommend a Ligurian white wine not well-known outside the region: Vermentino Riviera Ligure Ponente—delicately fruity, with mineral nuances and a yellow fruit aroma.

Carpaccio di Cedro

Citron Carpaccio

Serves 2 to 4

PREP TIME
20 minutes

INGREDIENTS

8 ¾ oz. (250 g) burrata cheese

A scant 3 oz. (85 g) pine nuts

1 citron (Cedro lemon)

3 ½ tbsp. (50 ml) robust extra virgin olive oil

1 red onion

Fine sea salt

Freshly ground black pepper

3 ½ oz. (100 g) prosciutto di Parma DOP, aged for at least 16 months

One special thing about the large, quaint-looking citron, also sometimes called Cedro lemon, is that you can eat every part of it. This carpaccio demonstrates this best. Citron also tastes very good uncooked as a salad served with fried swordfish, for example. The thinner the slices, the better. This fruit is also refreshing as a warm side dish served with fish, seafood, and shellfish. Its lemon-like juice is popular in Italy and is used in lemon-flavored soft drinks. Today, citrons are mainly grown in Sicily and Calabria. Always marinate the citron slices for at least 10 minutes to ensure their texture gives you a pleasant mouthfeel. This will make the pith, the white layer between the peel and the flesh, also called mesocarp or albedo, more uniform.

Drain the burrata in a strainer. In a skillet, toast the pine nuts without using oil. Rinse the citron in hot water, then dry it and cut it into thin slices. Place the slices on a plate and marinate them in olive oil for about 10 minutes. Slice the onion into thin rings. Tear the burrata into two pieces.

Arrange the citron slices carpaccio-style on two large plates, season with salt and pepper. Then place a burrata half on each plate of citron slices. Arrange the onion rings on top and drizzle the olive oil left over from marinating the citrons over the plates. Finally, arrange the thinly sliced prosciutto on top and add a little coarsely ground black pepper. Serve the carpaccio with white bread and a bottle of olive oil.

OUR TIP The best way to cut the slices thinly and evenly for the carpaccio is to use an electric food slicer.

Agrumi

Citrus Fruits

Even Goethe was fascinated by them, immortalizing the original Italian citrus fruits in his famous poem *Mignon*: "Know'st thou the land where the lemon-trees bloom?" It is hard to imagine the cuisine of this country without these remarkable fruits.

Their name dates back to ancient times. The Latin name *citrus* comes from the Greek word *kédros* for cedar, indicating the origin of the more than 1,500 different varieties of citrus fruit. They all come from the three original species: the grapefruit, the mandarin orange, and the citron, or Cedro lemon. Over the course of thousands of years, natural and intentional hybridization led to the incredible variety of citrus fruits, collectively known in Italy as *agrumi*.

Alongside their extremely high vitamin C content and sometimes more and sometimes less sour taste, they all have one thing in common. Everything about them smells irresistible—their fruit, their leaves, and even the wood of their trees. The people of ancient China, where citrus fruits were accepted as tribute payments over 4,000 years ago, were not the only ones enchanted by their fragrance. Alexander the Great was also so taken with them that he brought them back with him from Persia to the ancient Near East. There they were of particular religious importance to Jews, and after Jerusalem was conquered in the year 70 CE, migrants began cultivating them in Italy.

In Europe, citrus fruits were first used as perfume and as medicine against the plague. This is probably why they are also associated with death; convicts carried a lemon in their hands on the way to execution. It was only later that they came to symbolize luxury and wealth in the Renaissance gardens of wealthy Italian families.

Citrus fruits not only add an extra dimension to many dishes, but they are also incredibly healthy. Their vitamin C supports the immune system and improves the mood, while their juice has an antibacterial and antiseptic effect and lowers blood sugar levels. Although people in the 17th century were not aware of all this, they gradually discovered that lemon juice was an effective remedy against scurvy, the typical disease among sailors.

Citrus fruits did not find their way into Italian cuisine until later, but once they did, they were used all the more broadly—in cakes and drinks, with fish and pasta, or as a snack. One of the many secrets entails bringing out their special flavor even better with a little olive oil. Perhaps this is what inspired Goethe.

"When people get sick, they want chicken soup; I want spaghetti with parmesan cheese, olive oil and a bit of lemon zest. It makes me feel better every time."—Isabella Rossellini

Citrus fruits retain their flavor best when they are stored in a cool, dark, dry place—but not in the refrigerator, where it is too damp for them. Unlike other fruits, they do not continue to ripen after being picked. The color of the peel does not matter—if they feel firm and heavy, then they are perfectly ready for use.

Although citrus fruits grow in all warm regions, Amalfi lemons, Calabrian bergamot oranges, and Sicilian oranges are true Italian originals. With its rainy winters and dry summers, Sicily is actually not very well-suited to growing citrus fruits. However, irrigation systems, some dating back to Roman times, make it possible to cultivate the finest-tasting varieties.

Limone What an incredible waste! Initially, this extremely successful cross between the citron and the bitter orange was not cultivated for its taste, but instead as a decorative plant. Lemons not only add visual appeal to any dish, but their fruity, sweet acidity also adds the finishing touch taste-wise—from the northernmost lemons in Italy, the Limoni del Garda, used to make the very delicious Limoncello liqueur, to the legendary ancient Limoni di Sorrento, still harvested by hand to add the finishing flourish to any risotto. Botanically speaking, many fruits sold today as lemons are actually limes; they have more juice and pulp, but often not quite as much flavor as genuine lemons. Yet that flavoris precisely what makes them so perfect with pasta, risottos, *pesche*, *frutti di mare*, *dolci*, gelato, sorbetto, and so much more.

Limone sfusato This world-famous Amalfi lemon, or Sfusato Amalfitano IGP, has been cultivated on the slopes of the Amalfi coast for over 800 years. Beneath its particularly thick, extremely aromatic peel lies exceptionally sweet, juicy flesh, making it the perfect choice for desserts and drinks. Or for eating plain, on its own—with a drop of good olive oil, of course—and also to enhance seafood dishes and pasta.

Arancia Born some 4,000 years ago from a cross between the grapefruit and the mandarin orange, the name for this happy fluke comes from the Persian word *nārang* by way of Latin and French. Today, oranges are regarded as the most widely cultivated fruit in the world and are so well-known that a color has even been named after them. The orange first came to Italy in the 15th century, where it quickly made a name for itself in the kitchen—as *marmellata* and in salads, often combined with fennel to outstanding effect. Additionally, oranges are essential in Italian desserts like cannoli and gelato, showcasing their versatility.

Mandarino The mandarin orange is one of the world's oldest cultivated plants and was mainly considered a fruit of the wealthy in China, hence its name, as mandarins were high-ranking officials in ancient China. In Europe, however, this fruity gem has only been known since 1805. Since then, it has been a delightfully juicy gift around Christmas every year. Mandarin oranges get their bright orange color from the cold, which breaks down the chlorophyll, bringing out the orange-colored carotenoids. Because of their sweetness, mandarin oranges are usually eaten fresh or as *marmellata*. But Sicily's Tardivo di Ciaculli variety demands to be paired with Modica chocolate.

Bergamotto Bergamot oranges are grown almost exclusively in Italy, on a narrow coastal stretch in Calabria. The climate here is ideal for this truly exclusive fruit. And it is all about the peel, which contains a prized essential oil with a pleasant fragrance that is particularly sought after by the cosmetics industry. However, it also lends its distinctive essence to the esteemed Earl Grey tea, exquisite hard candies, and many a cocktail.

Cedro The citron, or Cedro lemon, was thought to have been brought back by Alexander the Great from ancient Media, and called the "Median apple." It is considered the first citrus fruit to be cultivated in Europe, giving its name to the entire family. This fruit holds great ritual significance because of its fragrance, in Buddhism as an altar offering and in Judaism at the Feast of Tabernacles. Often given as a New Year's gift, in China it stands for health, luck, and happiness. Yet its taste is equally enchanting—not because of its flesh or juice, but rather its peel and incredibly fine *pane di limone*, the white mesocarp, also called pith or albedo, that surrounds flesh inside. Thinly sliced and drizzled with olive oil, it is a revelation as citron carpaccio.

Lime Limes and lemons share name origins: Arabic *limah*, or "citrus fruit," from the Persian *limun*, or "lemon." Limes' origins are unclear due to their quick cross-breeding. Their high juice content makes them popular in cocktails.

Chinotto We do not recommend eating this fruit raw—the chinotto sour orange tree fruits truly are sour. But in jam and drinks, the Ligurian *Chinotto di Savona* is a real classic: the eponymous drink by the same name is also known as "the Italian cola," but it has much more flavor and is much healthier than cola.

"*We only use our special shears for the harvest—and always include a piece of the stem, as this helps the fruit retain its flavor longer.*"—Giuseppe Santangelo

Italy transforms its citrus fruits into authentic, choice specialties:

Caramelle The juice and essential oils bring out the full flavor of citrus fruits in these legendary hard candies. If you prefer something healthier, do as the Sicilians do and try lemon wedges with a little salt straight from the fridge.

Gelato Italian lemon ice cream is certainly the epitome of summer, the beach, and la dolce vita. In its original recipe, it is made with the juice of fresh lemons and is uniquely refreshing.

Limoncello Anyone who has ever been to Italy is likely familiar with this sweet lemon liqueur made from an infusion of ripe fruit and transformed by hand into a juicy and fruity liqueur. Poured over ice, it is a true delight, and not just when accompanying desserts.

Chinotto Made from citrus fruit extract, this caramel-colored Italian national beverage tastes wonderfully bittersweet and wonderfully refreshing, making it a welcome and natural alternative to conventional soft drinks.

Cedrata On the western shore of Lake Garda, the citron, or Cedro lemon, is used to make a fantastic sparkling soft drink. This fresh yellow-green thirst quencher has been around since 1886 and is now once again gaining popularity, not just among children.

Marmellata di Arancia rossa Blood oranges boast a rich, deep flavor profile, balancing lower acidity with subtle bitter notes. Like other citrus fruits, their preparation often involves boiling the whole fruit, peel included, with a touch of sugar to ensure their flavor dominates. The resulting *marmellata* not only tastes delightful on bread; it wonderfully enhances the flavor of sauces as well.

Miele di Arancio In Sicily and Calabria, orange groves buzz with bees collecting nectar from the blossoms each spring. Their honey is fragrant and rich, tasty on a buttered *cornetto* or to add a special touch to vinaigrettes, sauces, cocktails, and baked treats. A true taste of Italian sunshine!

Olio al Limone Made by pressing olives together with flavorful lemons, this oil is perfect for seasoning fish and seafood, and gives salads a particularly fresh taste. It is also delightful with beef carpaccio, scaloppine, and chicken. When buying it, be sure to check that the olives and lemons were actually pressed together in the making of the oil.

Le Arance Piu Gusto

Polenta abbrustolita

Grilled Polenta

Serves 4

PREP TIME
20 minutes plus 35 minutes refrigeration

COOK TIME
15 minutes

INGREDIENTS

2 cloves garlic, finely chopped

3 tbsp. extra virgin olive oil

1½ cups + 1 tbsp. (375 ml) vegetable stock (see p. 267)

1 bay leaf

1½ cups + 1 tbsp. (375 ml) milk

1¼ cups (185 g) fioretto polenta

Fine sea salt

1 small chile pepper, finely chopped

4¼ oz. (120 g) Parmigiano Reggiano DOP cheese, finely grated

3 sprigs rosemary, chopped

Polenta was long the most important staple food in the Veneto, Lombardy, Friuli, Trentino, and Piedmont regions of northern Italy, beginning in the 16th century. The merchants of Venice originally brought corn to Italy, where it was first cultivated in the country's northern regions. It was called Granoturco, *the grain of the Turks, because it came from far away. Owing to the limited resources of peasant cuisine, or cucina povera, polenta was eaten from morning to evening, resulting in the creation of numerous polenta variations, including storing the finished polenta under a cloth for later grilling, as we do here. Today, grilled polenta is often made with cheese, salumi, mushrooms, or tomato sauce. Traditional polenta is cooked in a copper pot under constant stirring for about 50 minutes.* Fioretto *is more finely ground, so it needs much less time.*

In a pot, sauté the garlic in the olive oil. Add the stock, bay leaf, and milk, and bring to a boil. Add the polenta, stirring constantly, and simmer for about 3 minutes. Remove the pot from the heat, cover with a lid, and let the polenta stand for about 5 minutes to absorb the liquid. Remove the bay leaf, add the chile pepper, Parmesan, rosemary, and tomatoes, and combine thoroughly.

On a baking tray lined with baking paper, spread the polenta mixture to a height of about 1¼ inches (3 cm). Refrigerate for 35 minutes. Then cut the polenta into diamond shapes or any other desired shape and grill it on the grill or in a grilling pan.

OUR TIP Burrata, semi-dried tomatoes, and basil make a lovely garnish for the polenta portions. If you are in a hurry, you can also use pre-cooked instant polenta. It only takes 3 minutes and tastes very good.

Panzanella

Tuscan Bread and Tomato Salad

Serves 4

PREP TIME
20 minutes

BAKE TIME
15 minutes, plus: approximately 1 hour standing time

INGREDIENTS

1 loaf ciabatta bread

Fine sea salt

Freshly ground pepper

⅝ cup (150 ml) robust extra virgin olive oil

4 tsp. (20 ml) Balsamico di Modena IGP, aged

3 cloves garlic, finely chopped

1 medium Tropea onion

1 Cuore di Bue beefsteak tomato

2 Camone tomatoes

2 vine tomatoes

5 semi-dried tomatoes

8 artichoke hearts in olive oil

1 tbsp. capers in salt

3 tbsp. Taggiasca olives

1 tbsp. acacia honey

1 handful fresh basil leaves

In the old days, people in rural regions like Tuscany would bake only once a week. Stale bread was a common everyday food. The dishes of cucina povera *such as this recipe, along with* Pappa al Pomodoro, Ribollita, *and* Bucatine alle Briciole, *all originally prepared with dry bread, date from this period. Slices of bread were placed on vegetable stews like* Ribollita *or* Pappa al Pomodoro *tomato soup before serving, and the pasta dish* alle Briciole *was sprinkled with bread crumbs. Our recipe uses fresh ciabatta, making it a bit of a luxury, and combining it with choice ingredients such as balsamic vinegar, special kinds of tomatoes, artichokes, Taggiasca olives from Liguria, and good capers from Pantelleria to create a mouthwatering bread salad. But stale bread is always an option when making this salad as well!*

Preheat the oven to 355 °F (180 °C) using the convection setting. Cut the bread into cubes of about ¾ inch (2 cm). Spread on a sheet pan, season with salt and pepper, drizzle with approximately ½ cup (120 ml) of olive oil and half (2 teaspoons) of the balsamic vinegar, and sprinkle with the garlic. Roast in the oven until golden brown.

Slice the onion into thin strips. Cut all the fresh and the semi-dried tomatoes into cubes about ¾ inch (2 cm) in size. Cut the artichokes in quarters. Under running water, thoroughly rinse the salt from the capers.

Place the capers, tomatoes, onions, olives, and artichokes in a bowl. Season to taste with the remaining 2 teaspoons of balsamic vinegar, the acacia honey, salt, pepper, and olive oil and let stand for an hour to allow the flavors to infuse. Finally, fold in the ciabatta cubes, sprinkle the basil over the salad, and serve immediately.

OUR TIP This Tuscan classic pairs well with an equally classic red wine from Tuscany, such as a fruity Rosso di Montalcino DOC.

Panissa

Baked Chickpea Sticks

Serves 4

PREP TIME
10 minutes

COOK TIME
Approximately 1 ½ hours

INGREDIENTS

3 cups (300 g) besan (chickpea flour, gram flour, garbanzo flour)

2 tbsp. mild extra virgin olive oil

2 cups plus 4 tsp. (500 ml) vegetable oil

Fine sea salt

1 lemon

Simple, easy to eat and delicious, panissa *has become a popular Italian street food and preferred aperitif accompaniment in Italy in recent years. Lemon juice adds a wonderfully refreshing and typically Italian tartness to the fried food. This rustic snack can also be served on a deep plate and eaten hot as chickpea polenta, with plenty of freshly ground black pepper, lemon juice, and a dash of olive oil. Another variation of panissa uses the basic batter the following day, like cornmeal polenta, with the batter, now somewhat solidified, being cut into slices and fried with onions. The recipe comes from Liguria, as does its cousin, farinata (**see p. 136**), a pancake that is also made from chickpea flour and eaten with your hands after being baked on large copper trays in a wood-fired oven. Farinata chickpea pancakes are also popular in Tuscany and Sardinia, where they go by the names* cecina *or* fainè.

Place the chickpea flour in a large bowl. Add 4 ½ cups (1 L) of lukewarm water and combine carefully, making sure there are no lumps. Stir in the olive oil and let the mixture stand for a few minutes.

Place the batter in a large pot and simmer at a low temperature for about 60 minutes. Using a wooden spoon, stir continuously until nothing sticks to the inside of the pot. Then spread the mixture on a cool surface, about ¾ inch (2 cm) thick. Once it has cooled, cut it into pieces ¾ inch (2 cm) wide and a little over 3 inches (8 cm) long.

Heat the vegetable oil in a pot and deep-fry the chickpea sticks. Drain on paper towels, season with salt, and sprinkle with a little lemon juice.

OUR TIP These fries also taste great with cold dips, like in our recipes on pp. 262 and 264.

Tagliere con la Giardiniera

Meat and Cheese Platter with Pickled Vegetables

Makes 4 jars, approximately 16 oz. (500 ml) each

PREP TIME
30 minutes

COOK TIME
Approximately 60 minutes

INGREDIENTS

2 carrots

1 small cauliflower

12 red shallots

1 red bell pepper

10 radishes

4 ½ cups (1 L) white wine vinegar

1 tbsp. sea salt

1 tbsp. sugar

4 bay leaves

1 tbsp. peppercorns

SELECTION FOR THE TAGLIERE

Pecorino al Pistacchio (Tuscan pistachio cheese)

Spianata (chile pepper salami)

Toma Piemontese DOP (Piedmont cheese)

Prosciutto grigliato con Rosmarino (grilled ham with rosemary)

Mostarda di Pere (mustard-pear preserve)

Capocollo di Martina Franca (Apulian ham)

Camembert di Bufala (buffalo-milk cheese)

Nuts, Focaccia

Tagliere *is the ultimate Italian charcuterie board, with selected* salumi *(cold cuts) and formaggi (cheeses), bread, fresh vegetables, and pickled sweet and sour treats. It features a rich variety of meats and cheeses, often including olives, caper berries, and* la giardiniera, *of course: Summer vegetables are cooked al dente and then pickled sweet and sour. Just as you can choose from a vast selection of endless regional variations of salumi and cheese for your tagliere, you are free to decide on the combination of vegetables for your* giardiniera. *Simply pick your favorite vegetables, ensuring they are fragrant and ready to harvest. Aim for a colorful mix!* Tagliere *(which means "cutting board" in Italian) is enjoyed with friends and family over an aperitif or a glass of wine.*

Wash and trim the vegetables, removing any inedible parts. Cut the carrots into slices slightly less than ½ inch (1 cm) thick. Break the cauliflower into small florets. Cut the shallots in half lengthwise. Cut the peppers into long strips, then cut the radishes in half.

Pour the white wine vinegar into a large pot with 4 ½ cups (1 L) of water. Add the salt, sugar, bay leaves, and peppercorns to the pot and bring to a boil. Cook each vegetable variety separately in the boiling liquid, removing them while they are still al dente. Use a slotted spoon to remove the vegetables and place them on a clean dish towel to cool. Repeat the process for each variety of vegetable. Next, allow the liquid to cool somewhat, then pour it through a fine mesh strainer. Remove the bay leaves and set aside.

Have four sterilized canning jars ready. Divide the cooled vegetables among them, varying the arrangement in each jar. Place one bay leaf in each jar so it is visible from outside the jar. Pour the strained liquid into each jar until all the vegetables are covered. Carefully close the lids. To sterilize the jars, place the finished jars in a water bath and simmer for another 20 minutes.

In addition to the giardiniera, marinated olives and vegetables such as *pomodori semisecchi* (semi-dried tomatoes), fresh fruit, and nuts go well with the *tagliere*, and for the cheese you will want to include mostarda, elegant mustard sauces made from fruit, like *mostarda di pere*, which is made from pears.

OUR TIP *La giardiniera* tastes even better after a few weeks, when it has had time to absorb the flavors. You may want to make some extra jars to stock up on, because a taste of *tagliere* is sure to leave you wanting more.

Prosciutto e Salumi

Hams and Cold Cuts

The essence of Italian cuisine, particularly when it comes to prosciutto and salumi, lies in combining tradition and just a few ingredients. Epitomized by the motto of one producer of Parma ham, *Natura, Salis et Tempus*, the creation of an authentic product that embodies the pride of an entire region relies on just three essential elements: nature, salt, and time. Throughout Italy, each area takes immense pride in its unique cold cut specialties, with production methods that have remained unchanged for centuries, treated as sacred traditions.

The Italian art of meat processing traces its roots back to ancient times, with the Romans crafting sausages like the thin *Lucanica*, which gave legionaries strength and stamina during their campaigns.

Historically, meat was a luxury rarely consumed fresh, prompting the development of preservation techniques to extend its longevity. Even in modern times, Italian prosciutto and salumi benefit from the country's mild, dry climate, relying almost exclusively on salting and air-drying, eschewing the smoking process. This approach, which accentuates the natural flavors of the meats, is reflected in their names: Prosciutto comes from *perex suctum*, Latin for "literally dry," and salume from *sallere*, meaning to salt.

The Italian umbrella term for meat specialties that are salted and aged over an extended period, "salume", or the plural version "salumi," encompasses a diverse array of cold cuts. This includes not only salami, but also other products steeped in tradition and made with minimal ingredients, such as ham, bacon, coppa, and mortadella.

"My kingdom for a mortadella, huh?"
—Tony Soprano

The land of prosciutto and salumi has produced a wealth of treasures—and a few genuine classics you are sure to encounter at every well-stocked meat and deli counter.

Mortadella The heart of Italy's cured meat region, Bologna is the birthplace of this iconic delicacy. Its recipe was set in stone by the 13th century, with one minor tweak. Before black pepper reached Europe, mortadella was seasoned with myrtle berries, hence its original name, *myrtatella*. Initially reserved for aristocracy, it now graces tables worldwide, though often in subpar industrial quality. But authentic Mortadella Bologna IPG, a protected product, practically melts in your mouth when sliced ultrathin. It can be enjoyed on its own, in sandwiches, or as part of a charcuterie board, showcasing its rich flavor and delicate texture.

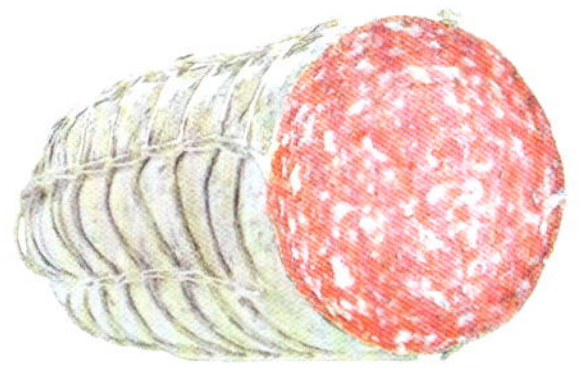

Salame Salami, with over 40 air-dried varieties hailing from various Italian regions and cities, is quintessentially Italian. Modena once reigned as the salami capital. As you head south, the regional products become smaller, coarser, and, notably, spicier. The Milano and Felino salami varieties have gained particular renown. Felino salami, marinated in white wine and originating near Parma, is quite popular among Italians. Meanwhile, the Milano variety has inspired imitators around the world, but they can only claim to be "Milan-style," as none can even come close to the genuine article's perfectly balanced seasoning, fresh aroma, and artful combination of lean meat and delicate morsels of bacon. It is often enjoyed with a variety of cheeses and crusty bread, making it a staple in antipasto platters.

Prosciutto crudo While the pig's hind quarters provide the basis, the artful combination of salt, air, and ample time transforms this humble leg into a delectable masterpiece. The secret lies in using minimal salt while allowing abundant air and time to work their magic. The hams mature with windows open, allowing air to circulate unhindered, for at least a year, resulting in a magnificent cut of meat, with a pinkish hue, fine grain, and indescribably hearty flavor. Only a third of these hams leave Italy, with the rest ending up in Italian bellies, often as a starter paired with fresh figs. When buying prosciutto crudo, it is important to note the origin of the pigs. Italian-born and raised pigs give the producer better control over the supply chain and quality, as well as preventing the pig from being too lean. Insufficient fat accelerates curing, hindering the development of the desired flavors, ranging from hazelnut and melon to salty and spicy notes.

Prosciutto cotto After being salted, typically by injecting a seasoned brine, then cooked gently at 160 °F (70 °C) for roughly 16 hours, the hind leg of the pig remains remarkably succulent. As a delicate slice of this tender, incredibly mellow meat dissolves in your mouth, you will find yourself utterly captivated. it pairs beautifully with a variety of wines and cheeses.

Porchetta Legend has it that an Etruscan from Rieti, a town in the Lazio region, conceived the idea for porchetta when pigs perished in a fire caused by burning herbs. Regardless of its origins, this suckling pig dish is a staple at festivals in cities, towns, and villages across Italy. The pig is generously stuffed with a medley of spices, spit-roasted for up to 8 hours, and then sliced; to be savored hot, cold, on its own, accompanicd by side dishes, or nestled in a sandwich.

Lardo In the world of Italian cuisine, bacon, speck, and lard reign supreme, enhancing countless main courses and starters. In this land of indulgence, the finest pork fat is a culinary delight of the highest caliber. Delicate, fatty morsels are carefully cut from the back, belly, and cheeks, then cured, seasoned, air-dried, and finally enjoyed. Lardo, or fatback, dissolves in your mouth when thinly sliced; pancetta is a popular companion to poultry, fish, and vegetables; and guanciale is a crucial component in the authentic pasta dishes *amatriciana* and carbonara.

"It is a matter of returning to a more authentic approach, without the limitations of intensive farming, with respect for the animal and its natural rhythms."—Nicolò Savigni

While it is impossible to list all the authentic salumi specialties, some originals do stand out in particular and represent the unique facet of Italy's rich tradition:

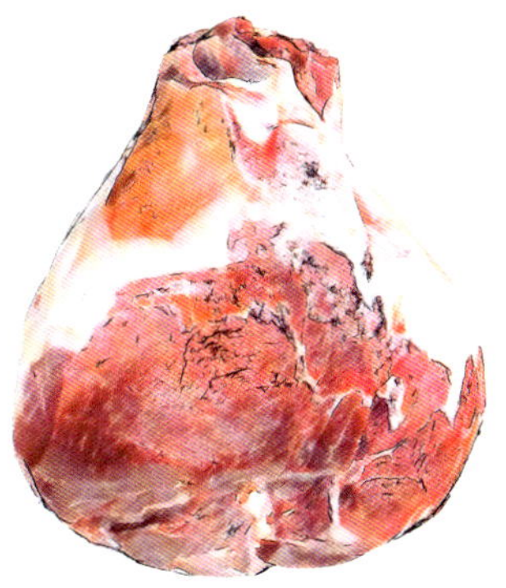

Prosciutto di Parma DOP The namesake of an entire category hails solely from the vicinity of the small town of Langhirano in Emilia Romagna. It is aged for 12 to 36 months in distinctive halls with expansive open windows, allowing the natural airflow to enhance its flavor. The ham is then sliced razor-thin (*sottilissimo!*) and wrapped around grissini.

Prosciutto di San Daniele DOP Along the banks of the Tagliamento River in Friuli, Italy's other prominent ham is aged for 14 to 24 months in the crisp mountain air. Alpine breezes mingle with Adriatic warmth here. Sliced razor-thin, this ham's delicate pink hue hints at a nutty, subtly sweet flavor. San Daniele rivals Parma ham in quality, offering a slightly finer, drier profile. This culinary masterpiece stands alone, requiring no accompaniment save perhaps a glass of Franciacorta or a slice of fresh bread for an unforgettable taste.

Culatello di Zibello DOP Arguably the crème de la crème of Italian hams, Culatello di Zibello is produced in just seven villages along the Po River. Nera Parmigiana and Mora Romagnola pigs, which spend their entire lives outdoors, subsist solely on what they forage in the wild. Their hind legs are rubbed with red wine and garlic, then aged for two years in humid cellars with open windows. Words cannot describe the bliss you experience when eating it.

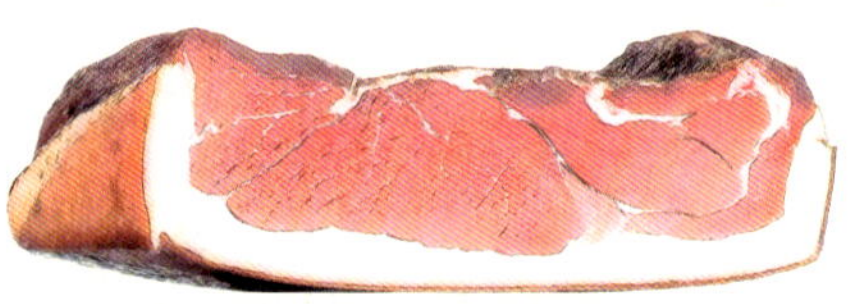

Speck dell'Alto Adige IGP Here, the hind legs are lightly cold-smoked, rubbed with rosemary, juniper, bay leaves, salt and pepper, and then air-cured for a minimum of 22 weeks. The salt content of the resulting speck may not exceed 5%. Together with bread and wine, this speck forms the centerpiece of the quintessential South Tyrolean snack known as "*Marende*," served alongside hearty bread and robust wine.

Bresaola IGP Made near the Swiss border using the inner hind quarter of beef, Bresaola IGP is cured for a relatively short time, just five weeks, before it disappears into your mouth as carpaccio with olive oil, lemon juice, shaved Parmesan, and arugula. This air-dried beef offers a tender texture and a deep, concentrated flavor, perfect for a light and sophisticated appetizer.

Nduja This spreadable sausage from Calabria is made from pork, offal, fennel, and a generous helping of chiles. It is indeed fiery hot, but tastes divine on toasted white bread, preferably accompanied by a beverage to quell the flames. This fresh sausage is also suitable for spicy dishes, as its full flavor blossoms when heated. It adds flavor to pasta sughi and vegetable and meat fillings, plus it makes a very popular pizza topping.

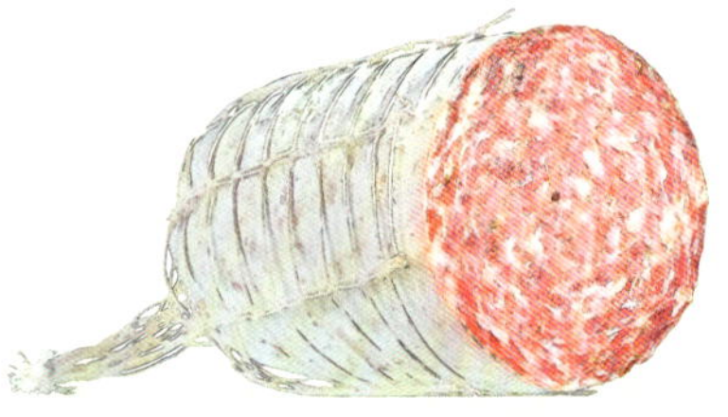

Salame Finocchiona This coarsely ground, soft salami is a typical Tuscan charcuterie specialty. Its distinctive seasoning includes wild fennel seeds, garlic, salt, pepper, and sometimes red wine. Its softer texture calls for thicker slices, amplifying the fennel's flavor. Finely diced fat contributes to its rich taste. In Tuscany, particularly around Florence, it is an essential component of any antipasti spread. Its robust taste pairs beautifully with a fruity red wine, enhancing the salami's aromatic profile and making it a perfect choice for a traditional Italian appetizer.

Salame spianata piccante This spicy, chile-flavored salami from Calabria has no mold casing and is pressed flat, a practical response to the warm climate in southern Italy, where a round salami cannot age as well as it can in the cooler, humid climate of northern Italy. Thinly sliced, this spicy delicacy tastes good as an antipasto, on panini with arugula, and on pizza.

Salame montanaro Coated with edible mold and seasoned with garlic marinated in white wine, this classic mountain salami from Tuscany develops a unique flavor profile.

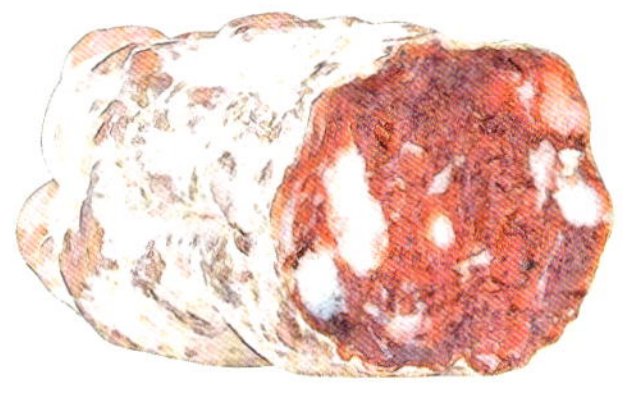

Salame di cinghiale Made from wild boar native to the Chianti region, this salami variety is a Tuscan quintessential.

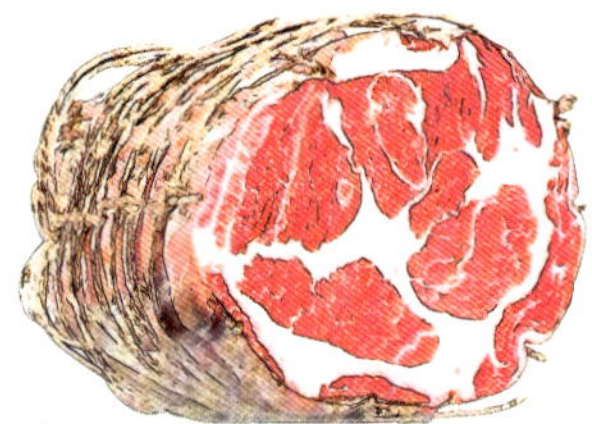

Coppa IGT This age-old Italian delicacy traces its roots to Piacenza. The neck of the pig is rubbed with pepper, salt, and nutmeg, then left to dry in a mesh casing for a minimum of 6 months.It is often served thinly sliced as part of antipasti or in sandwiches.

Capocollo di Martina Franca This Apulian relative of coppa is salted, peppered, immersed in *vincotto*, a syrupy concoction of unfermented grape must, for several hours before being cold-smoked over oak and almond wood, and cellar-aged for 3 months.

Panino con Porchetta

Roast Pork Belly and Loin on a Roll

Serves 4 to 6

PREP TIME
20 minutes

COOK TIME
4 hours

INGREDIENTS

4 ½ lbs. (2 kg) pork belly with loin, pre-ordered from the butcher

2 tbsp. fresh rosemary needles, chopped

1 tbsp. fennel seeds

4 cloves garlic

2 tbsp. white wine

Coarse sea salt

Freshly ground pepper

2 tbsp. robust extra virgin olive oil

Several bread rolls

Kitchen tools:

Butcher's twine and a meat trussing needle with a large eye

Porchetta, pork belly and loin roasted with herbs and garlic, is often found in Italian markets on a spit, purchased as a hearty snack on the go. Arricia, a town close to Rome, is famous for its porchetta. It also maintains the IGP status there, meaning its geographic origins have a protected designation. While its roots trace back to the Lazio region, this recipe has earned admiration across many other regions in northern and central Italy. In addition to the strong seasoning, two things are very important for this cibo di strada, *or Italian street food: the crispy outside crust of the roast on the spit and a good bread roll, crunchy on the outside but soft on the inside, able to absorb the juices from the meat. The people of Rome took it even further, crafting their own delectable interpretation by adding braised onions and endive leaves to the meat in the roll. Porchetta is also often sliced razor-thin and eaten cold in a sandwich.*

Using a mortar and pestle, coarsely crush the chopped rosemary with the fennel seeds, garlic, and wine. Cut the pork belly down the middle, starting from the meat side through the layers of fat down to the rind, but do not cut completely through it. Then fold it open. Season the meat with salt and pepper and spread the crushed herb mixture on top. Roll up the meat and sew together with butcher's twine and a meat trussing needle (with a particularly large eye). Rub the roast with olive oil and salt. Preheat the oven to 320 °F (160 °C) using top and bottom heat. Cut the roast so it is even on both sides, making sure nothing is sticking out.

Roast the porchetta on a rack in the middle of the oven, placing a baking tray underneath to catch the juices and fat. If the rind bubbles and it is brown and crispy, remove the roast from the oven and let stand for 10 minutes. Using a sharp knife, cut it into slices about ¾ inch (2 cm) thick.

Cut open a bread roll without cutting through completely and drizzle the inside with the juices collected on the tray. Place a slice of porchetta in the roll and enjoy your first mouthwatering bite.

OUR TIP We don't have a tip. We just hope you really enjoy eating this delicious treat. Although, come to think of it, we do recommend drinking a beer or an acidic white wine with it, such as a Grechetto from Umbria.

Tramezzino con Prosciutto cotto

Tramezzino Sandwiches with Cooked Ham

Serves 4

PREP TIME
5 minutes

TOAST TIME
1 to 2 minutes

INGREDIENTS

4 slices white tramezzini crustless bread or white sandwich bread with the crusts cut off

4 thin slices prosciutto cotto (cooked ham)

Freshly ground pepper

2 thin slices of scamorza affumicato cheese

1 tsp. fresh rosemary, chopped

Tramezzo *means something like "between," aptly naming this sandwich that is simply enjoyed as a mid-morning snack or with an aperitif. The secret lies in the simplicity of its filling—just a few good-quality ingredients that harmonize perfectly. Popular choices include Parma ham & pickled artichokes, eggs & tuna salad, Milano salami & arugula, and prawns & green cucumber, with fresh homemade mayo or pesto. Originating in Turin, they are now ubiquitous in Italian bars, beloved for their simple appeal.*

Top two bread slices with two slices of ham, crinkling the ham; season with pepper. Add a slice of smoked *scamorza* on top; sprinkle with rosemary. Top each with a slice of bread; press down. Preheat the contact grill, then toast the two *tramezzini* until the cheese melts. Cut diagonally.

OUR TIP A sparkling wine goes very well with *tramezzini*, such as a *frizzante*, a *spumante*, or in this case a bubbly *lambrusco*, the deliciously fruity *frizzante* from Italy's Emilia region. As a vegetarian alternative, you can prepare the *tramezzino* with grilled peppers, mushrooms, and *stracciatella di bufala* cheese.

Focaccia alla Genovese

Genovese-Style Focaccia

Serves 4

PREP TIME
10 minutes plus 1 ½ hours to rise

BAKE TIME
20 to 25 minutes

INGREDIENTS

½ tsp. sugar or 1 tbsp. honey

2 cups + 4 tsp. (500 ml) water

1 ¾ cups (250 g) flour Italian type 00

1 ¾ cups (250 g) Manitoba flour

1 ½ tsp. (7 g) dry brewer's yeast

4 tsp. fine sea salt

A scant ½ cup (100 ml) mild extra virgin olive oil

2 sprigs fresh rosemary, chopped

FOR THE BRINE
A scant 3 ½ tbsp. (50 ml) extra virgin olive oil

2 tsp. fine sea salt

Focaccia is the star of everyday life in Liguria, an authentically Genovese and delicious yeast bread made on a tray in the oven, with good olive oil dripping down your chin as you eat it, because that's how the locals say it tastes best: "Noi la fügassa la vogliamo bassa, ünta e bisünta." *Translated from the local dialect, this means, "We like it thin and very oily." In Genoa, you can eat the specialty they call* Fügassa *all day long, right up until dinnertime. It makes its first appearance of the day early on when it is enjoyed at breakfast with cappuccino. You can buy it in bakeries and from specialized focaccia makers. Baked at home, its savory saltiness makes it ideal to enjoy with an aperitif. This flavorful bread serves as an excellent accompaniment to meals, while also making for a tasty snack throughout the day with ham, tomatoes, or cheese. It is worth the effort to bake a whole trayful and use a very good extra virgin olive oil, made from Ligurian Taggiasca olives. This gives your focaccia even more of an authentic taste.*

Dissolve the sugar or honey in a scant 1 ½ cups (350 ml) of lukewarm water. Combine the flour and brewer's yeast in a bowl. Gradually pour in the water with the dissolved sugar or honey and add the salt; knead everything well. Next, work in 3 ½ tablespoons (50 ml) of olive oil until the dough is elastic and smooth. Cover the bowl and let the dough rise in a warm, draft-free place for 30 to 40 minutes.

Roll the dough out on a floured surface and place on a baking tray greased with oil. Place the tray in the cold oven and let the dough rise for another hour.

Now it is time to make the *salamoia*, the brine, for the dough's surface. Combine ⅝ cup (150 ml) of water with the olive oil and 2 teaspoons of salt. The easiest way to do this is to pour it all into a screw-top jar and shake well. Pour *salamoia* over the still-rising dough on the tray. Take the tray out of the oven.

Preheat the oven to 390 °F (200 °C) using top and bottom heat. Spread your fingers and then use your fingers to press small indentations into the dough, about ⅜ inch (1 cm) apart. Place the tray in the oven. After about 10 minutes of baking time, pour the remaining olive oil over the dough. Sprinkle the chopped rosemary needles on top and bake the focaccia for another 10 to 15 minutes.

OUR TIP Along with rosemary, you can also sprinkle oregano on top of your focaccia, or place some onion rings on it, or cherry tomatoes and Taggiasca olives.

Sardenaira

Focaccia with Tomato Sauce, Olives, and Anchovies

Serves 4

PREP TIME
20 minutes plus 6 hours standing time

COOK / BAKE TIME
40 minutes

INGREDIENTS

FOR THE DOUGH

3 cups (400 g) flour, Italian 00

1 cup + 2 tbsp. (250 ml) water

¾ cup (100 g) Manitoba flour

A scant ½ oz. (12 g) fresh or 1¼ tsp. (7 g) dry brewer's yeast

1 tsp. fine sea salt

A scant 3½ tbsp. (50 ml) mild extra virgin olive oil

FOR THE SAUCE

1 small onion

1 clove garlic

Olive oil for sautéing

2 cups (500 ml) tomato paste, double concentrated

Fine sea salt

1 tsp. sugar

1 tbsp. Taggiasca olives in oil, pitted

1 tsp. capers in salt, rinsed

1 tsp. anchovy paste

1 tsp. white wine vinegar

FOR THE TOPPING

5 to 10 anchovy fillets

1 tbsp. capers in salt, rinsed

2 tbsp. Taggiasca olives in oil, pitted

Their spicy, appetizing aroma wafts through the carruggi, the narrow streets of the coastal city of San Remo and those of many other coastal towns on the Riviera di Ponente in western Liguria. Inspired by classic focaccia, the taste of Sardenaira *is reminiscent of a northern Italian pizza marinara. Given Liguria's proximity to France, its culinary landscape transcends borders:* Sardenaira *is similar to* Pissaladière, *a treat found in the South of France. Sardenaira dough is soft and high, and when you sink your teeth into it, it's not easy to keep your nose from dunking into the flavorful medley of tomatoes, capers, anchovies, and Taggiasca olives blanketing this treat. If you choose, you can also bake it with unpeeled garlic cloves. Or you can sprinkle a few fresh oregano leaves on top of the finished* sardenaira *before eating it. This Italian street food variety, or cibo di strada, invites you to take a seat on the sand and enjoy it while gazing at the waters of the Mediterranean.*

Pour the two flours into a deep bowl. Add 1 cup plus 2 tablespoons (250 ml) of lukewarm water, the brewer's yeast, and the salt. Mix with a food processor or mixer using a dough hook or alternatively by hand. Pour in the olive oil and continue kneading until the dough has a soft consistency. Brush the dough with olive oil, cover the bowl with plastic wrap, and let it stand at room temperature for 3 hours. Roll the dough out on an oiled baking tray 12 × 16 inches (30 × 40 cm), and let stand in an unheated, closed oven for another 3 hours.

To make the sauce, peel and finely dice the onion and the garlic clove and sauté in a skillet in olive oil until soft. Add the tomato paste, salt, and sugar, and stew for a few minutes. Finely chop the Taggiasca olives and the capers. Add to the sauce along with the anchovy paste, stir well. Season with the vinegar. Remove the skillet from the heat and cover with a lid. Let stand until cold, giving the flavors time to infuse.

When the dough is done rising, spread the sauce on top, making sure to leave a bit of space free around the edges. Top with anchovy fillets, capers, and Taggiasca olives. Drizzle with olive oil and bake in a preheated oven at 425 °F (220 °C) using top and bottom heat for around 30 minutes.

OUR TIP Like any other simple recipe, it is important to use particularly good quality olive oil, as it has a strong impact on the taste. For this typical Ligurian recipe, it would be ideal to use extra virgin olive oil made from Taggiasca olives, such as Riviera Ligure DOP.

Pinsa Romana

Roman Flatbread

Serves 4 to 6

PREP TIME

Approximately 1 hour, plus at least 48 hours to mature

BAKE TIME

12 minutes

INGREDIENTS

A scant 3 cups (350 g) wheat flour, Italian type 00

A scant ½ cup (50 g) whole-grain spelt flour

A scant ½ cup (75 g) rice flour

25 g besan (chickpea flour, gram flour, garbanzo flour)

A generous ½ tsp. (2 g) fresh yeast

1¼ cups (300 ml) of ice-cold water

5 tsp. (25 g) liquid sourdough starter

A generous tsp. (5 g) fine sea salt

1 tsp. (5 ml) mild extra virgin olive oil

Oil to grease the dough proofing box

Flour

It might not be obvious to the uninitiated at first glance, but a pinsa *is not a pizza. Even its appearance is different: It is oval, fluffier, and thicker than pizza.* Pinsa *makes a good evening meal, with its hot, delicious base only having its toppings added shortly after baking. Unlike most Italian dishes, it is quite a young creation. The recipe was developed by a Roman baker named Corrado di Marco in 2001. To make it even more Italian, di Marco created a kind of history, or* storiella, *of its origins. He borrowed from a word used by ancient Romans to refer to the stamping of grain by foot,* pinsere, *bestowing the sacred status of traditional Italian cuisine on* pinsa. *His creation has become a delightful success story beyond Roman city limits, expanding delicious Italian culinary simplicity, marketing notwithstanding.*

Combine the four flours well. Dissolve the yeast in the ice-cold water and let stand for about 5 minutes. Add the water and yeast and the sourdough starter to the flour mixture and knead in a food processor with dough hooks on medium speed for about 6 minutes. Add the salt and knead for another 2 minutes. Add the olive oil and continue to knead for about 20 more minutes.

Cover the dough and let stand for about 30 minutes, pulling it from the edge to the center and folding it toward the center every 10 minutes. Then place it in an airtight, greased dough proofing box with a lid and let it mature in the refrigerator for at least 48 hours.

Two hours before you plan to work with it, remove the dough from the refrigerator and, using a dough scraper, cut it into 4 to 6 pieces. Preheat the oven to 465 °F (240 °C) using top and bottom heat. Flour your hands, then take a piece of dough, pull it, fold it over, and shape it into a long, oval patty. Repeat for the remaining pieces of dough. Bake in the preheated oven for about 12 minutes. Serve immediately and top as desired.

OUR TIP The cold ingredients for topping are placed on the flatbread after baking, making a meal of *pinsa* somewhat of a social event. You can make lots of different toppings and place them on the table for everyone to choose from to top their *pinsa*. Topping choices include diced tomatoes, young spinach, artichokes, various kinds of ham—prosciutto di Parma or prosciutto cotto—mozzarella or taleggio cheese, and so much more.

Impasto della Pizza alla Napoletana

Neapolitan-Style Pizza Dough

Makes 4 pizzas

PREP TIME
30 minutes plus 24 hours standing time

INGREDIENTS

7 ⅓ cups (1 kg) flour Italian type 00

A scant ½ tsp. (2 g) dry brewer's yeast

Approximately 2 cups + 4 tsp. (500 ml) ice-cold water

A generous 4 tsp. (25 g) fine sea salt

4 tsp. (20 ml) mild extra virgin olive oil

The special thing about this dough is its long dough-making process. It requires very little yeast and must be made at low temperatures. It should never be allowed to reach a temperature above 73 °F (23 °C) and should mature in the refrigerator at 37 °F to 39 °F (3 °C to 4 °C). The outcome is a particularly digestible and exceptional-tasting crust with a lot of holes and a mouthwatering aroma. La Vera Napoletana *is an association that aims to promote and protect* Pizza Napoletana *as a name and a product, and if you want to bake true* pizza napoletana *as they do, you are going to need this dough. To make the pizza shape, it is stretched until thin in the middle and the rim around the outside is pulled up. After baking, this rim is actually more reminiscent of bread. The production method of this pizza dough is protected under the designation* Vera Pizza Napoletana, *and if you have the time and the desire, you can even travel to Naples and attend one of their seminars—taught by the strict instructors and protectors of this pizza tradition, who dictate all the ingredients, along with the steps and method of preparation. Then all you need is an authentic pizza oven. However, this recipe also tastes good in a regular oven with top and bottom heat.*

Place the flour in a deep bowl, then use a whisk to fluff it up. Add the brewer's yeast. Gradually add around 2 cups + 4 teaspoons (500 ml) of ice-cold water over the next 15 minutes, mixing slowly using a mixer with dough hooks. Add the salt and some water until the dough has reached the right elasticity and is no longer sticky. The amount of water depends on the protein content of the flour and may be as much as a scant ½ cup (115 ml). Then knead in the olive oil using the high-speed setting of the mixer. Place the dough in an oiled dish and let stand for 15 minutes. Then divide into balls of pizza dough each weighing 8 ¾ oz. (250 g). Cover and refrigerate for 24 hours.

Remove from the refrigerator and let stand at room temperature up to 2 hours before use. The dough is now soft and elastic and can be laid on a work surface dusted with durum wheat flour and pulled into the right shape without applying pressure. Do not use a rolling pin, as this destroys the structure of the dough.

OUR TIP For the best dough consistency (not too firm and not too runny), using the right balance of flour and water is crucial. How much water the flour can absorb depends on the type of flour. It is important to keep this in mind and adjust the amount of water where necessary.

Pizza Margherita

Pizza with Tomato Sauce, Buffalo Mozzarella, and Basil

Makes 3 pizzas

PREP TIME
15 minutes plus 2 hours standing time at room temperature

BAKE TIME
10 to 15 minutes

INGREDIENTS

A scant 1 ¾ lbs. (750 g) fresh pizza dough (see p. 70), for 8 ¾ oz. (250 g) per pizza

1 14-oz. (400 g) can San Marzano tomatoes

½ tsp. fine sea salt

2 tbsp. robust extra virgin olive oil

8 ¾ oz. (250 g) buffalo mozzarella cheese from Campania

Flour for the work surface and dusting the dough

Durum wheat semolina for the work surface

1 handful fresh basil leaves

Pizza, including the renowned pizza Margherita, *is widely known to have originated in Naples. This recipe pays homage to Queen Margherita, who visited Naples with her husband, King Umberto I, in 1889. The colors of this pizza—white, red, and green—mirror those of the national flag of Italy, itself a nation since 1870. The traditional Neapolitan Margherita and Marinara pizzas are crafted by skilled pizzaioli, specialized pizza makers whose craft was added to the UNESCO Intangible Cultural Heritage List in 2017. However, pizza's immense popularity all over Italy and around the world can be attributed to a detour via the United States. Many southern Italians had immigrated to America, and in 1905, the first pizzeria began serving customers in New York, where pizza rapidly gained popularity among the public. When some of these emigrants returned to Italy, pizza gradually spread northward, eventually becoming a beloved street food throughout the country.*

Remove the pizza dough from the refrigerator and let it stand at room temperature for 1 to 2 hours. Meanwhile, place the San Marzano tomatoes in a bowl and finely crush using your hands. Season with salt, add some olive oil, and combine well. Drain the mozzarella in a sieve to remove the excess moisture and make sure the pizza stays crispy.

Sprinkle the flour and durum wheat semolina on the work surface, divide the pizza dough into three parts, and shape them into balls. Lightly flour the dough balls, cover with a towel, and let stand for 30 minutes. Gently applying pressure with your hands, stretch and flatten each ball of dough in a circle from the inside out until each one is approximately 11 inches (28 cm) in diameter, forming a rim ½ to ¾ inch (1 to 2 cm) wide.

Preheat the oven to the maximum temperature using the top and bottom heat setting with the baking sheet on the bottom rack. Prebake each pizza, one after another, on the baking sheet lined with baking paper for approximately 3 minutes. Remove from the oven, spread 3 to 5 tablespoons of the tomato sauce on each pizza, then top with mozzarella as desired. Bake each pizza in the oven again, one after another, for 5 to 7 minutes each, immediately dividing the finished pizzas into pieces. Tear the basil into pieces and sprinkle it over the pizzas, then drizzle with the remaining olive oil.

OUR TIP For the best results in a conventional oven, use a pizza stone. The porous structure absorbs moisture for a delightfully crispy crust.

Pizza Emilia Romagna

Pizza with Mortadella and Pistachios

Makes 4 pizzas

PREP TIME
10 minutes plus 2 hours standing at room temperature

BAKE TIME
Approximately 10 minutes

INGREDIENTS

A generous 2 lbs. (1 kg) pizza dough (see p. 70), for 8 ¾ oz. (250 g) per pizza

1 14-oz. (400 g) can of yellow Marzanella tomatoes

Fine sea salt

Freshly ground pepper

8 to 10 tbsp. extra virgin olive oil

8 ¾ oz. (250 g) fior di latte mozzarella cheese

12 large, thin slices of mortadella

6 tbsp. pistachio pesto

4 tbsp. dried capers

1 organic lemon

Flour for the work surface and dusting the dough

Durum wheat semolina for the work surface

Yellow Marzanella *tomatoes from southern Italy are a delightful addition to Italian tomato cuisine, offering a subtle sweetness that complements various dishes. As a sauce, these tomatoes pair well with the delicate cow's-milk* fior di latte *mozzarella and the fragrant mortadella, the authentic version of which does not include pistachios. Pistachio pesto adds a delicately tangy note here. This recipe combines both unusual and familiar elements. When it comes to salumi, such as sausage and ham products, it is often advisable to add them to the pizza after baking. This helps maintain their pleasant texture and taste, preventing them from becoming dry. Moreover, baking salumi on pizza can sometimes result in an overly salty flavor.*

Remove the pizza dough from the refrigerator and let it stand at room temperature for 1 to 2 hours. Preheat the oven set to the highest possible temperature using the top and bottom heat setting. Sprinkle the flour and durum wheat semolina on the work surface, divide the pizza dough into four parts, and shape them into balls. Gently applying pressure with your hands, stretch and flatten each ball of dough in a circle from the inside out until each one is approximately 11 inches (28 cm) in diameter, forming a rim ½ to ¾ inch (1 to 2 cm) wide. Pre-bake each of the four pizzas, one after another, for around 3 minutes in the preheated oven.

Meanwhile, place the tomatoes in a bowl, add salt, pepper, and olive oil, and crush the tomatoes with your hands until you have a relatively smooth sauce. Tear the mozzarella into small pieces. Spread 4 tablespoons of tomato sauce on each pizza, then distribute the mozzarella evenly on top. Bake the pizzas one after another for 4 to 6 minutes each.

After baking, top each pizza with 4 slices of mortadella, spread the pistachio pesto on top, sprinkle with dried capers, and season with pepper once more. Rinse the lemon in hot water and grate the zest over the pizzas. Finally, drizzle with olive oil.

OUR TIP Drain the *fior di latte* mozzarella in a fine sieve beforehand to keep the pizza from getting soggy.

Pizza ai cinque Formaggi con Rosmarino

Five-Cheese Pizza with Rosemary

Makes 4 pizzas

PREP TIME
10 minutes plus 2 hours standing at room temperature

BAKE TIME
Approximately 10 minutes

INGREDIENTS

A generous 2 lbs. (1 kg) pizza dough (see p. 70), for 8 ¾ oz. (250 g) per pizza

4 ¼ oz. (120 g) Buffalo mozzarella cheese

4 ¼ oz. (120 g) Fontina cheese, cubed

2 oz. (60 g) Gorgonzola piccante cheese, cubed

2 oz. (60 g) Scamorza cheese, cubed

1 oz. (30 g) Parmigiano Reggiano DOP cheese, grated

2 stems fresh rosemary, crushed

Freshly ground pepper

Flour for the work surface and dusting the dough

Durum wheat semolina for the work surface

A pizza bianca, *or white pizza, is made without using tomato sauce; this pizza is not very common but exceptionally delicious. Instead of the tomato sauce defining the Mediterranean flavor profile here, it is the other high-quality ingredients. In our recipe, the pizza showcases various types of cheese, along with capocollo, an air-dried meat made from the neck of the pig that is only added to the pizza after it has finished baking. This ensures it will taste completely authentic and having the flavor baked out of it. The blend of fresh mozzarella; aged* scamorza; *tangy Gorgonzola; buttery, nutty fontina; and tangy, salty Parmigiano creates a complex and flavorful taste experience. The result is something like a particularly piquant, hot cheese sandwich.*

Remove the pizza dough from the refrigerator and let it stand at room temperature for 1 to 2 hours. Preheat the oven set to the highest possible temperature using the top and bottom heat setting. Sprinkle the flour and durum wheat semolina on the work surface, divide the pizza dough into four parts, and shape them into balls. Gently applying pressure with your hands, stretch and flatten each ball of dough in a circle from the inside out until each one is approximately 11 inches (28 cm) in diameter, forming a rim ½ to ¾ inch (1 to 2 cm) wide. Pre-bake each of the four pizzas, one after another, for around 3 minutes in the preheated oven.

Spread the cheeses evenly on top of each. Bake each pizza for another 4 minutes, then sprinkle the rosemary on top. Bake each pizza for 1 more minute. Remove from the oven. Arrange the capocollo on top and season with pepper.

OUR TIP Smoked Capocollo di Martina Franca goes perfectly with this recipe, but if it is not available, we recommend substituting very thinly sliced coppa, another cured meat from the neck. Coppa, however, is not smoked. Or, if you prefer a vegetarian option, you can forgo the meat and enjoy the pizza with just the cheese.

Farina e Polenta

Flour and Polenta

Le chiacchiere non fanno farina, or "Talk doesn't make flour." That's what they say in Italy, and yet the perfect flour is a source of endless debate in Italian bakeries. What everyone agrees on, however, is that *farina* is used more in northern Italy and *semola* in southern Italy. *Farina* is flour made from soft wheat and *semola* is semolina made from durum wheat. Italians do not differentiate between semolina and flour, they just call everything *semola* that is ground from *grano duro*, durum wheat.

Both are made from wheat and primarily comprise two essential elements: starch and protein. Gluten, the important binding protein, is produced when protein is combined with water. It acts as a kind of fine web that holds the water and gases produced during fermentation in the dough. The more gluten develops, the better the dough rises.

However, which flour is the right one for which authentic Italian dish comes down to judgment and experience. Especially as the Italian names are a little peculiar: The *tipo*, or type, indicates the mineral content, but only for farina, the soft wheat flour. *Tipo 00* is the finest; it corresponds roughly to pastry flour in the United States, although you can usually also find 00 here as well. It is particularly soft with the fewest minerals and is mainly used for the dough of the original *Napolitana Pizza*. *Tipo 0* is similar to all-purpose flour; it is used for cakes and quiches. *Tipo 1* and *Tipo 2* (roughly equivalent to high gluten flour and first clear flour) are used for baking bread. *Integrale*, the whole-grain flour, still has all the minerals, but it is very coarse and therefore requires more leavening agent and a longer baking time.

In contrast, there is no classification system for *semole*, flours made from durum wheat, in Italy.

They are simply classified according to the size of the grain, from very coarse to very fine: *semola grossa*, *semola*, and *semola rimacinata* (sometimes also called *farina di grano duro*). The latter is—and for once there is no difference of opinion in Italy—the right flour for dusting pizza counters. But even in this very traditional craft, Italy is following the trend of resurrecting old grain varieties.

And there are plenty of them to discover: The first Italian bread was baked in Paglicci Cave in Apulia 32,000 years ago, and used oat flour.

Wheat has only been around for 2,500 years. The goddess Demeter is said to have given it to the Sicilians as a gift because they once stood by her while she grieved. This is how Sicily became the breadbasket of the Romans. It was also the Romans who turned the humble art of baking into the *arte bianca*, the "white art," and developed *panem et circenses* (bread and circuses) as a strategy for maintaining peace in society. Since then, bread has always been an essential part of Italian culture. As have lively discussions.

"*Knowledge is flour, but wisdom is bread.*"—
Austin O'Malley

It is worth knowing that flour should not be stored in direct sunlight and should be stored in dark containers. This is because it is quite sensitive and bleaches very quickly.

Flour dust, on the other hand, can hardly be avoided when using flour. However, please do not use it near an open flame—the mixture of flour dust and air is highly combustible.

To this day, Sicily and Apulia are famous for their grain—especially durum wheat, which needs a lot of sun and dryness. But other varieties are also cultivated here as well.

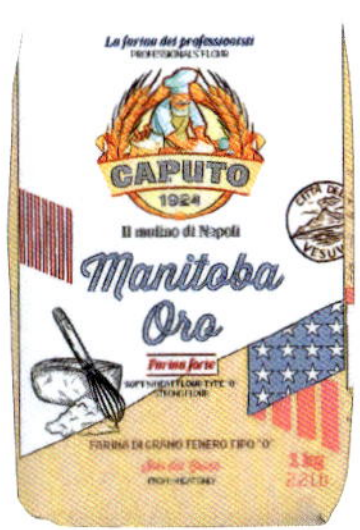

Grano tenero Soft wheat is one of the oldest cultivated plants in the world and the most economically significant type of wheat today. It has a much softer, flourier grain and a lower protein content than durum wheat. As a result, it forms less gluten and is ideal for bread and other baked goods—in other words, anything that does not need to be very firm to the bite. The Manitoba variety is particularly popular, at least for *Pizzaioli*.

Grano duro Durum wheat is rare, but particularly high in protein, making it perfect for elastic dough for making authentic Italian pasta. It is characterized by its rich yellow color and high gluten content, which ensures a good firm texture. This is not only valued when making pasta; it is also important for baked goods and for dusting your pizza counter—you get an extremely crispy pizza crust with it, because *semola* does not burn as quickly as ordinary flour.

Integrale After harvesting, only the awns and husks are removed from the whole grain. Fiber, vitamins, oils, and minerals are retained—they are particularly important for a healthy diet. In Italy, whole-grain flour is made from soft wheat, and particularly well suited for making short crust pastry for fruit tarts, biscotti, quiches, and other tarts. This flour is not ideal for making pasta the Italian way, but then again, healthy eating is becoming quite trendy in Italy these days.

Farina di mais Hominy grits, Turkish flour, is another name for hominy grits in Italy, although Italian explorers brought it back from America. And it is still very popular, especially in northern Italy. Hominy grits usually have a beautiful yellow color, but Veneto has a specialty called polenta bianca, made from hulled corn kernels of a very light color that shines a brilliant white.

"Whether the flour is good or not depends on what you want to do with it."
—Antimo Caputo

Pane Perhaps it owes its existence to happenstance. Maybe a dollop of cereal porridge did not end up in the mouth of a Stone Age man, landing instead on a hot stone where it baked into flatbread. One thing is certain, however, and that is that bread was already being baked systematically 15,000 years ago. Thanks to a series of inventions and discoveries—the oven, yeast, and later, sourdough fermentation by the Egyptians, and the mill by the Romans—the art of baking bread has been continuously refined. The best bread in the world, at least according to the great Latin poet Horace, is Pane Altamura from Apulia, a durum wheat bread with natural sourdough. The same region is home to the famous Pane Pugliese with its moist, holey crumb—a bread made from semola, the flour used to make pasta. Pane Carasau is the bread of Sardinian shepherds, paper-thin, plus it keeps for a year. The classic ciabatta from Veneto was actually not invented until 1982 by a resourceful miller using a new type of flour that is able to absorb a lot of moisture.

Grissini Legend has it that these thin, crunchy breadsticks from the Piedmont region were invented in 1675 by baker Antonio Brunero for Vittorio Amedeo II of Savoy, who was suffering from digestive problems, and they soon gained popularity in aristocratic circles around the world. Today, no Italian table is complete without them—the best ones are *stirati a mano*, or "stretched by hand," easily recognized by their twisted shape.

Focaccia Even the Romans knew it. This typical Ligurian flatbread made from yeast dough was a by-product of bread baking, used to test whether the oven had reached the right temperature. It is not only popular in Genoa; there are different versions and variations throughout Italy. Last but not least, it also gave rise to pizza. Focaccia comes alive with good olive oil, dripping down your chin as you bite into it. Genoa is the birthplace of focaccia, known locally as *fugassa*. Traditionally, bakers create dimples in the dough with their fingertips, forming perfect little pockets for olive oil. While this simple method of preparation is iconic, focaccia comes in many different varieties. As a focaccia roll, it offers a hearty alternative to panini and tramezzino. One particularly delicious warm filling is stracchino, a sourish cream cheese rarely found outside Italy, and used to make *focaccia di recco*.

Pizza Perhaps the most Italian of all foods was first created in the mid-18th century, when the tomato became popular in southern Italy. Pizza became famous when a particularly patriotic version with green basil, white mozzarella, and red tomato sauce was created in Brandi pizzeria in Naples on June 11, 1889, in honor of Queen Margherita. The original Napolitana pizza remains unchanged to this day: A thick crust surrounds a thin interior roughly 8½ to 14 inches (22–35 cm) in diameter without excessive toppings, baked until crispy at 800–900 degrees Fahrenheit (430–480 degrees Celsius).

Pasta Italy without pasta is unthinkable. And while pasta may not have been invented here, it has still had a significant influence on Italian culinary traditions. Pasta has its own dedicated course in the Italian meal sequence: the *primo piatto*. And each type of sauce has its own pasta shape. But they all have one thing in common, though. They are made from *semola*, which gives them their appetizing golden yellow color.

Biscotti Italian biscotti are famous for their simplicity. Just a few ingredients create maximum flavor. And they can be enjoyed for breakfast, too. Just dunk them in your coffee, and your day is off to a great start.

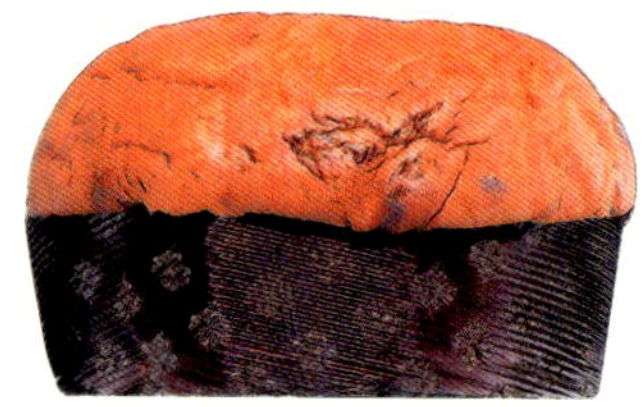

Panettone What would Christmas be without this authentic Milanese cake? It is traditionally made from wheat sourdough with a long fermentation process, giving it its wonderful flavor. It gets its typical domed shape thanks to special baking paper shells. The wheat sourdough starter is often a family heirloom passed down for decades. This precious ingredient, ideally combined with a four-day maturation process, ensures the cake's signature airiness. While juicy raisins and candied citrus are traditionally added, modern variations incorporate chocolate, apples, or Amarena cherries. A sparkling wine is always a perfect match.

Torta Italians can also make cakes. One legendary cake is the *Torte della Nonna*, a delicacy made from short crust pastry and filled with custard cream. The fresh *Torte al Limone* with ricotta filling and the simple but amazing orange wreath cake are also true gems of Italian baking.

Polenta A predecessor of polenta was already popular with the Romans. However, it was not made from hominy grits, as they did not come to Italy until the Renaissance. Polenta is so popular in northern Italy that southern Italians somewhat disparagingly call their northern compatriots *polentoni*, or polenta eaters. Polenta is still delicious the next day, either cold or cut into wedges and fried.

Ostia For something as revered as the body of Christ, this wafer has rather mundane origins. The host consists solely of water and pure wheat flour, and was initially the everyday bread that the faithful brought along themselves. Only later were strict regulations issued for the baking of the host, regulations which could generally only be observed in convents.

Pasta Fresca

Pasta Dough with Durum Wheat

Serves 4

PREP TIME
10 minutes plus ½ hour refrigeration

COOK TIME
2 minutes

INGREDIENTS

A scant 2 ¼ cups (365 g) durum wheat semolina flour

½ tsp. salt

1 tsp. mild extra virgin olive oil

⅔ cup (165 ml) water

Basically, all you need to make pasta dough is durum wheat semolina and water. But olive oil adds another level of flavor to the pasta, giving it a more supple taste as well as a smoother dough. Homemade pasta is a philosophy to live by, and it can elevate your cooking if you are not afraid to tackle the making of fresh dough. When you begin, you can choose to be a purist or you can build on your new skill, find your own preferences and routine, and use your rolling pin or pasta maker to easily whip up the basis for a really big meal like a spaghettata *(a table full of pasta and sauces) or a primo.*

Combine the semolina flour, salt, and oil with the water. Knead the dough for 5 to 7 minutes, then refrigerate for half an hour. Take the dough out of the refrigerator and briefly knead again. Then work it using a pasta maker, a pastry wheel, or a *chitarra* pasta cutter. A *chitarra* is a tool made of a wooden frame and wires; the pasta dough is pressed through it to make long, spaghetti-like noodles, but with square cross-sections instead of round noodles.

OUR TIP *Pasta secca* is just fresh pasta without eggs, hence *secca*, or dry. The freshly made pasta can be cooked immediately, which is the most delicious option. If you have any uncooked pasta left over, you can dry it in the oven at a low temperature (below 95 °F / 35 °C) to use later. Any leftover cooked pasta can be frozen.

Pasta all'Uovo

Pasta Dough with Eggs

Serves 4,
makes a little over 2 lbs. (1 kg)

PREP TIME
10 minutes plus 1 hour standing time

COOK TIME
1 to 2 minutes, or longer if stuffed

INGREDIENTS

3 ¾ cups (450 g) flour Italian type 00

4 eggs

2 egg yolks

Fine sea salt

2 tbsp. extra virgin olive oil

⅓ cup (50 g) fine durum wheat semolina flour

Fresh pasta made with eggs is used in northern and central Italy, especially in the Piedmont, Liguria, Emilia, Tuscany, Umbria, and Marche regions. The people of the Piedmont region enjoy their bright yellow local tajarin *pasta with truffles and the little* Agnolotti del Plin *stuffed with meat for soup. Ligurians are known for ravioli, in Emilia the stuffed pasta ranges from tortellini to tortelloni; there you will also encounter the famed* Tagliatelle all'Uovo *with* Ragù alla Bolognese. *In Tuscany, people love to eat pappardelle, the particularly wide flat noodles, with braised meat, and in Umbria, it is* strangozzi, *a long, thick pasta rolled by hand. In the Marche region, angel hair pasta—very thin, long noodles—is often used for soups, but also makes a lovely side dish for seafood. The taste of egg pasta goes very well with creamy, rich sughi made with meat, cream, and truffles, as well as with butter. If you don't have a pasta maker, you can cut long shapes with a knife, separate them with a pastry wheel, or use cutters or stamps to make special shapes.*

Pour the type 00 flour in a bowl and make a well in the center. Break the eggs, then place the whole eggs and egg yolks in the well. Whisk continuously using a fork or small whisk, incorporating more and more of the flour. While doing so, add the salt and olive oil as well; knead everything together to form a smooth dough. Shape the dough into a ball, wrap in plastic wrap, and let stand at room temperature for an hour.

Sprinkle the durum wheat semolina flour on the work surface and, always working from the center outward, use a rolling pin to roll the dough out to a thickness of about ⅒ inch (2 to 3 mm).

OUR TIP We recommend using very fresh free-range organic eggs. The egg yolk is more intense when the chickens have eaten grass because of the carotenes found in grass.

Tajarin con Burro e Parmigiano Reggiano

Piedmont-Style Egg Noodles with Butter and Parmesan

Serves 4

PREP TIME
70 minutes

COOK TIME
15 minutes

INGREDIENTS

14 oz. (400 g) tajarin pasta (the name for tagliarini in the Piedmont dialect) (see p. 84)

Fine sea salt

10 ½ oz. (150 g) butter

3 ½ oz. (100 g) Parmigiano Reggiano DOP cheese, finely grated

Tajarin is an exquisite pasta delight: thin, golden egg noodles with the perfect length, elasticity, mouthfeel, and taste, not to mention how beautifully they twirl on your fork. In Piedmont, where they are made, they are the preferred pasta to eat with truffles, which are easy to add to this recipe too, making it a bit more of a pricey undertaking. This everyday version with butter and Parmiggiano Reggiano could not be simpler or more delicious. It is basically a children's favorite that caters to adult taste buds. You can make the finest tajarin right on your kitchen table, using quality Italian type 00 soft wheat flour and fresh egg yolks. Italy has very fine cream butter, but you can also use French varieties or local artisanal butter here. With its milky sweetness and subtle tanginess, however, the Parmiggiano Reggiano DOP is not open to discussion.

Cook the fresh tajarin in salted water until they are not too soft, but soft enough that they can be easily twirled onto a fork. Melt the butter slowly in a pot over low heat. Drain the pasta and reserve a good ½ cup (150 ml) of the pasta water. Gradually add some pasta water to the butter, stirring to form a creamy emulsion. Next, stir in the Parmesan in small portions as well, keeping the temperature low. Depending on the desired consistency, continue adding pasta water. Once the emulsion has a creamy consistency, add the tajarin and combine well.

OUR TIP If making the tajarin pasta from scratch seems too time-consuming yet the recipe's simplicity and flavors are too alluring to pass up, you can substitute quality tagliolini made by quality pasta producers. It is essential, however, that you avoid using pasta from industrial mass production here.

Spaghetti alla Carbonara

Spaghetti with Guanciale and Egg

Serves 2

PREP TIME
15 minutes

COOK TIME
30 minutes

INGREDIENTS

A generous 2 ¾ oz. (80 g) guanciale (cured meat from pork cheek)

1 clove garlic

1 organic egg

1 organic egg yolk

Fine sea salt

Freshly ground black pepper

Nutmeg

8 ¾ oz. (250 g) spaghetti

A generous 2 ¾ oz. (80 g) Pecorino Romano cheese, finely grated

2 sprigs flat-leaf parsley

The recipe for Spaghetti alla Carbonara, an icon of Roman cuisine, is less than a century old. The invention of this pasta dish is said to be attributed to the American soldiers during the occupation in Rome, who did not want to do without their breakfast of eggs and bacon. So they traded some of their food rations for egg powder and bacon on the black market, the Mercato carbonaro, *which later gave the dish its name. The soldiers asked trattoria proprietors to make them pasta with eggs and bacon, likely giving birth to this recipe, which was subsequently refined Roman-style. It is now so popular around the world that there are hard rules in place to protect the original recipe when it comes to the ingredients. The cardinal rules are to never use cream and to always use guanciale, a type of cured bacon from pork cheek with herbs and wine, a traditional ingredient in Roman cuisine. Tangy Pecorino Romano cheese is also a must; its flavor is not as harmonious and milky as that of Parmigiano Reggiano cheese, so it lends a bit of excitement to the sauce.*

Remove the rind from the guanciale and cut into cubes slightly smaller than ½ inch (1 cm). Fry the guanciale cubes in a skillet without oil until the meat has released all of its fat. Let the cubes fry in this fat at a low temperature for another 15 minutes. Finely chop the garlic and add just before the end of the cooking time. Set the skillet aside.

Whisk the egg and egg yolk together thoroughly and season with salt, pepper, and nutmeg. Bring salted water to a boil and cook the spaghetti until al dente, approx. 9 minutes. Drain and allow to cool briefly. Add the spaghetti and the egg mixture to the skillet with the guanciale cubes, along with half of the grated pecorino. Cook briefly over low heat, stir well, and divide between two plates.

Finely chop the parsley leaves and sprinkle them over the carbonara, along with the remaining pecorino. To round it off, coarsely grind some pepper over the pasta.

OUR TIP For a really creamy carbonara sauce, stir in some of the pasta water.

Trofie liguri al Pesto

Ligurian Pasta with Pesto

Serves 2

PREP TIME
20 minutes

COOK TIME
20 minutes

INGREDIENTS

2 big waxy potatoes

5 ¼ oz. (150 g) green beans

Salt

8 ¾ oz. (250 g) trofie pasta

3 tbsp. Pesto alla Genovese (see p. 262)

1 ½ oz. (50 g) Parmigiano Reggiano cheese

Black pepper

Olive oil

The Ligurians have always been a seafaring people, some of them traders and some fisherfolk, not to mention a few pirates along the way. Even in past centuries, this meant having little time to cook and wanting to invest the least amount of energy possible in doing so. Recipes requiring a single pot and—apart from the fresh beans—made only from preserved and non-perishable ingredients were very practical. Trofie, *which are short, rolled pasta, are typical of Liguria, as is basil pesto, whose finest primary ingredient grows on the Riviera di Ponente near Genoa: a flavorful basil variety with a Protected Designation of Origin that boasts a delicate sweetness. This traditional recipe can be served as a starter or as a vegetarian second course, as the combination of pasta and potatoes makes it very filling.*

Peel the potatoes and cut them into cubes slightly smaller than ½ inch (1 cm). Wash the beans, cut off the ends with the stems, and remove any strings. Cut the beans in half lengthwise.

In a large pot, cook the trofie, potato cubes, and beans together in salted water for approximately 5 to 8 minutes until al dente. While they are cooking, be sure to regularly check the consistency of all three ingredients to ensure they reach the ideal al dente stage at the same time.

Put the basil pesto in a bowl, add some pasta water, and stir until combined. Using a strainer, drain the trofie, beans, and potatoes, then return them to the pot. Add the pesto sauce and combine thoroughly. Season with salt and pepper to taste. Sprinkle each plated portion with grated Parmesan before serving. Place mild Taggiasca extra virgin olive oil from Liguria on the table for added flavor.

OUR TIP To make sure the trofie are cooked to the perfect doneness, you can also cook the pasta separately from the potatoes. However, this means that the potato and pasta starches will no longer blend together, resulting in a somewhat less creamy dish.

Ravioli alle zucchine con Mandorle tostate

Zucchini Ravioli with Toasted Almonds

Serves 4

PREP TIME
1½ hours plus 1 hour standing time

COOK TIME
Approximately 15 minutes

INGREDIENTS

2¼ lbs. oz. (1kg) pasta dough all'Uovo (see p. 84)

10½ oz. (300g) zucchini

5 tbsp. extra virgin olive oil

2 shallots

1 clove garlic

1 organic lemon

A scant 3 oz. (80g) buffalo ricotta cheese

4¼ oz. (120g) Parmigiano Reggiano DOP cheese

Fine sea salt

Freshly ground pepper

Pesto piccante (see p. 263)

FOR THE TOPPING
A scant 3 oz. (80g) almonds

½ tsp. cane sugar

Fine sea salt

2 tbsp. balsamic vinegar, aged

1½ oz. (40g) Tuscan pecorino, aged

The hearty flavors used to make this ravioli make the usually rather reserved zucchini a true Sicilian knockout. Combined with flavorful pesto, roasted almonds, and pecorino, zucchini becomes a gourmet treat and reveals its hidden strengths. If we were in Liguria, we would use the firm, aromatic Zucchini di Trombetta, a variety that does not contain as much water. We prefer to source the almonds from Sicily. Buffalo ricotta is truly a revelation; if you were not a fan of ricotta before, you certainly will be after this! Pecorino is definitely the right cheese to use here, as it is saltier than Parmigiano Reggiano and gives savory recipes quite a kick.

Make the pasta dough according to the recipe. Dice the zucchini. Heat the olive oil in a skillet and sauté the zucchini. Finely dice the shallots and garlic clove, add to the skillet, and sauté until soft. Move the contents of the skillet to a bowl, add the lemon zest, buffalo ricotta, and Parmesan, and combine. Season with salt and pepper to taste.

Roll the dough out and use a spoon to place small mounds of the filling 2 inches (5cm) apart on one half, fold the other half over it, and use a ravioli cutter or pastry wheel to cut out the individual ravioli.

Prepare the Pesto piccante according to the recipe on page 261.

Chop the almonds and roast them in a skillet. Sprinkle the sugar and a pinch of salt over the almonds. Let them caramelize, then deglaze with the balsamic vinegar.

Cook the ravioli in salted water for approximately 2 minutes. Add them to the almonds in the skillet and stir well. Serve with the pesto and place the grated pecorino on the table.

OUR TIP Pesto piccante also tastes very good with grilled meat, cheese made from sheep's milk, carrots, and cabbage. Why not make some extra to use later?

Spaghetti spezzati in brodo

Short Pasta in Beef Stock

Serves 4

PREP TIME
20 minutes

COOK TIME
3 hours

INGREDIENTS

6 ½ cups (1.5 L) beef stock (see p. 268)

1 carrot

1 stalk celery with celery greens

2 spring onions

Approximately 18 oz. (500 g) short pasta, such as casarecce or spaghetti spezzati (broken spaghetti)

This recipe is cooked by people all over Italy, especially in the winter. Broken spaghetti is often used as pasta—although the breaking of spaghetti is actually purported to be a sacrilege committed only by non-Italians. But Italians actually do this too! For this soup, they break their long spaghetti noodles, usually twirled so elegantly with a fork, and, it goes without saying, without a spoon. In Naples, people also like to use pasta mista, *a combination of different short pasta shapes that was created to use up leftovers. If any of the various pasta noodles were left over, they were combined, resulting in this curiosity. Pasta mista is often used in soups and stews, and its mouthfeel is intriguing, not to mention its appearance. This combination is certainly an appealing alternative to* casarecce *or broken spaghetti.*

Peel and julienne the carrot. Remove the threads from the celery stalk and also julienne. Trim the spring onion and slice into thin rings. Bring the stock to a boil and cook the carrots, celery, and onions in it until al dente. Check whether more salt is needed. Add the pasta and cook until al dente. Garnish with some celery greens and serve.

OUR TIP Place medium extra virgin olive oil and grated Parmigiano Reggiano DOP on the table.

Bucatini con le Sarde

Bucatini with Sardines

Serves 4

PREP TIME
20 minutes

COOK TIME
20 minutes

INGREDIENTS

6 anchovy fillets packed in oil

A scant 1¼ oz. (30 g) golden raisins

20 saffron threads

3 sprigs wild fennel or the greens from 2 fennel bulbs

Stale white bread sufficient for 3½ oz. (100 g) breadcrumbs

1 medium onion

A scant ½ cup (80 ml) medium extra virgin olive oil

A scant 3½ tbsp. (50 ml) dry white wine

8 fresh sardine fillets or sardines packed in olive oil

A generous 1 oz. (30 g) pine nuts

10½ oz. (300 g) bucatini pasta

Fine sea salt

Freshly ground pepper

The flavors of Sicily: The blend of raisins, pine nuts, and saffron is reminiscent of the historical Arab influences in the region. Wild fennel grows everywhere, just waiting to be picked, and sardines swim circles around the island. In the event there were no sardines to be had, people improvised and cooked Pasta con le Sarde a Mare, *which translates as pasta with sardines that are still swimming in the sea. Sicilian olive oil is among the best olive oils Italy has to offer. This recipe is a piece of history, and also proves that combining available culinary treasures is a tasty idea. Breadcrumbs are part of cucina povera, or peasant cuisine; instead of cheese, breadcrumbs were sprinkled over pasta. This underscores the deep reverence for bread in Sicilian culture. Breadcrumbs are still around, not just out of tradition, but because they taste especially good and their crunch is very appealing.*

Dab the sardine fillets from the oil dry with a paper towel and finely chop. Soak the raisins in water. Also steep the saffron in a little warm water. Finely chop the fennel greens. Grate the white bread and toast the grated breadcrumbs in a skillet without oil over medium heat.

Finely dice the onion and sauté in ¼ cup (60 ml) of the olive oil until soft. Add the anchovies and stir until they disintegrate. Add the wine and bring to a boil, allowing the alcohol to evaporate. Coarsely chop the fresh sardine filets and add along with the raisins, pine nuts, saffron, and wild fennel. Combine carefully, season to taste with salt and pepper, and simmer for another 10 minutes. If fresh sardines are not available, add sardines that were packed in oil to the sauce just before the end of the cooking time to warm them up.

Cook the bucatini in plenty of salted water until al dente and drain, reserving some of the cooking water. Add the pasta to the sardine sauce and combine. Add some of the cooking water. Drizzle with the remaining olive oil and sprinkle with the toasted breadcrumbs.

OUR TIP If you don't have fennel in your garden and don't know a good gardener who grows fennel, you can also use one teaspoon of fennel seeds that have been soaked in water for a few hours beforehand.

Spaghetti alle vongole

Spaghetti with Clams

Serves 4

PREP TIME
1–2 hours to soak

COOK TIME
25 minutes

INGREDIENTS

A generous 2 lbs. (1 kg) clams

9 tbsp. mild extra virgin olive oil

2 cloves garlic

1 chile pepper, de-seeded and chopped

1 bunch flat-leaf parsley

⅓ cup (75 ml) dry, mild white wine

Fine sea salt

14 oz. (400 g) spaghetti

Spaghetti alle Vongole *should be the first thing you eat when you visit the Italian coast. Although the recipe originally comes from Campania, it has become a specialty across the nation. Some versions use a little bit of tomato, and whether the white wine might interfere with the delicate clam flavor is the subject of debate. There are countless opinions about which restaurant or trattoria serves the absolute best* Spaghetti alle Vongole. *If you have a fish market nearby whose clams are really fresh, you are very fortunate, because this means you can bring the taste of the ocean to your own dining room table. The wafting fragrance and the delicious clam broth are truly enchanting. The wine used to make this dish should be really mild and subtle, or you can just use water instead. The rule for this pasta recipe is the same as for all combinations with fish and seafood in Italy—you never sprinkle Parmesan on top.*

Sort the fresh clams. Remove any damaged, opened, and sand-filled clams, then rinse the remaining clams under cold running water. If they have not been cleaned yet, you will have to soak them yourself. To do this, place the whole, unopened clams in a bowl of cold salted water (1 ¼ oz. salt per 4 ½ cups water / 35 g salt per 1 liter water). Change the water as many as three times, then carefully lift the clams out of the water after 1 to 2 hours. This removes any remaining sand.

Slightly crush one garlic clove. In a large skillet, heat 4 tablespoons of olive oil with the garlic clove and add the clams. As soon as they open, remove the skillet from the heat and discard any unopened clams. Remove the garlic clove. Pour the liquid from the skillet through a sieve, reserving the liquid. Heat another 4 tablespoons of olive oil in the skillet, add the chile pepper, the other clove of garlic, and a few stalks of parsley. Deglaze with the white wine, let it reduce somewhat, then add the reserved clam water and the clams. Briefly cook on low heat with the lid on. Remove the garlic clove and parsley stalks. Finely chop the remaining parsley. Remove the clam meat from three quarters of the clamshells and add the meat to the clam broth. Stir in the chopped parsley. Cook the spaghetti in salted water until al dente, then add to the skillet with the clams. Finally, drizzle a bit of olive oil over the top; serve immediately.

OUR TIP A Vermentino di Gallura DOCG wine from Sardinia pairs well with this dish. It is creamy and floral, and has a lower acidity—the ideal wine to enjoy while you dine on clams.

Tagliatelle con Ragù alla Bolognese

Flat Egg Noodles with Bolognese-Style Ragu

Serves 4

PREP TIME
20 minutes

COOK TIME
2 to 2 ½ hours

INGREDIENTS

5 ¼ oz. (150 g) pancetta

¼ cup (50 g) butter

1 ¾ oz. (50 g) carrot, finely diced

1 ¾ oz. (50 g) celery stalk, finely diced

1 ¾ oz. (50 g) onion, finely diced

10 ½ oz. (300 g) ground beef, coarse

A scant ½ cup (100 ml) dry red wine

¾ oz. (20 g) triple concentrated tomato paste, or 5 tbsp. tomato sauce

Beef stock if needed (see p. 268)

A scant ½ cup (100 ml) milk

Fine sea salt

Freshly ground pepper

Ragù alla Bolognese *with pasta is much loved yet often misunderstood. It is actually a stew, and it should never be drowned in tomato sauce. It is also advisable not to use only ground beef, as it usually gets dry. Pancetta adds some juiciness. The pig is the favorite animal of Italy's Emilia region, the region that gives us this recipe. In 1982, a version of this recipe was filed with the Bolognese Chamber of Commerce by the municipal delegate of the Italian Academy of Cuisine, or* Accademia Italiana della Cucina, *basically making it a "protected species." Our recipe adheres to the current authentic Bologna version. It is worth following the traditional guidelines here, and, in the process, doing without oregano, which is often found in poor imitations.*

Dice the pancetta and finely chop with a mezzaluna, or crescent cutter. Melt the butter in a thick aluminum skillet about 8 inches (20 cm) in diameter and lightly fry the chopped pancetta in it. Add the carrots, celery, and onions, and sauté. Add the ground beef, stir to combine everything, and use a ladle to press the meat to the bottom of the pan to ensure it cooks evenly. Pour in the red wine and let it evaporate. Then stir in the tomato paste. Stir again to ensure everything is combined well, add the lid, and let simmer over low heat for 2 to 2 ½ hours. Add some beef stock if necessary. Just before the end of the cooking time, add the milk. Finally, season with salt and pepper to taste.

OUR TIP You will definitely want to eat this sauce with tagliatelle made with eggs (see p. 84), preferably freshly made, and combine the hot sauce with the pasta as soon as the sauce is ready.

Lasagne al Ragù

Lasagna with Meat Ragu

Serves 6 to 8

PREP TIME
2 hours

COOK TIME
Approximately 1 hour

INGREDIENTS

FOR THE RAGU
1 small onion

1 small carrot

1 stalk celery

4 tbsp. mild extra virgin olive oil

A generous 1 ½ lbs. (700 g) ground beef

10 ½ oz. (300 g) ground pork

¾ cup plus 4 tsp. (200 ml) red wine

A scant 18 oz. (500 g) canned San Marzano tomatoes, chopped

2 tbsp. tomato paste

Fine sea salt & ground pepper

Vegetable stock (see p. 267)

FOR THE BÉCHAMEL SAUCE
⅓ cup (80 g) butter

⅔ cup (80 g) flour

4 ½ cups (1 L) milk

Fine sea salt & Nutmeg

FOR THE LASAGNA
1 tbsp. butter, softened

10 ½ oz. (300 g) lasagna sheets all'Uovo (see p. 84)

A scant 3 oz. (80 g) Parmigiano Reggiano DOP cheese, grated

Creamy béchamel, spicy ragu, golden pasta, and melted cheese: Lasagna satisfies all these culinary cravings and then some. It is the steaming heart of the dinner table, with its sturdy casserole dish positively exuding the feeling of certainty that there is more than plenty to go around. It is a meal for a large group of family and friends, which is easily well-prepared and is sure to delight every single guest. Naturally, this successful approach can also be used to create variations with vegetables. One special favorite is lentil lasagna, where the meat is replaced with fine, small lentils simmered with soffritto, San Marzano tomatoes, and bunches of herbs. Umbrian mountain lentils are perfect for this. Pecorino cheese is used as an alternative to Parmigiano Reggiano for lentil lasagna.

To make the ragu, finely dice the onion, carrots, and celery, giving you your soffritto (see p. 266). Heat the olive oil in a skillet and sauté the diced vegetables for a few minutes until soft. Add the ground pork and sauté over medium heat for several minutes. Pour in the red wine and let it evaporate. Stir in the chopped San Marzano tomatoes and tomato paste, season with salt. Stir well, then reduce the heat. Simmer for about one and a half hours. Add some vegetable stock if necessary. Season to taste with salt and a generous amount of pepper; set aside.

To make the béchamel sauce, melt the butter in a pot and use a whisk to stir in the flour. Gradually pour in the milk and continue to whisk over medium heat until the sauce has the desired consistency and creaminess. Season with salt and nutmeg.

Preheat the oven to 360 °F (180 °C) using top and bottom heat. Grease the bottom and sides of a large, rectangular casserole dish with the butter. Spread some béchamel sauce on the bottom and place the first layer of lasagna sheets on top. Place a few spoonfuls of ragu on the sheets, spread with béchamel sauce, and sprinkle with Parmesan. Repeat the whole process. When you are finished, there should be about six layers, ending with lasagna sheets. Generously spread béchamel sauce on the top lasagna sheets. Sprinkle the remaining Parmesan on top, about 1 ¾ oz. (50 g). Bake in the preheated oven for approximately 1 hour. If the cheese starts to get too brown, cover the lasagna with baking paper.

OUR TIP Let the lasagna stand for a few minutes before cutting. This makes it easier to cut and serve.

Ravioli al Brasato con Ragù

Ravioli with Roast Filling and Ragu

Serves 4 to 5

PREP TIME
20 minutes plus 1 hour standing time

COOK TIME
4 minutes

Emilia is a paradise of rich and elaborate cuisine: People there eat lavishly with sophisticated spices, meat, and sausages, dining on mortadella, fresh egg pasta, and butter. Its capital city of Bologna has been dubbed La Grassa, *"the fat one," and its cuisine is warm, caring, and generous, giving you the feeling of being in an Italian mamma's kitchen. One specialty is stuffed pasta, which is very practical to use up leftovers in a particularly delicious way! This ravioli recipe makes use of* brasato *leftovers, combined with tasty ingredients to make a filling, served with a zesty ragu, as Bologna itself sets the standard here with its renowned* Ragù alla Bolognese. *The secret of Emilia's feel-good cuisine is braising, and many dishes are actually a Sunday meal, because they require a lot of time to both make and enjoy. As long as you do not shy away from the task of preparing fresh pasta dough, Emilian cooking will be easy for you.*

INGREDIENTS

2 ¼ lbs. (1 kg) pasta dough all'Uovo (see p. 84)

FOR THE FILLING
2 shallots / 2 cloves garlic

3 tbsp. extra virgin olive oil

5 ¼ oz. (150 g) brasato (see p. 184)

⅓ cup (75 g) butter, softened

2 tbsp. parsley, chopped

2 ½ oz. (70 g) Parmigiano Reggiano DOP cheese

3 tbsp. Crema di Balsamico vinegar

2 tbsp. pine nuts

A scant ½ cup (100 ml) beef stock (see p. 268)

FOR THE RAGU
1 carrot / 1 stalk celery / 1 medium onion

3 tbsp. medium extra virgin olive oil

1 tbsp. butter

8 ¾ oz. (250 g) coarsely ground beef

1 bay leaf / 2 cloves / 1 pinch nutmeg

⅝ cup (150 ml) red wine

⅝ cup (150 ml) beef stock

Fine sea salt & ground pepper

Peel and finely chop the shallots and garlic, then sauté in the olive oil in a skillet. Tear the leftover roast into small pieces; add to the skillet. Heat for 2 to 3 minutes, then puree in a tall container using an immersion blender. Add the other ingredients and combine everything to create an even, but not too fine mixture, making sure the structure of the meat is still visible. Season the filling to taste and fill into a piping bag with a large nozzle.

Roll the dough out until thin, then pipe small dabs of the filling onto one half of the dough, ¾ inch (2 cm) apart. Place the other half of the dough on top, press the pastry lightly around the filling, and use a pastry wheel to cut out square ravioli. To whip up the ragu, peel and finely dice the carrot, celery, and onion. Heat the olive oil in a skillet, add the butter, and sauté the diced vegetables. Add the ground beef and the bay leaf, cloves, and nutmeg. Season with salt and pepper. Add the red wine and let the alcohol evaporate. Then add the beef stock and let simmer for an hour. Add a bit more stock if necessary. When finished, season with salt and pepper to taste.

Add the ravioli to salted boiling water and cook for 4 minutes. Strain, then serve with the ragu on warmed plates.

OUR TIP Place some Parmesan on the table. Serve with a salad containing lots of wild greens. Heading out to the meadows to pick wild greens is a popular Italian pastime.

Spaghetti all'assassina

Braised Spaghetti, "Female Assassin-Style"

Serves 4

PREP TIME
10 minutes

COOK TIME
20 minutes

INGREDIENTS

7 oz. (200 g) tomato paste

Fine sea salt

3 dried chile peppers

2 cloves garlic

3 tbsp. extra virgin olive oil

5 ¼ oz. (150 g) passata (tomato puree)

A scant 18 oz. (500 g) spaghetti

5 sprigs flat-leaf parsley

This spaghetti dish is an Apulian specialty that originated in the city of Bari. Its bizarre name should actually be all'Assassino, *or "male assassin-style," since it was male restaurant chef Enzo Francavilla who was accused by a guest of attempting to murder him with this spicy dish, thus creating the legend behind this recipe. Aside from its spiciness, which is customizable as desired, what makes this recipe distinctive is that the pasta is not cooked in water as it usually is. The uncooked noodles are simmered in tomato broth, becoming caramelized and crispy in the process. Now a cult classic in Bari, throughout Italy, and even around the globe, this pasta dish exemplifies the sophistication of Italian cuisine with minimal use of ingredients. The spiciness epitomizes the fondness Apulians have for pepperoncini: The region's pepperoncino olive oil is also renowned for its quality, as the chiles used in making it are also grown there.*

First, make a tomato broth using water and the tomato paste. To make the broth, dissolve the tomato paste in approximately 4 ½ cups (1 L) of boiling water and season with salt to taste. Keep the broth warm. Finely chop the chiles. In a large cast-iron pan with a diameter equal to the length of the spaghetti, sauté the garlic cloves, and chile peppers in the olive oil. Add the passata and season with salt to taste. Next, add the uncooked spaghetti to the pan. Using a wooden spoon, gently move the spaghetti back and forth until the sauce covers the pasta. If the pasta sticks to the bottom of the pan, as it should, add a little tomato broth. When the broth has been completely absorbed, add some more. Carefully turn the spaghetti over, so that the top side of the pasta is now simmering on the bottom of the pan. Repeat this process until the pasta is al dente. The spaghetti should be crispy and slightly browned, but not burned!

Finely chop the parsley and sprinkle over the plated pasta portions.

OUR TIP Even though it appears easy to make, this recipe requires your undivided attention and careful handling of the pasta. The pasta should not be moved too often, or it won't be able to steep and soak up the flavors. This dish pairs well with a Sangiovese from the Marche region, with its aromas of red fruits such as blackberries and fresh plums and firm but soft tannins.

Pomodoro
Tomatoes

Hardly any other fruit (though classified by the US government as a vegetable in 1893) is as synonymous with authentic Italian cuisine as the tomato. And hardly any other fruit boasts such a rich history, transitioning from a status symbol for the few to a national treasure for all.

It all begins with the plant. The tomato is a member of the nightshade family, a family of plants that has a somewhat bad reputation, and is a close relative of belladonna, mandrake, and tobacco. The tomato plant forms bright yellow blossoms and brightly colored fruits which, thanks to their high concentration of lycopene, develop a vibrant red, a rich yellow, or an intense orange. Until just about 50 years ago, it was still pollinated by hand, but these days bumblebees have thankfully assumed responsibility for performing this task.

Even the name reflects the fascination that this fruit inspires. For a long time, it was known in Europe primarily as the love apple, paradise apple, or even golden apple (*pomo d'oro* in Italian), because the first varieties were golden yellow. Tomatoes were used as love apples for magic potions in France in the 16th century because they were believed to have an aphrodisiac effect. This is actually somewhat true; two of the substances they contain, tyramine and serotonin, actually possess mood-enhancing properties. It was not until the 19th century that the tomato was given its current name in many languages, derived from *xītomatl*, which means "belly button of fat water" in the Aztec language.

Hernán Cortés brought the tomato from the Aztecs to Europe as a souvenir for the Spanish royal family and, by way of their territories such as Sardinia and Naples, to Italy. So it was that on October 31, 1548, Tuscan Grand Duke Cosimo de Medici held a basket of tomatoes in his hands for the first time—and probably did not know exactly what to do with them. Admittedly, these fruits were rare and were planted as exotic treasures in the gardens of the upper classes, as they testified to the wealth of their owners while impressing visitors. However, they were considered poisonous, and it was probably exactly this that aroused the interest of the Medici family. They carried out certain experiments with the nightshade plant, but these failed to produce the desired outcome when used on their adversaries. It was not until a century later that the fruit ended up on the plate of the Spanish Viceroy of Naples. His chef Antonio Latini composed the first recipes with tomatoes, which quickly caught on and became famous as *alla spagnola*, or "the Spanish way." So, it was the Italians who played the biggest role in the triumphant introduction of the tomato to the kitchens of the world. Not only do we have them to thank for an extremely versatile and tasty ingredient, tomatoes are also really healthy. Although tomatoes are made up of 95% water, they are chock full of vitamins, including A, B1, B2, C, E, and niacin, and also have an antioxidant effect, boosting the immune system. If only the Medicis had known!

"It would take a lifetime to know everything about tomatoes."—Ferran Adrià

But there are a few things you should know:

Fresh tomatoes are best stored separately from other fruit and vegetables, as they release ethylene during storage, causing neighboring fruits to ripen and spoil more quickly. They should not be stored in the refrigerator as they lose their flavor and become mealy. Tomato plants themselves are quite sensitive. In addition to color, smell, and shape, they also signal stress through sounds, which, however, are in the ultrasonic range and not audible to humans.

It is claimed that the best tomatoes ripen in Apulia. And in Sicily. And on Mount Vesuvius. And certainly elsewhere too. There are more than 3,100 varieties worldwide and at least as many varieties again that have not been registered and do not have their own specific name. However, the most important varieties are the following:

San Marzano "Campania's red gold" grows at the foot of Mount Vesuvius, around the village of San Marzano. This variety has been cultivated ever since Ferdinand de Bourbon received it as a gift from Spain in 1770. Unfortunately, by the 1980s, this variety had almost completely disappeared because it had to be harvested painstakingly and individually by hand, but thanks to a team of researchers, several farmers, and the slow food movement, it was rediscovered and now graces authentic Neapolitan pizzas. San Marzano tomatoes develop their full flavor—a strong bitter-sweet taste with balanced acidic nuances—in cans when they are gently preserved in a water bath at exactly 212 °F (100 °C). San Marzano DOP is the perfect base for sauces, salsa, and traditional pizza.

Piennolo These little treasures are cultivated on the slopes of Mount Vesuvius. The sun is merciless here and the soil particularly rich in minerals, giving the tomatoes a firm skin, plenty of minerals, and a very special sweetness. Immediately after harvesting, they are tied together by hand to form the eponymous *piennoli*, the large grape-like clusters, which will keep for a whole year. This is also why these tomatoes have been depicted in the famed Neapolitan nativity scenes since the 18th century—they are a traditional ingredient in the local cuisine at Christmas time. The Piennolo del Vesuvio DOP is perfect for enhancing seafood dishes, pizza, bruschetta, and buffalo mozzarella, offering a rich, tangy flavor.

Corbarino Those who like it very tangy and flavorful will be delighted with this historic variety from the Naples region. Grown in the Corbara hills of the Campania region, these egg-shaped cocktail tomatoes are firm, very flavorful, and easy to slice, making them ideal for salads and appetizers. They are also wonderful as a finishing touch in baked fish dishes or pasta bianca, pasta dishes without tomato sauce, with these fresh tomatoes adding a burst of flavor.

Ciliegino Despite its diminutive size, the cherry tomato is considered the ancestor of the modern cultivated tomato and is believed to have first been domesticated in Mexico. The earliest mention of it in Europe was in the year 1623 in Swiss botanist Caspar Bauhin's standard work *Pinax theatri botanici*. Thriving in the mineral-rich volcanic soil at the base of Mount Etna, these Sicilian tomatoes develop an exceptional flavor. Harvested at the peak of ripeness, they are made into sughi and bruschetta spreads. If you are lucky enough to find them at your local vegetable shop, you can savor them in a salad, paired with buffalo mozzarella, or simply as fresh tomatoes atop bruschetta.

Cuore di bue This distinctive oxheart tomato is thought to have originated in Russia in the late 19th century, and quickly found its way to Italy. It is undoubtedly the heavyweight among tomatoes, and not just in terms of taste. Its firm flesh and considerable size (up to 2+ pounds or 1,000 grams!) make it the number one choice in Italian kitchens. They are preferred to be eaten raw and still slightly green, as the acid to sugar ratio is ideal in terms of taste at this stage. That's what makes *Cuore di bue* the centerpiece of salads and starters. Ideal for summer feasts, this tomato adds a flavorful touch to any meal.

Datterino This small but immensely flavorful date tomato originally comes from Sicily. It is characterized by its fine fruitiness and distinct sweetness. *Datterino* tomatoes are ideal for creating elegant sauces, pairing beautifully with tender shrimp, or enhancing vegetable dishes.

Grappolo This tomato, which is usually purchased still attached to the vine, is one of the most popular varieties in Italy and abroad. Its strong and hearty flavor has earned it a regular place on our plates. *Grappolo* tomatoes are best served in salads or with starters.

Perino In its native region of southern Italy, this extremely successful cross between the zesty date tomato and the sweet cherry tomato is considered the best of all small tomatoes, adding a very special touch to sauces, bruschetta varieties, and salads.

Pachino This variety has been cultivated in the Sicilian town of the same name for around 100 years. According to the locals, it also grows in slightly salty soil, which gives it a very special taste. Pachino IGP are perfect for adding the final zing to exquisite sauces, pasta dishes, and salads.

Roma This plum tomato is a real success story—it can be found all around the world, but nowhere is it as good and as flavorful as in Italy. With its thin skin and characteristic sweetness, the Roma tomato is particularly suitable for tomato sauces, canning, or making dried tomatoes.

"The tomato must always be relaxed. Just like the hand that touches it."
—Filippo D'Acunzi

One reason why the tomato is probably one of the most popular ingredients in the kitchen is because it inspires creativity and has such versatility, as attested to by the various following forms:

Passata Fresh, ripe tomatoes are pureed together with their juices to create a thick mixture for *primi piatti*, sauces, and tomato soups.

Polpa Tomatoes are peeled, cut into small pieces, and combined with passata to form a base for bruschetta, sauces, meat, fish and, of course, pizza.

Pelati Whole tomatoes are blanched, peeled, and preserved in their juice. Later, they are crushed during cooking to give fast dishes the perfect amount of freshness.

Concentrato To make tomato paste, the tomatoes are crushed and cooked, filtered, and then further reduced until they are perfect for seasoning and adding color to stews and legumes.

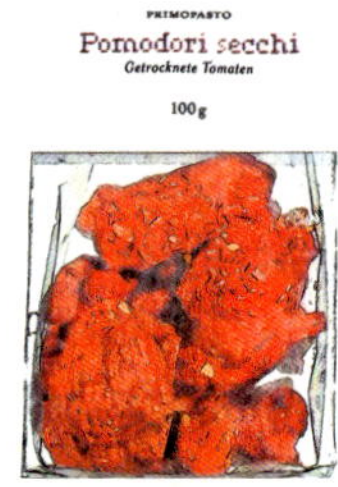

Secchi To preserve tomatoes, they are cut in half, salted, and left to dry in the hot Italian sun. These sun-dried tomatoes lend their wonderfully hearty flavor to antipasti.

Semisecchi / al forno Unlike secchi, these tomatoes are not dried in the sun; they are dried gently in the oven at low temperatures, allowing them to retain much of their freshness and a balance of sweetness and acidity.

Sugo Classic Italian tomato sauce is the base for many traditional recipes. Fresh tomatoes are cooked with celery, carrots, onions, and garlic.

1876

Tortelloni con Lenticchie

Tortelloni with Lentils and Wild Boar Salami

Serves 4

PREP TIME
30 minutes plus 70 minutes dough prep

COOK TIME
35 minutes

INGREDIENTS

2 ¼ lbs. (1 kg) Pasta all'Uovo dough (see p. 84)

14 oz. (400 g) spinach

1 shallot / 2 cloves garlic

5 tbsp. extra virgin olive oil

7 ¾ oz. (220 g) buffalo ricotta cheese

1 lemon

1 tbsp. pine nuts, roasted

½ tsp. peperoncino

Fine sea salt

Freshly ground pepper

FOR THE LENTILS AND SALAMI

3 tbsp. robust extra virgin olive oil

1 handful sage leaves, fresh

1 onion / 1 clove garlic / 1 carrot

3 ½ oz. (100 g) Umbrian mountain lentils

A scant 3 cups (700 ml) vegetable stock (see p. 267)

1 bay leaf

Fine sea salt

A generous 2 oz. (60 g) wild boar salami

2 tbsp. balsamic vinegar, aged

This dish with lentils and wild boar salami is hearty and perfect for fall. The deep-fried sage and balsamic vinegar give this recipe even more flavor. A strong red wine such as a Chianti Classico or a Montepulciano d'Abruzzo pairs well with this tasty dish. But you can just as easily eat this tortelloni stuffed with spinach and ricotta in the summertime. It tastes delicious with a simple sauce of browned butter with deep-fried sage leaves, black pepper, and plenty of Parmigiano Reggiano. Anyone who has ever made fresh homemade filled pasta will appreciate the difference compared to store-bought pasta. If you enjoy making fresh pasta, it is a good idea to buy a pasta maker or, get a long, thin rolling pin like those used in Italy. There are various sizes; for this recipe we recommend one ranging up to 30 inches (80 centimeters) in length.

Rinse the spinach. Finely dice the shallot and garlic. Heat the olive oil in a pan; sauté the shallot and garlic. Add the wet spinach, cover with the lid, and let briefly wilt.

Place the ricotta in a large bowl. Drain the spinach in a sieve, squeezing well to remove any excess liquid, and add to the ricotta. Use a zester to zest the lemon. Finely chop the pine nuts. Add the zest and pine nuts to the ricotta, generously season with the peperoncino, salt, and pepper to taste, and fill into a piping bag with a large nozzle, if you have one. If not, you can also use a tablespoon.

Roll out the dough thinly, then use a pastry wheel to cut squares slightly larger than 3 × 3 inches (8 × 8 cm). Place filling in the center of the squares using the piping bag or tablespoon. Moisten the dough edges, fold each square diagonally to form a triangle, and press down. Twist the ends around your finger to form the tortelloni. Place on a board dusted with durum wheat semolina flour.

To make the lentils, heat the olive oil in a skillet and fry the sage leaves until crispy, then remove. Finely dice the onion, garlic, and carrot; sauté in the sage oil for two minutes. Add the lentils and vegetable stock and simmer with the bay leaf for around 30 minutes uncovered, until the stock has cooked off. Remove from heat; season with salt. Thinly slice the wild boar salami.

Cook the tortelloni in salted water for 4 to 5 minutes. Arrange on deep plates with the lentils, wild boar salami, and sage leaves. Season with balsamic vinegar.

OUR TIP *Tortelloni* are a good size for beginners when it comes to shaping filled pasta. Tortellini, the smaller version, are a little more challenging.

Nero

Penne con Salsiccia

Penne with Italian Sausage

Serves 4

PREP TIME
20 minutes

COOK TIME
Approximately 2 hours

INGREDIENTS

1 small onion

2 cloves garlic

1 small carrot

1 stalk celery

1 bunch parsley

A scant 18 oz. (500 g) salsiccia

2 tbsp. (30 ml) extra virgin olive oil

1 bay leaf

1 tsp. dried chile

1 tbsp. seasoned tomato paste

A scant ½ cup (100 ml) red wine

28 oz. (800 g) San Marzano tomatoes (can)

1 pinch cinnamon

1 pinch ground cloves

1½ oz. (40 g) Parmigiano Reggiano

14 oz. (400 g) penne pasta

Salt, pepper

OUR TIP We recommend a dry, fruity red wine that does not contain a lot of tannins, such as a Montepulciano d'Abruzzo DOC.

This recipe is easy and quick to make, but takes a while to cook. The result is an incredibly flavorful sugo, or tomato sauce, with a deep, well-seasoned flavor. The secret is a pinch of cinnamon. It rounds off the taste and takes the acidic edge off the tomato sauce. But the star of the show is salsiccia, a fresh Tuscan sausage made from coarsely ground pork and seasoned with fennel and herbs. High-quality ingredients are all the more important in simple recipes, so we recommend shopping at an Italian supermarket for your salsiccia, and your tomatoes too: Canned whole San Marzano tomatoes, picked in Campania at peak ripeness and immediately processed, have a more intense flavor than any fresh tomato. They are cooked in a water bath before canning, helping them later develop their full flavor in the can. The harmony between sweetness and acidity is unparalleled, making a simple sugo a gourmet food.

Finely dice the onion and garlic. Trim, peel, and finely dice the carrot. Trim the celery, remove any strings, and finely dice. Finely chop the thick bottom sections of the parsley stalks; set aside. Finely chop the parsley leaves and the rest of the stalks.

Remove the sausage from its casing. In a large frying pan, heat the olive oil and brown the sausage meat on all sides. Using a wooden spoon, break it apart into pieces and sauté for about 5 minutes until it is evenly browned (avoid sautéing too long, as this will make the meat too dry). Using a slotted spoon, remove the meat from the pan and set aside.

In the fat in the pan, fry the onions, garlic, carrots, celery, parsley stalks, bay leaf, chile, and tomato paste. Season with salt and cook over medium to high heat for about 10 minutes, stirring regularly. Deglaze with red wine and cook until the liquid is almost gone. Add the tomatoes and season with the cinnamon, cloves, and pepper.

Cover and simmer gently over low heat for 30 minutes. Add the sausage meat to the sauce and continue to simmer for an additional 30 minutes.

Cook the pasta in salted boiling water until al dente, then drain well in a sieve.

Add the chopped parsley leaves to the finished sauce. Coarsely grate the Parmesan. Combine the pasta and sauce; arrange on preheated pasta dishes. Sprinkle with Parmesan and serve immediately.

Minestrone alla Genovese

Genovese Vegetable Soup

Serves 4

PREP TIME
20 minutes

COOK TIME
50 minutes

INGREDIENTS

1 bunch chard (approx. 12 ¼ oz. / 350 g)

3 ½ oz. (100 g) spinach leaves

4 leaves cavolo nero (also known as Tuscan kale)

3 small zucchini

1 eggplant

1 ¾ oz. (50 g) pumpkin

3 small waxy potatoes

1 small carrot

2 stalks celery

1 onion

3 ½ oz. (100 g) peas

3 ½ oz. (100 g) green beans

3 ½ oz. (100 g) borlotti beans (cranberry beans)

Fine sea salt

4 tbsp. robust extra virgin olive oil

5 ¼ oz. (150 g) small pasta, such as Sardinia's maloreddus or cocciule pasta

4 tbsp. (60 g) Pesto alla Genovese (see p. 262)

8 tbsp. (60 g) Parmigiano Reggiano DOP cheese, freshly grated

The Ligurians love vegetables, and there are certainly plenty of them here. Paired with Pesto alla Genovese *(see p. 262), this recipe is a quintessential staple of traditional Ligurian home cooking. The ingredients may vary, rice can be added to the soup instead of pasta, or the pesto can be added right to the pot. This hearty minestrone is a lavish dish, reminiscent of a grandmother patiently making it with bountiful produce from her own garden. The name minestrone is derived from the word* minestra, *meaning "soup," but colloquially it also means "hodgepodge." This gives vegetable lovers the flexibility to select vegetables based on seasonal availability and their personal preference. But the soup should always be nice and green, and pesto is an integral part. Chard, an essential vegetable in Ligurian cuisine, is definitely the Viani family's go-to vegetable.*

Clean and trim all the vegetables and finely dice or cut into coarse strips (chard, spinach, cavolo nero). Fill a large pot with 9 cups (2 L) of water, add salt and 1 tablespoon of olive oil. Add the vegetables to the cold water, then simmer for 30 to 40 minutes. When the vegetables are almost cooked and still somewhat al dente, remove half of the soup from the pot, puree it, and return it to the pot. Season to taste with salt. Bring the soup to a boil and add the pasta to cook. Pour the portions in heated soup plates. Before serving, add a dash of olive oil, and 1 tablespoon each of *Pesto alla Genovese* and Parmesan to each serving.

OUR TIP As not all vegetables are always readily available or may have a short season, you can use canned borlotti beans, for example, and add them later, toward the end of the cooking time.

Linguine al limone

Linguine with Lemon

Serves 4

PREP TIME
10 minutes

COOK TIME
Approximately 8 minutes

INGREDIENTS

Fine sea salt

2 organic Sicilian lemons

12 ¼ oz. (350 g) linguine

½ cup plus 2 tbsp. (150 ml) lemon-flavored extra virgin olive oil

Freshly ground black pepper

1 ¾ oz. (50 g) Parmigiano Reggiano cheese, grated

1 tbsp. flat-leaf parsley, chopped

This recipe from Sicily combines two of the island's wonderful foods in an especially straightforward way: olive oil and lemons. Ripe Sicilian lemons are in a class of their own. Along with their acidity, they also have a pleasant, sweet fruitiness, and the lemon oils made by pressing olives and lemons are a specialty of the island's oil mills. This simple recipe, with its fresh lemon zest, is a minimalist pasta dish that pays tribute to Sicily and epitomizes Italy's culinary culture, alongside classics like Aglio, Olio e Peperoncino, Cacio e Pepe, *and* Burro e Parmiggiano Reggiano. *The lemons should have a smooth, firm peel and the zest should be fine and small, making it easy to distribute it well throughout the pasta. The result is a mouthful of Sicily at its purest.*

In a large pot, salt the water and bring to a boil. Meanwhile, rinse the lemons in hot water and use a zester to scrape the zest off. In a large bowl, combine the oil with the zest, black pepper, and some Parmesan. Once the water boils, add the linguine to the pot and cook until al dente. Reserve some of the cooking water and add it to the bowl along with the pasta. Combine well, then fold in the parsley. Divide between four deep plates and sprinkle the remaining Parmesan on top.

OUR TIP Good lemon oil comes from good millers. They press the lemons together with the olives, allowing the flavors of the fruit to instantly infuse into the oil. Nothing is added after pressing. It is worth choosing a high-quality lemon oil, making sure to read the label carefully!

Ravioli del Plin con Ricotta al forno

Little Ravioli with Baked Ricotta

Serves 4 to 6

PREP TIME
30 minutes plus dough prep

COOK TIME
20 minutes

INGREDIENTS

A scant 18 oz. (500 g) Pasta all'Uovo dough (see p. 84)

10 ½ oz. (300 g) fresh whole spinach

FOR THE FILLING
14 oz. (400 g) wild herbs

A scant 4 oz. (110 g) grissini breadsticks, finely grated

3 tbsp. whole milk

A scant ⅓ cup (70 ml) robust extra virgin olive oil

A generous ⅓ cup (80 g) butter

1 ¾ oz. (50 g) pecorino cheese

Fine sea salt & ground pepper

FOR THE SAUCE
⅔ cup (150 g) butter

5 ¼ oz. (150 g) buffalo ricotta cheese

1 organic lemon / 1 sprig rosemary

Fine sea salt & ground pepper

5 tbsp. robust extra virgin olive oil

7 oz. (200 g) Datterino tomatoes

8 to 10 basil leaves

2 sprigs flat-leaf parsley

1 ¾ oz. (50 g) capers in sea salt, rinsed

1 tbsp. balsamic vinegar, aged

Stuffed pasta is a veritable playground for the taste buds. It is important to ensure the ingredients' consistency and seasoning harmonize with the sauce, whether it is a simple butter and sage sauce or a more elaborate variety. Overcoming any fear of making homemade filled pasta opens up a realm of possibilities to experiment with an array of creative fillings, such as vegetables, salad greens, herbs, mushrooms, meat, ham, and various cheeses. This recipe is Mediterranean in nature, with capers, tomatoes, herbs, and the more intense buffalo ricotta cheese. Any pasta filling needs a lot of seasoning if it is to be the focus of the primo; or all your work will have been in vain. The dough itself can also be varied by using spinach, basil, nettles, wild garlic, or tomatoes.

Rinse and puree the raw spinach, then knead it into the pasta dough.

Rinse the wild herbs (such as borage, nettles, ground elder, and dandelion); remove the woody and fibrous stems. In a medium pot, bring salted water to a boil, add the herbs to briefly soften. Drain the herbs in a sieve, rinse in cold water and finely chop. Soak the grated grissini in the milk and olive oil until you can form shapes. Add the softened butter, finely grated pecorino, and wild herbs; combine well. Season well with salt and pepper.

Roll out the pasta dough thinly; cut into long strips 4 ½ inches (11 cm) wide. Place filling on half the dough strips ¾ inch (2 cm) apart, 2 inches (5 cm) from the edge. Place the plain dough strips on top of the strips with filling. Moisten the edges; press together. Separate the ravioli with a pastry wheel, then press the edges together. Place on a board sprinkled with semolina flour; set aside.

In a skillet over medium heat, brown the butter for 10 to 15 minutes without burning, set aside. Preheat the oven to 375 °F (190 °C) using top and bottom heat. Zest the lemon and finely chop the rosemary; combine with the ricotta. Season with salt and pepper. On a baking tray, spread the ricotta ⅜ inch (1 cm) thick, drizzle with olive oil and bake for 15 minutes.

To make the sauce, juice the zested lemon. Quarter the tomatoes, tear the basil leaves into pieces; finely chop the parsley and half of the capers. Combine the tomato, basil, parsley, and chopped capers; season with olive oil, lemon juice, and balsamic vinegar.

Boil the ravioli in salted water for 2 minutes, sauté briefly in the browned butter. Combine with the sauce. Crumble the baked ricotta and sprinkle it on top. Sprinkle with the remaining capers.

Tortellini alla panna

Tortellini in Cream with Blue Cheese Filling

Serves 4 to 6

PREP TIME
10 minutes plus 70 minutes dough prep

COOK TIME
10 minutes

INGREDIENTS

A scant 18 oz. (500 g) Pasta all'Uovo dough (see p. 84)

8 ¾ oz. (250 g) buffalo milk blue cheese

1 ¾ oz. (50 g) Piedmont hazelnuts IGP, chopped

4 ¼ oz. (120 g) ricotta cheese

1 egg yolk

1 tbsp. fresh flat-leaf parsley, finely chopped

½ organic lemon

Whole milk, optional

Fine sea salt

Freshly ground pepper

⅝ cup (150 ml) whipping cream

Tortellini in a cream sauce certainly make the most obvious statement possible about Emilian cuisine: We are not afraid of fat; we love it! Added to that is the finesse of a filling encased in the finest of egg pasta. An erotic culinary legend tells the tale of how tortellini came by its unusual shape. A beautiful traveler, who, unbeknownst to her hosts was actually the goddess Venus herself, was staying at an inn in Bologna and, as she lay down naked to rest, the cook peeked through the keyhole and caught a glimpse of her navel. Inspired by this, he went straight to his kitchen and fashioned the first tortellini based on the navel of Venus. The production of tortellini is said to date back to the 12th century, with the earliest known written recipe appearing around 1300. Even today, tortellini remains a dish for festive family occasions in Italian households.

Finely dice the blue cheese. Stir in the hazelnuts. Fold in the ricotta and egg yolk. Add the parsley. Rinse the lemon in hot water and use a zester to peel off a thin layer of zest, add to the mixture and stir in. If the mixture seems too dry, add milk. Season with salt and pepper to taste.

Roll out the pasta dough thinly. Use a pastry wheel to cut it into squares 2 ½ × 2 ½ inches (6 × 6 cm). Using a teaspoon or piping nozzle for dough, place the filling in the center of the squares. Fold the dough squares diagonally to form a triangle. Brush the edges with water and press down, then roll up the tortellini and fold the outer corners over your finger.

In a pan, heat the whipping cream for cooking the tortellini and bring to a boil. Add the tortellini after 3 minutes and cook for around 5 minutes.

OUR TIP This recipe is wonderfully simple and can be made with many different tortellini fillings. A bit of Parmigiano Reggiano on top makes it even more special.

Pasta

Pasta

Pasta is serious business, especially in Italy, where it is exclusively reserved for the second course of an authentically Italian meal. But above all because every region, every town, and every village, no matter how small, has its own pasta tradition, which is usually based on some legend or another. Anyone who dares to combine the ingredients incorrectly is guilty of an almost unforgivable crime.

Most original pasta dishes do not appear to be particularly challenging to make, given their minimalistic ingredients. But it is precisely this simplicity that makes the details all the more important.

To be more specific, it is about the feel, look, and shape of the pasta, because they all have a significant influence on how the taste is experienced. As the structure of a pasta determines how much sauce clings to it, there is an ideal pasta variety for every sauce. Long pasta shapes such as spaghetti, linguine, and bucatini are particularly suitable for sughi that are smooth yet rich. A meat ragu is usually served with wide, textured egg noodles, and never with spaghetti, please. Vegetable sughi, on the other hand, are best served with penne, rigatoni, or *tortiglioni* and other short forms, as the heavy pieces of vegetables get caught in the holes and the sauce is trapped in the grooves of the pasta. The larger pasta shapes such as lasagna, cannelloni, and *conchiglioni*, are primarily designed for oven-baked dishes because they are easy to fill and bake.

One thing is certain though, around 2,000 years ago, noodles were not only eaten by the Chinese; the Greeks and Etruscans dined on them too. In any event, strings made from wheat were cooked in Sicily in the 12th century, and were so popular that they were exported to the entire Mediterranean region. Pasta soon became so important that prices were regulated and pasta makers were exempt from taxes and customs duties. Yet pasta was still being trampled underfoot. Before there were food processors and pasta machines, the firm pasta dough was worked by being stomped on by foot.

Another very important factor for high-quality pasta is slow drying at low temperatures, a process that can sometimes take several days. This preserves its proteins and starch better, which not only makes the pasta easier to digest, it also gives it a much better flavor—indicated by the "*Lenta Essiccazione*" label on the packaging.

Properly dried, pasta secca will keep forever. If it doesn't end up in the pot at some point, that is. Stirring it every now and then is enough to prevent it from sticking together—oil should never be added to the pasta water! Because this is something that is also sacred to Italians—a good sauce needs good pasta water to get creamy and cling to the pasta.

And when the perfect harmony of textures and flavors spreads in your mouth, it becomes clear that pasta makes people happy. Seriously.

"It will be maccheroni, I swear to you, that will unite Italy."—Giuseppe Garibaldi

But all pastas are not equal. There are not only major differences in appearance, but also in the way they are made:

Pasta secca Durum wheat pasta is made without eggs. Its only ingredients are water and *grano duro*, which has extra sticky properties and only grows in southern Italy. This gives spaghetti, penne, trofie, orecchiette, and many others their typical firm, al dente texture and beautiful golden yellow color.

Pasta all'uovo In northern and central Italy, pasta is made from soft wheat flour. Here, eggs add even more of a binding effect, so that the dough for tagliatelle, pappardelle, lasagna, ravioli, and the like can be made wafer-thin and sometimes even feel like tissue paper on your tongue.

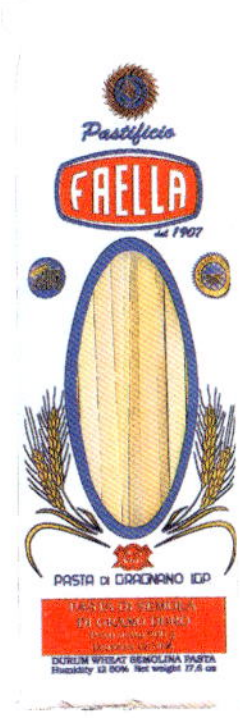

Pasta di Gragnano The world's only pasta with an IGP seal is made exclusively with flour from local durum wheat and fresh water from the nearby Lattari mountains and shaped using special bronze dies. This gives the pasta its typical rough surface, which is retained even after cooking.

However, the drying of the pasta has always been of the utmost importance. In the mid-19th century, the streets in Gragnano were even planned in such a way that the wind from the sea could easily reach the pasta drying in the open air, ensuring optimal texture and flavor.

Gnocchi These little dumplings, also called *Nocken* in Alpine countries, originated in northern Italy. The version popular in Southern Italy uses wheat. Potatoes are used to make the famed *Gnocchi di patate*. There are also countless local variations.

Pizzoccheri In the Valtellina valley in Lombardy and in the neighboring Val Poschiavo and Lake Como, pasta is made from buckwheat and wheat flour. It is typically combined with savoy cabbage and potatoes, then served with cheese.

Croxetti The round coins are a special expression of the unique pasta culture from Liguria. Aristocratic families there used to have stamps with their coat of arms, which they used to mark the pasta they made themselves. Croxetti pair very well with creamy sauces, such as salsa di noci.

"The pasta factory is right in the middle of the fields. Because that way we are always close to our wheat."—Massimo Mancini

Every sauce has its pasta. The Italians have come up with an almost inconceivable number of shapes and sizes for their pasta. Here is just a selection:

Bavette This typical Ligurian pasta is shaped to release a lot of starch into the pasta water. It is perfect for pesto, as its rough surface absorbs the oily sauce well. If bavette is unavailable, trofie pasta is the only alternative to eat *Pesto alla Genovese* with.

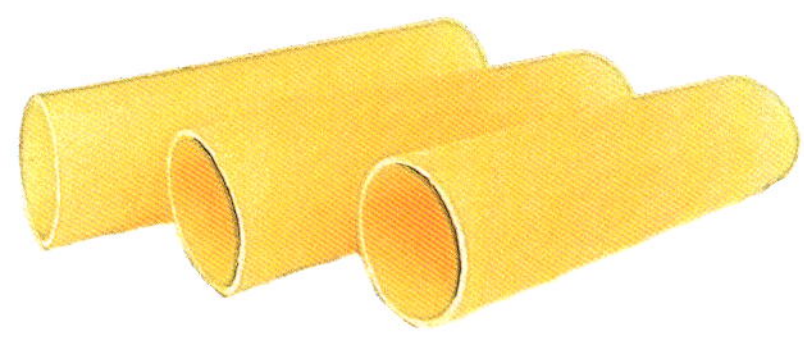

Cannelloni These large tubes are pre-cooked, then filled with ragu or ricotta and spinach, and baked with béchamel sauce and Parmesan cheese.

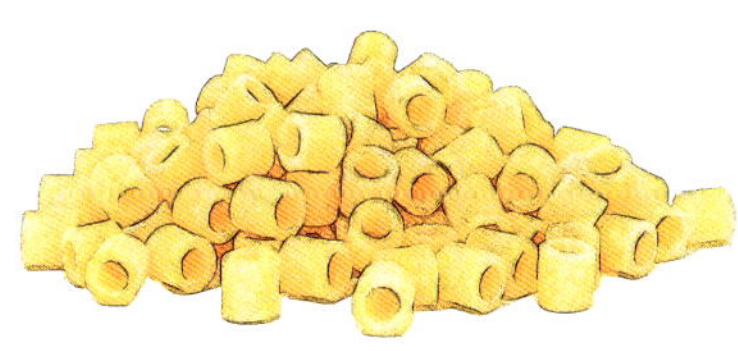

Ditali This thimble-shaped pasta is mainly found in southern Italy, where it is primarily used in soups and stews such as minestrone, *Pasta e Fagioli*, and so on.

Fregola sarda In Sardinia, these small, irregular balls are rolled in a large clay bowl and roasted in the oven. This gives them their distinctive flavor and hearty wheat taste. Perfect for sottos, soups, and stews.

Fusilli Sicily and Sardinia are at odds with the rest of southern Italy over the copyright to this spiral-shaped pasta. In the past, strings of dough were wound around knitting needles by hand. Today, this pasta, also known as *spirelli*, is so popular because its shape makes it perfect for almost any type of sauce.

Penne The name comes from *penna*, the Latin word for quill (like the English pen), because the ends are always cut at an angle. This is also why it goes well with almost any chunky sauce, as smooth *penne lisce* or *penne rigate* with ridges.

Tortellini This pasta specialty from Bologna, filled with all sorts of things and expertly folded from a single piece, is known the world over. It was invented in Bologna at an inn that Venus, the goddess of beauty and love, is said to have visited herself. The chef caught a glimpse of her navel through the keyhole of her room and, impressed by its beauty, created tortellini in her honor.

Lasagne The Romans were already fond of *lagana*, which was baked in a thin layer and topped with varioussweet and savory ingredients. Lasagna as we know it today has only been around since the 13th century.

Ravioli First mentioned in Bocaccio's *Decameron*, ravioli is not folded like tortellini, but instead sealed with a second sheet of dough. The most wonderful fillings can be found inside—from meat or fish to vegetables or cheese.

Trofie The name for this small, twisted pasta with tapered ends goes back to the Genovese word *strofissià*, which refers to the scrubbing motion of the hands when forming it. This pasta shape was not invented until the late 18th century, and is the only permissible alternative to bavette for eating with pesto.

Maccheroni Maccheroni or bucatini, as the long version of the tubular pasta is called, is thought to have originated in Sicily. At the very least, it was described in 1154 by an astonished Islamic scholar in his notes on the customs of the Sicilian population.

Spaghetti Originally from Sicily, these strings are now a classic all over Italy for *Pomodoro*, *Aglio Olio*, or *Carbonara*. What you should never do, no matter where you are, is to break the spaghetti before cooking!

Vermicelli The first dishes with these "little worms" appeared in ancient Rome. Over time, vermicelli became synonymous with a special type of thin pasta sold north of the Alps by 18th-century Tyrolean traders. Today's version has a much rougher surface than spaghetti and absorbs a lot more water when cooked, making it much thicker.

Orecchiette These "little ears" from Puglia are typically shaped by rolling a small piece of dough over a wooden board or table using your thumb. In the narrow streets of Gallipoli, they are primarily made by nuns.

Tagliatelle The *Accademia Italiana della cucina* in Bologna has kept a perfect tagliatelle pattern in gold since 1972—all tagliatelle must be made to the millimeter according to this pattern to be entitled to bear this name. This classic pasta from Emilia-Romagna is perfect for thick ground meat sauces.

Pasta e Lenticchie

Pasta with Lentils

Serves 4

PREP TIME
20 minutes

COOK TIME
Approximately 40 minutes

INGREDIENTS

A generous 1 oz. (30 g) pancetta (pork belly) or guanciale (cured meat from pork cheek)

2 tbsp. mild extra virgin olive oil

1 to 2 stalks celery, finely diced

1 red chile pepper, de-seeded and chopped

1 clove garlic, peeled and crushed

4 ½ to 5 oz. (120 to 140 g) Umbrian mountain lentils

2 cups + 4 teaspoons (500 ml) vegetable stock, warmed (see p. 267)

1 tbsp. triple concentrated tomato paste

Parmigiano-Reggiano rind, optional

1 bouquet garni, with fresh rosemary, thyme, and sage

Fine sea salt

A generous 6 ¼ oz. (180 g) pasta mista (mixed small pasta shapes)

1 bunch flat-leaf parsley

Freshly ground pepper

Parmigiano Reggiano, as desired

Italy's cucina povera, or peasant cuisine, has long enjoyed popularity. Its simplicity is often lauded by those who have the means to indulge in more extravagant fare. But there was a time when it really was what its name suggests: cuisine for the less fortunate. One good example of this is pasta mista from Naples, a combination of pasta remnants from pasta manufacturers that we also use in this recipe. Everything that was left over from the production was tossed together and sold by weight. The city of Naples endured great poverty, prompting many of its residents to emigrate to America. During this period, pasta dishes adding ingredients like legumes and potatoes became prevalent in the city. With simple ingredients such as chile peppers, herbs, and, in the best case, a bit of bacon, the improvisation and cooking skills of housewives and mothers during that period made sure we could continue to enjoy these tasty dishes today.

Cut the pancetta or guanciale into thin slices. Heat the olive oil in a large pot and fry the meat. As soon as it turns a nice color and gets a little crispy, add the celery, chile pepper, and garlic. Simmer over low heat for 2 to 3 minutes. When the garlic takes on color, remove it. Add the lentils and simmer for another 2 to 3 minutes. Add about 3 ladlefuls of vegetable stock, dissolve the tomato paste in a little stock and add it as well, then add the Parmesan rind (if desired). Add the herb garni and some salt. Cook for around 20 minutes on low heat.

When the lentils are still al dente but softened, remove the herbs and add the pasta. Check whether more salt is needed. Add enough vegetable stock to cover the pasta. Cook the lentil and pasta mixture for approximately 10 minutes, stirring continuously. Its consistency should be thick and stew-like at the end. Finely chop the parsley and stir it in. Season with a little Parmigiano Reggiano and black pepper to taste.

OUR TIP Even if it appears easy to make, this recipe requires your undivided attention and careful handling of the pasta. The pasta should not be moved too often, or it won't be able to stew and soak up the flavors. This dish pairs well with a Sangiovese from the Marche region, with its aromas of red fruits like blackberries and fresh plums and firm but soft tannins.

Farinata di Ceci al rosmarino

Chickpea Pancakes with Rosemary

Makes 4 shallow baking trays, each 14 inches (36 cm) in diameter

PREP TIME
10 minutes plus at least 4 hours standing time

BAKE TIME
20 minutes

INGREDIENTS

5 cups (500 g) besan (chickpea flour, gram flour, garbanzo flour)

Fine sea salt

½ cup plus 2 tbsp. (150 ml) mild extra virgin olive oil

1 sprig rosemary

Olive oil for the trays

Freshly ground black pepper

Salt flakes

OUR TIP Instead of rosemary, you can use onion or leek rings, Gorgonzola, *stracchino* cream cheese, or *salsiccia*. Vermentino from Liguria and Vino rosato are refreshing wines to enjoy with your *farinata*.

Along with focaccia, farinata is the ultimate Ligurian street food, having originated in Genoa. This pancake made of besan, water, and olive oil is as simple as it is delicious; its crispiness and aroma are truly sensational. If you find yourself in Genoa or Savona in the wintertime, be sure to stop by a cozy sciamadda, *aglow with a wood-fired oven full of round farinata trays of galvanized copper.* Sciamadde *are takeaways and simple trattorias that specialize in farinata. They get their name from the word for flames in the Genovese dialect. The round farinata trays have a diameter of 14 or 16 ½ inches (36 or 42 cm) and are part copper to ensure the heat is distributed evenly. A rim around the outside of the tray comes in handy when it is time to use a wooden stick to pull the tray out of the oven. Of course, you can also prepare farinata in a pan. Although it will not come close to the original made in a wood-fired oven, it will still taste fantastic. Farinata is ideal for anyone on a gluten-free diet.*

Put the *besan* in a large bowl, then gradually add 6 ½ cups (1.5 L) cold water while whisking vigorously to prevent lumps. Stir in the salt and olive oil. Once the batter is creamy, cover and let stand at room temperature for at least 4 hours or refrigerate overnight to allow the flour to absorb the water. Skim off any foam that forms on top.

Preheat the oven to 480 °F (250 °C), or as hot as 575 to 660 °F (300 to 350 °C) if possible. Convection is not recommended if you want to achieve perfectly crispy results. Generously oil the farinata tray and spread the batter to a height of just under ½ inch (1 cm), or about 5 ladlefuls of batter per tray. Gently mix the batter with the olive oil already in the tray, creating lots of little droplets on the surface. Pluck the rosemary needles from the sprig and sprinkle evenly over the batter, pushing them down into the batter a bit to prevent burning. Carefully place the tray in the oven.

The farinata takes about 8 minutes to cook at very high heat, and up to 20 minutes at 482 °F (250 °C). After a few minutes, turn the tray to ensure it cooks evenly. It is done when a golden crust has formed on the surface and the inside is still creamy. Season with black pepper and salt flakes before serving; eat immediately. Tomato and onion salad tastes very good with farinata.

Zuppa tradizionale

Tuscan Peasant Soup with Legumes

Serves 4

PREP TIME
15 minutes plus at least 8 hours to soak

COOK TIME
Approximately 1 hour

INGREDIENTS

A scant 18 oz. (500 g) mixed dry legumes, such as cannellini beans, peas, lentils, chickpeas, and fava beans

1 porcini mushroom bouillon cube

1 clove garlic

1 onion

1 carrot

1 stalk celery

2 tbsp. medium extra virgin olive oil

1 tbsp. tomato paste

1 14-oz. (400 g) can San Marzano tomatoes

Fine sea salt

Freshly ground black pepper

Parmigiano Reggiano or aged Pecorino Toscano cheese

Aged balsamic vinegar

Fresh thyme

Robust extra virgin olive oil

This soup is the heart of rustic Tuscan cuisine. Bread and good olive oil complete the simple, hearty dish. Legumes of exceptionally high quality have grown on the high plains of Tuscany and Umbria for centuries. These legumes and the robust olive oil from Tuscany are what make this dish so rich. Historically, the vegetable proteins in legumes were a valuable resource for hard-working peasant farmers, who had a limited supply of meat throughout the year. Vegetables from the garden, bread baked once every few weeks, and the healthy olive oil were satisfying fillers, meeting the nutritional needs of farm hands. These recipes have been preserved thanks to and the country's positive spin on culinary conservatism and the thriving Italian agriculture.

Soak the legumes overnight or for at least 8 hours in a generous 3 cups (750 ml) of water. When they are finished soaking, use a large pot to heat up the legumes in the water they have been soaking in, and simmer for approximately 45 minutes. Add the porcini mushroom stock cube and briefly bring to a boil.

Finely dice the garlic and onion. Trim, peel, and finely dice the carrot. Finely dice the stalk of celery as well. In a pan, sauté the garlic, onion, carrot, and celery in the 2 tablespoons of medium extra virgin olive oil, add the tomato paste and continue cooking. Add the liquid from the tomatoes in the San Marzano can to the beans along with the vegetable and tomato paste combination from the pan, stir well. Finely chop the canned tomatoes and add them to the pot, stir well.

Let the soup simmer for another 15 to 20 minutes. The legumes should be softened but still al dente. Season with salt and pepper to taste.

When serving the soup, place the grated cheese of your choice, balsamic vinegar, fresh thyme leaves, robust extra virgin olive oil for added flavor, and bread on the table.

OUR TIP Pecorino Toscano and Pecorino Romano are tangy, salty cheeses made from sheep's milk that make good alternatives to Parmigiano Reggiano, which tends to have sweet caramel notes from cow's milk.

Risi e Bisi

Rice and Pea Soup

Serves 4 to 6

PREP TIME
1 hour

COOK TIME
30 minutes

INGREDIENTS

2 lbs. 3 oz. (1 kg) fresh peas

1 spring onion

A generous 2 oz. (60 g) pancetta

3 sprigs flat-leaf parsley

½ clove garlic

6 tbsp. (85 g) butter

2 tbsp. extra virgin olive oil

9 oz. (255 g) Vialone Nano risotto rice

Fine sea salt

Freshly ground pepper

2 ¼ oz. (65 g) Parmigiano Reggiano DOC cheese, grated

While the name Risi e Bisi *may sound like a children's dish, historically it was a very exclusive recipe served as an offering to the Doges of Venice on the feast of San Marco on April 25th. Today, it remains a specialty that graces menus in Venice and throughout the region of Veneto. Traditionally* Risi e Bisi *heralds the arrival of spring, its freshly harvested peas lending it a seasonal nature. But is it a soup, or more of a risotto? The outcome should not be too soupy or too firm. The term* minestra asciutta, *or thick dry soup, seems to fit best here. What's special about this recipe is that it uses the empty pea pods, cooking them to make a broth and then pureeing them, which is a good way to use the entire vegetable, whether it has pods or husks. You can use this method to avoid wasting any part of the vegetable when making other dishes as well. If you don't end up with enough pea pod broth, you can always add a little vegetable stock to achieve the desired consistency.*

Shell the peas and set aside in a bowl. Wash the pods, remove any stems and strings, and bring to a boil in a pot of cold water. Simmer over medium heat for about 45 minutes until the pods are very soft. Pour the contents of the pot through a fine mesh sieve, reserving the broth. Place the strained pods in a food processor and puree until smooth. If necessary, use a fine mesh sieve to strain the puree again to make sure all the woody bits have been removed. This should yield approximately 3 ½ cups (840 ml) of stock and approximately 2 cups (500 g) of puree.

Finely slice the spring onions into rings, finely dice the pancetta, and finely chop the parsley and garlic. In a medium saucepan, heat 3 tablespoons (45 g) of the butter along with the olive oil. Add the spring onions, pancetta, parsley, and garlic, and sauté over medium heat for around 5 minutes. Add the peas and cook for 2 minutes. Then pour in 3 ½ cups (840 ml) of the pea pod broth and add the rice. Let it simmer for 10 minutes while continuing to stir. Add the pea pod puree, continue stirring, and let it simmer for another 10 minutes, until the rice is softened but still somewhat al dente. Season with salt and pepper to taste. Stir in the remaining butter and the Parmesan; serve immediately.

OUR TIP Vialone Nano is the ideal risotto rice for *Risi e Bisi*, as it readily absorbs the stock and has an excellent starchy texture, making this dish particularly creamy.

Legumi

Legumes

Boring? Hardly. Beans, and their leguminous kin, are far from it. Not only are they a veritable superfood, they also epitomize exactly what is so characteristic of original Italian cuisine: uncomplicated, authentic happiness.

That is exactly why legumes fit so well in our modern world. They are a valuable, healthy, inexpensive source of protein, not to mention extremely sustainable. Since they can be grown locally almost anywhere, they have the lowest carbon footprint of all foods, plus they also bind nitrogen in the soil, which means the soil needs less fertilizer.

Legumes—or grain legumes, to use their full name, *legumi* in Italian—are actually seeds. They have a higher protein content than meat, but are lower in fat. They also contain a variety of vitamins and minerals such as magnesium, potassium, iron, phosphorus, and B vitamins. They help prevent cancer, cardiovascular disease, and diabetes, and because they are so undemanding, produce high yields, and can be stored for a long time, are the perfect food.

This was already evident in the Neolithic Age, according to archaeological discoveries in Asia Minor.

Even in the European Middle Ages, beans, as all legumes were commonly referred to, were the most important food and were dined on by peasants and kings alike. Nowadays, bean stews and lentil dishes are sometimes viewed disparagingly, but not in Italy, where peasant dishes are held in high esteem. Especially when served with pasta or bread, they not only fill you up quickly, they are also a quick serving of happiness.

"Beans have a soul."—Pythagoras

Most legumes are actually poisonous when eaten raw, but heating them to over 70 °C breaks down the poison they contain, called lectin. The protein released into the cooking water creates foam, which can quickly boil over, but this can be prevented by adding a little oil.

Fagioli Cannellini These white beans, one of the most popular legumes in Italy, have a shiny, smooth appearance. And they are perfect for enhancing the reputation of Italy's simple yet appealing cuisine. Their particularly mild, nutty flavor goes perfectly with short pasta types—such as *Pasta e Fagioli*—or with salsiccia or grilled meats. Or as a salad. Or, well, let's just say the list of foods these beans go well with is a long one.

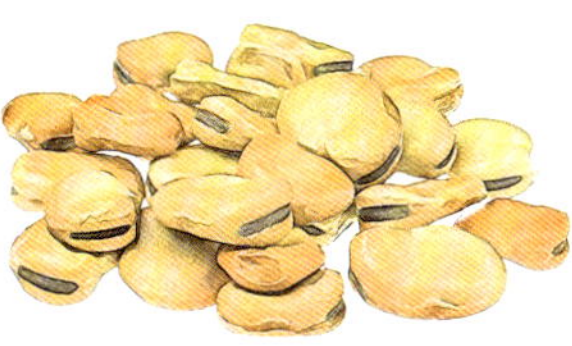

Fave Also known as broad beans, early forms were not very broad; remnants found in Stone Age settlements were rather small. Yet the fava bean became one of the most important European staples well into the 1700s. Nowadays, they are particularly popular as a puree, in risotto, with pasta, or fresh from the field with a chunk of pecorino cheese.

Fagioli Corona Magnificently plump and enormous, these giant beans are harvested meticulously by hand. They transform pasta, stews, soups, and salads into a tremendous treat, especially when served with tuna, oregano, and olive oil, or air-dried ham.

Fagioli Borlotti Their nutty taste and creamy texture make minestrone a classic. These beans also cut a *bella figura* in an antipasto salad with premium extra virgin olive oil.

Piselli One of the oldest staples in the world, peas are now usually purchased in cans or in the frozen food aisle, as the fresh version of these little vegetables does not have a very long shelf life. However, peas are a must as a side dish in soups or pureed.

Ceci Chickpeas have been farmed (and loved) for over 8,000 years. In Italian cuisine they make their appearance as puree, in stews, salads, as a pasta garnish, or even in the form of flour for the famous Ligurian farinata. Chickpeas are a beloved ingredient in both traditional and modern recipes. This bean is also known by another name, the garbanzo bean.Versatile and nutritious, chickpeas are celebrated for their rich flavor and high protein content, making them a staple in various culinary traditions worldwide.

Lenticchie Little yellow, red, brown, or black lentils have always been highly prized. In the Bible, Esau sells his birthright to his younger brother Jacob for a dish of lentils. To this day, they are still considered a bringer of good luck in Italy, and it is believed they will increase your wealth if you eat them on New Year's Eve, preferably in a hearty stew or with pasta. The most classic pairing, however, is with cotechino, a hearty fresh pork sausage. And the more lentils you eat, the greater your financial blessings will be in the new year. For vegetarians, we recommend a tasty lentil salad with dried tomatoes, red onions, and an abundance of herbs.

Lenticchie di Montagna Very small and from very high up—mountain lentils grow at an altitude of over 3,280 feet above sea level. And they are a true delicacy. Castelluccio di Norcia IGP, lentils from a small village in the Umbrian mountains with a nutty flavor, and Lenticchia di Altamura IGP, lentils from Apulia with an al dente texture, offer the ultimate culinary enjoyment. With their incomparably delicate and elegant taste, they perfectly round off exquisite seasonal dishes featuring shellfish, salsiccia, and pancetta.

Cicerchia Also known by numerous other names such as grass pea, chickling vetch, and chickling pea, cicerchia are high in protein and make excellent purees. In Italy, they are enjoyed atop toasted bread, drizzled with the season's first pressing of olive oil, though they are most frequently found in soups. To make cicerchia, soak overnight, then simmer in fresh water the following day. During the cold winter months, warming and hearty soups with sage and pancetta are cooked with cicerchia, as are dishes using short pasta varieties like ditalini.

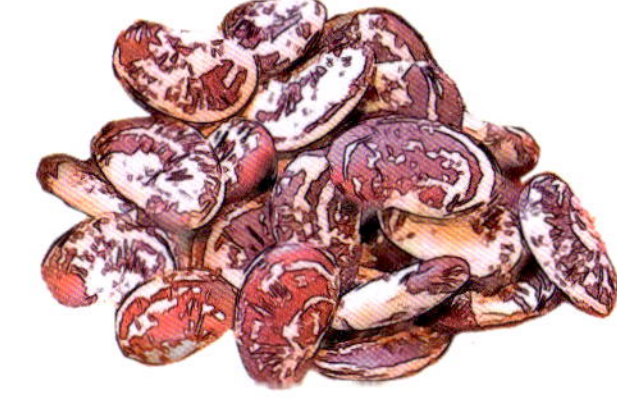

Fagioli di Lima Lima beans are particularly easy to digest and retain their attractive curved shape when cooked. As they prefer a warm climate, they are mainly cultivated in southern Italy. When cooked, lima beans do not get mushy, making them ideal for salads with tuna or seafood. Another popular use is in oven-baked stews with tomatoes.

Risotto alla Piemontese

Piedmont-Style Risotto

Serves 2

PREP TIME
10 minutes

COOK TIME
20 minutes

INGREDIENTS

1 shallot, finely chopped

1½ oz. (40 g) butter

1 clove garlic, finely chopped

11¼ oz. (320 g) arborio or carnaroli risotto rice

7 tbsp. (50 ml) white wine

3¼ cups (780 ml) vegetable stock (see p. 267)

3½ oz. (100 g) Piemontese Tonda Gentile hazelnuts IGP

5 sprigs of fresh marjoram

3½ oz. (100 g) Castelmagno cheese, grated

Castelmagno is a cheese from the Piedmont region which has a protected designation of origin and is made from the milk of cows, sheep, and goats. It ages in tufa caves and boasts a very special finely grained texture with a subtle flavor of essential mountain herbs, forest soil, and mushrooms. It can develop blue mold on a natural basis, but is not specifically inoculated with blue mold cultures. Castelmagno is very well suited for cooking. It is typically eaten with gnocchi after being enriched with cream and butter, a local specialty of Cuneo. But in this risotto, combined with Piedmont's widely known ambassador, the hazelnut, it also represents its region and regional palate magnificently. In Italy, risotto is considered perfect when it moves like an ocean wave when stirred with a wooden spoon, known as all'onda. *It is creamy, but not sticky, and the Castelmagno enhances its creaminess. Be sure to watch for this moment and then serve the risotto quickly after letting it stand for a short time:*

In a large pan, sauté the shallot in a generous 4 teaspoons (20 g) of the butter until translucent. Add the garlic and risotto rice. Stir continuously, making sure it gets hot but does not burn.

Deglaze with the white wine and stir vigorously until the liquid and alcohol have evaporated. Meanwhile, heat the vegetable stock. Reduce the heat somewhat and pour in just enough heated stock to barely cover the rice. Allow the liquid to reduce, then add another ladleful of stock. Repeat this process while stirring until the rice is all'onda; this will take about 18 minutes.

Coarsely chop the hazelnuts and toast them dry, without oil. Fold half of the hazelnuts, marjoram leaves from 3 of the 5 sprigs, the remaining butter, and the grated Castelmagno into the risotto and stir.

Turn off the heat, put the lid on, and let the risotto stand in the pan for 3 minutes. Garnish with the remaining marjoram and hazelnuts.

OUR TIP This dish is made even more delicious by adding freshly ground black pepper as a final touch.

Risotto ai Funghi porcini

Risotto with Porcini Mushrooms

Serves 2

PREP TIME
10 minutes plus soak time

COOK TIME
20 minutes

INGREDIENTS

A generous ¼ oz. (10 g) dried porcini mushrooms

1 shallot

1 clove garlic

1½ oz. (40 g) butter

7 oz. (200 g) arborio or carnaroli risotto rice

5 tbsp. (75 ml) white wine

1 porcini mushroom bouillon cube

1¾ oz. (50 g) Parmigiano Reggiano cheese

3 sprigs fresh oregano, or ½ teaspoon dried

Salt

Freshly ground pepper

You can make this flavorful classic dish from northern Italy whenever you feel like it, since dried porcini mushrooms are available at many grocery stores and from other food sellers all year round. To intensify the flavor, gradually pour the water used to soak the mushrooms into the risotto, plus you can use another wonderful little invention: the porcini mushroom bouillon cube. These cubes have long been available in supermarkets in Italy, and have always been a popular souvenir to bring back and use at home. Fortunately, good-quality bouillon cubes are now also exported. Although risotto is a simple dish made from just a few ingredients, it requires a lot of attention while you are making it. A topic passionately debated among chefs is whether and how often the simmering risotto is to be stirred: There are constant stirrers, restrained stirrers who only stir occasionally to prevent the rice from sticking to the bottom, and non-stirrers. This latter group of cooks just put the lid on and let the risotto cook over low heat for around 20 minutes. It's up to you!

Soak the dried porcini mushrooms in a generous 2 ¼ cups (550 ml) of hot water. When the mushrooms are soft, strain the water through a fine mesh sieve into a bowl and keep it hot.

Finely chop the garlic and shallot, and sauté together in a pan with the risotto rice in half of the butter. Finely chop the porcini mushrooms. Deglaze the rice with the white wine and add the bouillon cube and porcini mushrooms. Gradually pour in the porcini mushroom water and simmer the risotto for 18 minutes while stirring. Then fold in the rest of the butter and the grated Parmesan. Season to taste with the oregano, salt, and pepper, put the lid on, and let it stand for 3 minutes before serving.

OUR TIP Do not rinse the rice beforehand; doing so would strip the starch from the grains of rice, which gives the risotto its creaminess.

Risotto al Barolo

Risotto with Barolo

Serves 4

PREP TIME
5 minutes

COOK TIME
18 minutes

INGREDIENTS

1 small red onion

3 to 4 tbsp. mild extra virgin olive oil

6 ½ cups (1.5 L) vegetable or beef stock (see p. 267 and p. 268)

10 ½ oz. (300 g) carnaroli or arborio risotto rice

⅞ cup (200 ml) Barolo DOCG wine

1 bay leaf

Salt

Freshly ground pepper

1 ¾ oz. (50 g) butter

1 ½ oz. (40 g) Parmigiano Reggiano DOP cheese

The Piedmont region is a garden of paradise: It has truffles, a wonderful pasta culture, with many varieties using eggs and often filled, and baroque-style meals where numerous delicious little bites are served until you are absolutely satiated. These include carne cruda, *a steak tartare made from the meat of Piemontese cattle, and bagna cauda, a warm anchovy sauce to dip raw vegetables in. The Piedmont region's excellent red wines offer the perfect accompaniment to this cuisine with all its character. Barolo is a wine made from the Nebbiolo grape variety, characterized by its refinement, elegance, and a certain brittleness. It is a wine that begs to be mastered! A creamy risotto made with Barolo is a pleasant way to start. The quality of the wine plays an essential role here: A good wine is a must for this dish to come into its own. A trusted wine seller will be able to recommend one to you.*

Finely dice the onion. In a large pan, heat the olive oil and sauté the onion until translucent. Meanwhile, heat the stock in a smaller pan. Once the onions are translucent, add the risotto rice and sauté while stirring. When it is too hot to touch, it is time to pour in the Barolo and let it evaporate while stirring. Add the bay leaf. Then add enough heated stock to cover the rice, reduce the temperature slightly, and continue adding stock while stirring until it has been completely absorbed by the rice.

After half the cooking time, about 9 minutes, season with salt and pepper to taste. Once the rice is cooked but still al dente, remove the pot from the heat and stir in the Parmesan and butter. Let the finished risotto stand for another two minutes in the pot with the lid on. Remove the bay leaf. Put each serving on a heated plate.

OUR TIP This risotto is not only good as a starter; it is also a delicious side dish for goulash made with game or beef. Glazed carrots cooked in sugar and butter are a good vegetable to serve with this dish.

Risotto alla Milanese

Milanese-Style Saffron Risotto

Serves 4

PREP TIME
5 minutes

COOK TIME
18 minutes

INGREDIENTS

1 small onion

3 to 4 tbsp. mild extra virgin olive oil

6 ½ cups (1.5 L) chicken or vegetable stock (see p. 267)

10 ½ oz. (300 g) carnaroli risotto rice

A scant ½ cup (100 ml) dry white wine, such as Roero Arneis DOCG from the Piedmont region

1 tsp. ground saffron

Salt

Freshly ground pepper

1 pinch saffron threads

A generous 1 oz. (30 g) Parmigiano Reggiano DOP cheese

1¾ oz. (50 g) butter

1 tsp. fermented black garlic powder

Risotto alla Milanese *has enjoyed legendary status since becoming the trademark of Italy's most famous chef, Gualtiero Marchesi. A modern twist was used back in the 1980s: A piece of gold leaf lay atop the risotto. In traditional cuisine, saffron risotto is best known as a side dish for osso buco. The saffron lends it a wonderful fragrance and complex flavors. Carnaroli is the rice of choice here, as it cooks without losing its al dente quality on the inside, and texture plays a starring role with these minimalist ingredients. Risotto requires patience and attention to ensure that the timing is right: When does the rice need more liquid and when has it reached the desired consistency? The black garlic infuses the risotto with a warm, smooth flavor.*

Finely dice the onion. In a large pot, heat the olive oil and sauté the onion until translucent. While sautéing the onion, heat the stock in a smaller pot. As soon as the onions are translucent, add the risotto rice and sauté while stirring. When the rice is too hot to touch, pour the white wine over it and let it evaporate while continuing to stir. When the wine has evaporated, add enough heated stock to cover the rice and reduce the temperature somewhat. Continue adding stock while stirring until the stock has been completely absorbed by the rice.

About halfway through the cooking time, about 9 minutes, add the saffron and season the risotto with salt and pepper to taste. Once the rice is cooked but still al dente, remove the pot from the heat and stir in the saffron threads, Parmesan, and butter. Let the finished risotto stand for another 2 minutes in the pot with the lid on. Put each serving on a heated plate. Finely sprinkle each portion with the garlic powder and some pepper and serve immediately.

OUR TIP Like any other recipe that uses wine, the wine should be good enough to accompany the food and be one that the chef enjoys.

Riso e Grano

Rice and Grains

In Italy, people know that "rice is born in water and dies in wine," a saying that perfectly reflects the qualities of authentic Italian cuisine when it comes to making the best out of even the simplest of products.

Rice is probably the most uncomplicated of all staples, and one of the most important foodstuffs in the world. In many languages, the word "rice" also means "food" or "meal." The enormous diversity of varieties and crosses bred over thousands of years can be divided into two large groups: Indica, the long grain rice, and Japonica, the particularly sticky round grain rice that is essential in Italian dishes.

Rice is popular because it has a high yield—a single plant can bear almost 3,000 grains. Not originally an aquatic plant, over the millennia cultivation and natural selection enabled it to adapt to the flooding of the fields by simply washing away weeds and pests.

Rice was first discovered and cultivated over 8,200 years ago in the Chinese Pearl River Delta. From there, it reached the Roman Empire by way of Mesopotamia, where it was primarily known as a medicine and beauty product. In the Middle Ages, rice was mainly regarded as an exotic spice and ingredient for sweet dishes, until a resourceful Milanese duke recognized it as the ideal food for his subjects and ordered it to be planted over large areas in the Po Valley.

Italy is now the largest producer of rice in Europe. It is mainly grown in the Piedmont region around Vercelli and Novara, where approximately a third of Europe's rice is produced.

The harvest process is quite complex. First, the rice is threshed and dried, with some varieties even being dried for up to 12 months. Only then are the husks removed in the rice mill. The remaining grain of rice, including the outer layer known as the silver skin, is sold as brown rice, wholegrain rice, or natural rice. In a further step, the bran and germ are removed by milling. What remains is the classic white rice, which, although it has a longer shelf life, is less nutritious than brown rice. This milling procedure roughens the rice and causes it to quickly release starch into the cooking water, making it sticky. Finally, the grains of rice are smoothened by being rubbed against one another before they have the opportunity to shine brilliantly as polished rice in the most wonderful recipes.

The gentler this refining process, the longer the rice ages, and the purer the variety, the better the taste and appearance.

"It's tricky to make a truly great risotto, but it seems so simple that everyone tries."
—Bethany Turner

The most important rule is to wash the rice before cooking! Because regardless of the quality, rice plants draw arsenic from the soil. You can get rid of this by generously soaking the rice grains in water and stirring them thoroughly before cooking. This way, only a little starch is lost, and the rice grains retain their slightly sticky properties.

Experts disagree about which Italian rice is the best. One thing is certain; it definitely comes from the three main rice-growing regions of Lombardy, Piedmont, and Veneto.

"Rice has therapeutic benefits. Not just for the soul, but for the body too."—Silvia Tovo, Meracinque

Arborio The main growing area for the popular risotto rice bearing its name surrounds the small Piedmont town of Arborio. This rice is the most widespread and consists of large, round grains that are polished slightly more gently. This enables them to release more starch during cooking and bind the cooking liquid to make it particularly creamy. The rice still remains al dente, though—an important requirement for a perfect risotto.

Carnaroli The king of Italian rice; carnaroli is considered the best variety because it does not overcook. Thanks to a balanced ratio between its capacity for absorbing water and slow water migration, the grains do not release their starch as quickly during cooking—the risotto does not become mushy, and instead remains wonderfully creamy and yet deliciously al dente.

Baldo Baldo is one of Italy's younger rice varieties, and also one of the most interesting. It is ideal for salads and perfect for recipes that use sauces or dishes made au gratin, as these particularly large rice grains slightly expand and become sticky when cooked, binding all the ingredients together.

Vialone nano The perfect rice for the traditional dish favored by the Venetian Doges, *Risi e bisi*, comes from the northeast part of Veneto. The beautiful, round, small grains of vialone nano rice have a high starch content and more volume, not to mention a wonderfully nutty taste.

Venere This black rice from Vercelli in the Piedmont region is truly very special. It is the result of a cross between a local white rice and a black Asian variety believed to be an aphrodisiac in China. Its name is a reminder of this, coming from the goddess of beauty and love herself, Venus. Venere rice also has a beguiling aroma reminiscent of fresh bread and a slightly sweet but nutty taste. It tastes particularly delicious in salads, with fish, white meats, and vegetables.

Sant'Andrea Named for the patron saint of the Cathedral of Vercelli, the capital of rice cultivation in Europe, this rice variety is blessed indeed. It absorbs liquid very well during cooking and yet remains al dente, producing excellent risottos, soups, cakes, and side dishes.

Farro Emmer, also known as farro, is not rice, it is an ancient whole grain that was already eaten and appreciated back in Roman times, mainly for its nutty taste and slightly al dente texture. Its low gluten content makes it easy to digest, while its high fiber content is good for the immune system and for healing wounds. Today, the use of farro in northern Italian cuisine is on the rise, in soups, as an alternative grain in risotto, and even in desserts. The nutty-tasting grain is delectable when combined with herbs and vegetables and also makes a delicious summer salad. One well-known traditional recipe using farro is *Minestra Garfagnina*. Hailing from Tuscany's mountainous Garfagnana region near Lucca, this hearty winter dish is made with borlotti beans, farro, and sausages. Besides its culinary uses, farro is also known for its nutritional benefits, as it is rich in vitamins, minerals, and antioxidants.

Orzo perlato Pearl barley used to be a food that was popular because it was cheap and filling, but nowadays it is back in fashion in the kitchen—as a welcome change from rice. The hulled and polished barley pearls are prepared like rice as stews, salads, risottos, or soups, including, of course, the legendary *Minestra d'Orzo*. Originally from the Trentino region of the Alps, this hearty soup combines pearl barley with potatoes and bacon, starting with a soffritto base. The thick consistency of the dish blurs the line between soup and risotto, earning the moniker of orzotto. Risotto aficionados can explore countless variations of orzotto, preferably incorporating substantial ingredients such as cabbage, smoked sausage, and cheese.

Mezze maniche con Burrata e Funghi porcini

Mezze Maniche with Burrata and Porcini Mushrooms

Serves 4

PREP TIME
15 minutes

COOK TIME
20 minutes

INGREDIENTS

A scant 18 oz. (500 g) fresh porcini mushrooms

2 garlic cloves

2 tbsp. medium extra virgin olive oil

Fine sea salt

Freshly ground black pepper

10 sprigs fresh basil

14 oz. (400 g) mezze maniche pasta

A scant 18 oz. (500 g) burrata cheese from Andria, Apulia

Pasta in bianco *("pasta in white") enjoys its own recipe genre in Italy. This alternative to the usual tomato sauce version places the noodles themselves on center stage, so they should be very good quality.* Mezze Maniche *("half sleeves") are short, thick, tubular noodles. Popular bianco sauces in northern Italy include* ragù bianco, *the white counterpart to* Ragù alla Bolognese, *and olive oil-based sughi such as* Aglio, Olio e Peperoncino *in southern Italy. This recipe is a wonderfully minimalist example of pasta in bianco. Just a few ingredients, a soft cheese that melts into the sauce, and some pasta water make this dish a harmonious delight where it is not the sauce playing the main role, but instead the pasta, porcini mushrooms, burrata, and basil—basta.*

Use a paper towel and a brush to carefully clean the porcini mushrooms and remove any soil residue. Use a very sharp, thin knife to cut the mushrooms into thin slices. Peel the garlic cloves and press down on them. In a heavy pan, heat the olive oil, then sauté the mushrooms and garlic for a few minutes until golden brown. Keep turning them over, making sure they do not burn. When finished, season them with salt and pepper. Wash the basil and carefully shake it dry. Cut some of the basil leaves into strips and pluck some leaves off the stems.

Cook the pasta in salted boiling water until al dente. Drain the water, reserving about 5 tablespoons for the sauce. Put the hot pasta in a large bowl or casserole dish. Tear the burrata into small pieces and immediately fold it into the pasta. Remove the garlic cloves from the sautéed mushrooms and add the mushrooms to the pasta. Combine everything well and add the reserved pasta water to make the sauce creamier. Season the pasta with salt and black pepper to taste and sprinkle the basil over it. Serve immediately.

OUR TIP If you use a preheated bowl, the pasta will stay hot longer and the burrata will melt faster. You can either rinse the bowl in hot water or preheat it in the oven.

Uova strapazzate con Tartufo

Scrambled Eggs with Black Winter Truffle

Serves 4

PREP TIME
12 hours

COOK TIME
5 minutes

INGREDIENTS

6 organic eggs

A generous 1 oz. (30 g) black winter truffles

1 tbsp. tartufata (truffle cream)

Fine sea salt

Freshly ground pepper

⅔ cup (150 g) sweet cream butter

Cooks show that they understand truffles and know how to serve them to their guests so they will be enjoyed, by complementing them with simple, fatty accompaniments that don't overpower their flavor. Truffles and good butter are a dream team, just like truffles and eggs, truffles and flat egg noodles, or truffles and potatoes. This recipe uses butter, but fats in the form of cream and olive oil also flatter truffles and enhance their flavor. The mild Italian winter truffle, also known as the nutmeg truffle, is very flavorful, nutty, and spicy. It is in season from November to March. The choice of truffle is also a question of price; white Alba truffles are particularly flavorful and exquisite, but also expensive. This recipe offers a chance to learn to appreciate truffles and to gradually approach the subject, always keeping in mind that when it comes to truffles: the simpler, the better.

Crack the eggs into a bowl, add a third of the truffles and the *tartufata*, cover with plastic wrap, and refrigerate overnight.

The next day, remove the truffles from the eggs and finely chop. Return the chopped truffles to the eggs, season with salt and pepper, and whisk together.

Heat the butter in a non-stick skillet until it forms small bubbles. Then add the egg mixture and stir constantly with a wooden spatula until translucent. Turn off the heat, push the scrambled eggs together with the spatula, and let them set slightly. Divide between four plates and thinly shave the remaining truffle on top before serving.

OUR TIP A dry, fruity red wine from Piedmont such as Barbera d'Asti is recommended here.

Ravioli del Plin con Funghi porcini

Little Ravioli with Porcini Mushrooms

Serves 4

PREP TIME
40 minutes plus 70 minutes dough prep

COOK TIME
20 minutes

INGREDIENTS

A scant 18 oz. (500 g) Pasta all'Uovo dough (see p. 84)

FOR THE FILLING

7 oz. (200 g) Crescenza cream cheese (made from cow's milk)

7 oz. (200 g) sorrel

A scant ⅜ cup (80 ml) whole milk

A scant ⅜ cup (80 ml) robust extra virgin olive oil

1 egg yolk

5 stalks lemon thyme, crushed

1 tbsp. finely grated dry bread

Fine sea salt & ground pepper

FOR THE SAUCE

A generous 1 oz. (30 g) dried porcini mushrooms

1½ shallots / 1 clove garlic

3 tbsp. mild extra virgin olive oil

2 tbsp. (30 ml) dry Marsala wine

⅝ cup (150 ml) cream

Fine sea salt & ground pepper

1½ oz. (40 g) Parmigiano Reggiano cheese

3 stalks flat-leaf parsley

Ravioli al Plin *are a typical pasta style from the Piedmont region. The word "plin" refers to the final pressing of the dough between the index finger and thumb on both sides after the individual ravioli have been separated using a pastry wheel. They are often filled with cooked or roasted meat and served with gravy or melted butter. The size of these little ravioli make them a popular addition to broths and soups. They are often eaten on holidays, especially at Christmastime, and they can also be bought ready-made as fresh pasta, since the homemade version takes a lot of time to make and requires a certain amount of skill. Like many stuffed dumplings, they served as a resourceful way to repurpose leftovers. Their origins likely trace back to the ruling House of Savoy in Turin, where large feasts boasting numerous meat dishes were held. Afterward, the chefs were able to tuck the leftovers in the pasta dough.*

Take the *crescenza* out of the refrigerator and put it in a bowl an hour before you start making the filling to make it easier to handle. Rinse the sorrel, chop somewhat, and place in a tall container. Add the milk and olive oil, and very finely puree with an immersion blender, then stir it into the crescenza. Add the egg yolk and lemon thyme; combine into a smooth mixture. Season with salt and pepper to taste.

Roll out the pasta dough thinly; cut into long strips 4½ inches (11 cm) wide. Place the filling on half the dough strips ¾ inch (2 cm) apart, 2 inches (5 cm) from the edge. Place the plain dough strips on top of the strips with filling. Moisten the edges; press together. Separate the ravioli with a pastry wheel, then press the edges together. Place on a board sprinkled with semolina flour; set aside.

Soak the dried mushrooms in a generous ⅝ cup (150 ml) of hot water for 10 minutes. Peel and finely chop the garlic and shallot. Heat the olive oil in a skillet and lightly sauté the garlic and shallot. Deglaze with the wine, add the cream, and season with salt and pepper. Drain the mushrooms in a fine mesh sieve, reserving the water they soaked in. Semi-coarsely chop the mushrooms. Add the mushrooms, soaking water, and half of the Parmesan to the sauce; let it reduce somewhat. Add the ravioli and let simmer in the sauce for about 3 minutes. Arrange on plates, top with the remaining Parmesan and chopped parsley, and serve.

OUR TIP Stuffed ravioli freezes very well if you happen to have a bit extra. Just place the individual ravioli next to each other in a container, then cook directly after removing from the freezer, without defrosting.

Taglierini al tartufo

Tagliarini with Black Winter Truffles

Serves 2

PREP TIME
10 minutes

COOK TIME
10 minutes

INGREDIENTS

1 ¾ oz. (50 g) Parmigiano Reggiano cheese

About ½ oz. (10–15 g) black winter truffle

8 ¾ oz. (250 g) tagliarini pasta

Fine sea salt

1 ½ oz. (40 g) unsalted butter

Freshly ground black pepper

Truffles don't just add flavor: They are the stars of every dish they make an appearance in. What boosts their flavor is fats like butter and cheese, such as mild, creamy Fontina Val d'Aosta cheese from the Italian Alps, which is used in fonduta, *Italy's version of fondue. In the Piedmont region, truffle dishes use very few ingredients, leaving the major role to be played by the truffles. This version, called tajarin in the region and using thin egg noodles, butter, and Parmesan cheese, is a classic dish. The white truffle, the most expensive and elegant of all truffles, is shaved cold over dishes just before serving or sometimes even right at the table, with its fragrance being what captivates us. But the black winter truffle doesn't develop its flavor on the palate until warmed; it tastes earthy, full-bodied, and autumnal. It is so incredibly flavorful that any dish using it can be a full meal on its own. Black truffle season lasts from November to March, depending on the seasonal climate.*

Finely grate the Parmesan. Clean the truffle with a brush to remove any remaining soil.

Cook the tagliarini in salted boiling water until al dente. Drain the pasta, reserving a scant ½ cup (100 ml) of the pasta water.

Melt the butter in a large pan, finely shave the truffle, and sauté it in the butter. Add the cooked tagliarini and toss it in the butter. Add the Parmesan and enough pasta water to thicken the sauce and make it creamy. Season with salt and pepper to taste, if desired. Sprinkle with Parmesan and shave very thin slices of truffle on top.

OUR TIP The red wines from the Piedmont region pair perfectly with the flavor of the truffle. The Nebbiolo grape variety in particular, which is used to make Barolo wine, is able to hold its own with the impressive taste of such a minimalist dish.

Polenta con Funghi porcini

Polenta with Porcini Mushrooms

Serves 4

PREP TIME
1 hour

COOK TIME
30 minutes

INGREDIENTS

A generous 2 oz. (60 g) dried porcini mushrooms

1 onion

2 cloves garlic

5 tbsp. extra virgin olive oil

1 bay leaf

A generous ⅓ cup (80 ml) dry white wine

A scant ⅞ cup (200 ml) milk

½ cup plus 2 tbsp. (150 ml) beef stock (see p. 268)

2 ¾ oz. (75 g) instant polenta

3 ½ oz. (100 g) fresh porcini mushrooms

10 ½ tbsp. (150 g) butter

1 ¾ oz. (50 g) Fontina cheese

2 ½ oz. (70 g) Parmigiano Reggiano DOC cheese

Fine sea salt

Freshly ground pepper

Nutmeg

2 tbsp. parsley, chopped

Dried porcini mushrooms are the height of umami; their flavor offers a comforting roundness to enhance any dish. Combined with polenta and cheese, they make a delicious meal in the fall, when fresh porcini mushrooms are abundant, and even in the winter, if you happened to dry some mushrooms yourself to ensure their availability or you know a source for good mushrooms. This dish can be served as a main course with a fresh green salad like purslane in the winter, but it also makes an excellent side dish for brown stews. Polenta, or corn meal, is a specialty of northern Italy and its mountain regions, especially the Dolomites in Veneto and Trentino. Polenta is an under-appreciated ingredient which, in its finely ground white form with the outer skin of the kernels removed, also pairs exquisitely with fish and seafood, as evidenced by numerous Venetian recipes.

Soak the dried porcini mushrooms in a generous ½ cup (150 ml) lukewarm water for about 60 minutes and set aside. Peel and finely dice the onion and garlic, then sauté in a pot in 2 tablespoons of olive oil until translucent. Add the bay leaf and deglaze with white wine, allowing the alcohol to evaporate.

Drain the porcini mushrooms and reserve the water used to soak them. Finely chop the softened mushrooms. Add the milk and beef stock to the pot and bring to a boil. Quickly whisk in the instant polenta and simmer over medium heat for 3 minutes.

Clean and trim the fresh porcini mushrooms, cut into bite-sized pieces, and sauté in 5 ½ tablespoons (80 g) of the butter until golden brown. Add the remaining olive oil, the remaining butter, and the cheeses; stir until creamy. Remove the pot from the heat. Season to taste with salt, pepper, and nutmeg. Garnish with the fresh porcini mushrooms and chopped parsley.

OUR TIP We recommend a dry, fruity red wine that does not contain a lot of tannins, such as a Nero d'Avola from Sicily.

Tartufi e Funghi

Truffles and Mushrooms

Gioachino Rossini, the renowned composer and gastronome, hailed truffles as the Mozart of mushrooms. These prized delicacies have always been immensely popular, particularly among the upper echelons of society, even though authentic Italian truffle recipes tend to be rather uncomplicated. Regardless, truffles remain the most valuable mushrooms in both culinary and financial terms—these exceptionally rare tubers are brimming with flavors, myths, and mysteries. Pliny the Elder regarded truffles as a botanical marvel, as they grow without roots. Plutarch believed that a combination of water, heat, and lightning brought them into existence. The Greeks and Romans considered them an aphrodisiac, while in the Middle Ages, they were viewed as the epitome of sin. It wasn't until the Renaissance that truffles regained their popularity and became a staple at every distinguished table, including that of the Pope.

The allure of truffles lies in their scent, which appeals to the discerning palate, or rather the nose. With just 120 volatile organic compounds, truffles offer a limited flavor profile. However, the olfactory sense can detect the most incredible notes of nutmeg, wild berries, and musk. With a stuffy nose, the enjoyment of truffles is impossible. Wild boars can detect the scent of truffles through several inches of forest soil. After consuming truffles, they excrete the indigestible spores along with fertilizer, making wild boars the primary contributors to the spread of truffles, which grow mainly at the base of oak, poplar, and willow trees.

The use of pigs in truffle hunting is now prohibited due to the excessive damage they cause to the delicate root system. Instead, young dogs are trained from an early age, as they retire by the age of two when their noses lose sensitivity. This method of truffle hunting in Italy, where truffles grow in the regions of Umbria, Tuscany, and especially Piedmont, the home of the legendary white truffles, falls under the UNESCO Intangible Cultural Heritage.

The difficulty in finding these tubers and their resulting high prices make the market rife with fraud, particularly involving Chinese truffles, which closely resemble Italian truffles but lack flavor.

Despite their appearance, truffles are very delicate when not in the ground and can only be stored for a few days, ideally individually in dry paper towels, in a closed container, and refrigerated at 37.4°F to 44.6°F (3 to 7°C). A fresh truffle loses some of its weight and flavor every day, and gourmets are highly sensitive to these changes.

"I confess to having cried three times in my life: when my first opera was a failure, when I heard Paganini play the violin, and when a turkey with truffles fell overboard during a picnic on a boat."—Gioachino Rossini

While truffles share certain characteristics, there are significant variations in their appearance, aroma, and flavor. A common feature among all truffles is the marbled flesh within and the bark-like growths on the outer skin, the shape, color, and structure of which play a crucial role in identification:

Tartufo estivo Summer truffles, available from early May to late November, are dark in color and possess a slightly earthy aroma, accompanied by a mild and nutty flavor. To enhance their taste, people often add a touch of truffle oil or cook them in truffle butter. These truffles pair well with egg pasta, fish, meat, risotto, ravioli, and *ricotta di bufala*.

Tartufo autunnale This delightful variety of summer truffle is available from early October to late December. The aroma of autumn truffles is reminiscent of hazelnut and earth, while the flavor is more intense, with porcini mushroom notes. These truffles are best enjoyed combined with butter or cream, and while they can be heated slightly, they do not tolerate temperatures above 140 °F (60 °C). Briefly sauteed, they are perfect with poultry, in creamy ragouts, with cooked ham, in scrambled eggs, or in mashed potatoes.

Tartufo invernale The winter truffle, queen of truffles, can be found from mid-November to late March. Its faceted surface, marked by hexagonal warts, hints at the class of these tubers. Prized Italian specimens hail from Norcia and Spoleto in Umbria. Their scent is beguiling, with light cocoa notes, while the taste overwhelms with musk, nut, and humus aromas. This truffle demands a strong partner and quality fat to truly excel, pairing wonderfully with fine egg pasta.

Tartufo bianco This white gold, characterized by its thin, smooth skin and firm, compact body, is only available in late autumn, from early October to late December, and is exclusively found in the Piedmont's Alba region, although similar qualities can also be sourced from Umbria and Tuscany. The flavor of white truffles is exceptionally strong yet pleasant, with subtle notes of garlic, honey, and flowers. However, as its sensitivity to heat causes it to lose its flavor when cooked, this truffle is usually shaved raw over egg noodles or potatoes. The simpler the dish, the more this delicacy shines.

In addition to truffles, original Italian cuisine also makes delicious use of other exquisite mushrooms:

Ovolo Caesar's mushrooms, as their name suggests, were already revered by Roman emperors as an unsurpassed delicacy. Related to the fly agaric, this mushroom is extremely rare and only grows in deciduous forests south of the Alps. In some countries, it is strictly protected and cannot be picked. In Italy, it is enjoyed raw or very thinly sliced as a carpaccio to preserve its delicate flavor and is often featured in gourmet dishes.

Porcini Even the Romans named porcini mushrooms, "little pigs" in Italian, after pigs ("*suillus*"), but the reason behind this nomenclature for these prized edible fungi remains unclear. However, porcini mushrooms are among the most sought-after and widely picked edible mushrooms. Their popularity stems from an intense flavor that remains undiminished when dried or cooked, complementing braised meats, quality pasta, and hearty risottos. The only porcini with IGP status is Il Fungo di Borgotaro IGP from Emilia Romagna, prized for its intense flavor and clear aroma, devoid of any pungency.

Finferli Chanterelles are the most commonly cooked wild mushrooms in Europe and are also highly favored in Italian cuisine. They are often served as a sauce or side dish alongside hearty meat dishes, briefly sautéed with tagliatelle, tossed in butter with gnocchi, and, of course, featured in risotto.

Unfortunately, fresh truffles and mushrooms are not always readily available. However, there are a few authentic ways to enjoy them without having to forgo the flavor:

Olio al tartufo Truffle-infused extra virgin olive oil captures the unmistakable essence of truffles, allowing just a few drops to transform simple, humble dishes like scrambled eggs, mashed potatoes, cream sauces, and carpaccio into heavenly delights.

Porcini secchi When fresh porcini mushrooms are out of season, Italians turn to the dried variety. They retain most of their flavor and are excellent for preparing risottos or sauces, ensuring the taste year-round.

Burro al tartufo The combination of butter and truffles is extremely satisfying. Without overpowering other ingredients, the elegant truffle flavor elevates simple dishes to new heights. Truffle butter is delicious on toasted bread, adds depth to omelets, mashed potatoes, and risotto, and pairs beautifully with egg pasta.

Tartufi bianchi conservati High-quality preservation methods extend the availability of coveted white truffles beyond their brief season. These prized fungi are preserved in brine. Once dried, they can be shaved over dishes, just like fresh truffles. Like with all fresh mushrooms, simpler dishes allow the truffle's intricate flavors to have more of an impact and provide a gourmet touch to any meal.

Tartufata Truffle paste, a rich blend of truffles, mushrooms, and extra virgin olive oil, is a versatile multi-tasker that gives many dishes a wonderful truffle flavor. It complements meat, poultry, and fish dishes perfectly, can be used to create sophisticated sauces, and tastes fantastic added to egg pasta with a touch of cream.

Polvere di tartufo Truffle powder is the perfect way to add just the right amount of truffle flavor. Made from dark summer truffles and a little salt, it is a delicate seasoning that is perfect for egg dishes, sauces, and creams. Its use extends to fruit and desserts such as ice cream and mousses. For truffle aficionados, it is perfect to add gourmet flair to everyday cooking.

Gnocchi di patate

Potato Dumplings

Serves 4 to 6, makes a little over 2 lbs. (1 kg)

PREP TIME
30 minutes

COOK TIME
Approximately 10 minutes

INGREDIENTS

A generous 1¼ lbs. (600 g) yellow potatoes

1¾ cups (250 g) flour Italian type 00

3½ oz. (100 g) Parmesan cheese

1 egg yolk

Fine sea salt

Gnocchi are Italy's potatoes, in a refined and bite-sized form. It is believed they have been made with potatoes since the 17th century; prior to that, similar shapes were made using bread crumbs and cheese. Gnocchi make a good partner for winter dishes with braised beef or game, and Alpine cuisine with cheese. Pesto and other sauces cling to gnocchi very well, and they are also delicious with smooth, uncomplicated sauces like Pesto alla Genovese *or* Sugo al Pomodoro. *Or you can simply enjoy them with butter and sage, or butter and Parmesan. When deciding on gnocchi portions to serve as the primo course, it is important to keep in mind that they are more substantial than pasta. These little dumplings are more common in northern Italy, but they have relatives in Rome made with semolina,* Gnocchi alla Romana, *and in southern Italy with tomato sauce, mozzarella, and basil,* Gnocchi alla Sorrentina.

Rinse the potatoes thoroughly and boil them with skins on in salted water until soft. Peel while warm and lightly mash with a fork in a bowl. Let stand for approximately 5 minutes to allow the steam to evaporate.

Sift the flour into a bowl and make a well in the middle. Put the potatoes through a potato ricer into the well, add the remaining ingredients, and season with salt to taste. Quickly work it into a smooth, non-sticky dough. Roll the dough into logs approximately 1 inch (2½ cm) high, then use a flat spatula to cut each log into gnocchi ¾ inch (2 cm) long. To help the gnocchi hold more sauce, use a fork or gnocchi board to make grooves on the tops of the dumplings.

Bring a large pot of salted water to a boil and add the gnocchi a few at a time, not all at once. When the first ones have risen to the top, skim them off and add the next portion.

OUR TIP To give the outside of the gnocchi a crisp texture, rinse after cooking and briefly sauté in butter.

Gnocchi di patate con Gorgonzola e Uva

Gnocchi with Gorgonzola and Grapes

Serves 4 to 6

PREP TIME
40 minutes

COOK TIME
15 minutes

INGREDIENTS

25 oz. (700 g) fresh Gnocchi di Patate (see p. 168)

1 ¼ cups (300 ml) cream

7 tbsp. (100 ml) dry white wine

5 ¼ oz. (150 g) Gorgonzola dolce cheese

1 pinch cinnamon

7 oz. (200 g) dark grapes

2 tbsp. butter

Fine sea salt

Freshly ground black pepper

2 tbsp. balsamic vinegar, aged for at least 3 years

Gnocchi are very popular in Italy as a comfort food, and are traditionally served on Thursday as a filling dinner, Giovedi Gnocchi, *to fill you up before Friday, a meatless day for religious reasons. Gnocchi also has its own true devotees: The first Gnocco Club was started in Treviso, in the region of Veneto, and created over 40 recipes using these little potato dumplings. When gnocchi began to gain popularity in other countries, it was rumored that to check the consistency, you had to toss the gnocchi onto the ceiling: If they stuck, they needed a little more flour; if they fell off, they were ready for boiling. There's no telling how many gnocchi you might find still stuck to the ceiling anywhere the previous residents enjoyed these tasty Italian dumplings, but hopefully not many! Our gnocchi recipe combines a lot of typical northern Italian ingredients, including Gorgonzola and balsamic vinegar, and is a great recipe to make in late summer and fall.*

Make the gnocchi following the recipe on p. 168. Bring salted water to a boil, reduce the heat and let the gnocchi continue cooking. As soon as they rise to the surface, remove them with a slotted spoon and transfer to a dish, keeping them warm.

Meanwhile, heat the cream in a large saucepan and let it simmer. Add the white wine and let it continue simmering until all the alcohol has evaporated. Cut the Gorgonzola into small cubes, then gradually add it to the saucepan and let it melt, stirring constantly. Season the Gorgonzola sauce with cinnamon to taste.

Wash the grapes and cut them in half. In a pan, melt the butter and braise the grapes in it over low heat for 1 to 2 minutes. Season with salt and pepper and deglaze with the balsamic vinegar. Add the gnocchi to the Gorgonzola sauce. Plate the gnocchi and sauce, garnishing with the grapes.

OUR TIP Chopped roasted Piedmont hazelnuts are delicious as a topping on this northern Italian recipe, giving it a delightful crunch.

Saltimbocca alla Romana

Veal Escalope with Parma Ham and Sage

Serves 4

PREP TIME
5 minutes

COOK TIME
10 minutes

INGREDIENTS

8 thin veal cutlets, about 2 ½ oz. (70 to 80 g) each

8 slices Prosciutto di Parma DOP

8 sage leaves

3 scant tablespoons (40 g) butter

A scant ½ cup (100 ml) white wine

Fine sea salt

Freshly ground pepper

This recipe already finds mention by Pellegrino Artusi, whose cookbook La scienza in cucina e l'arte di mangiar bene *(Science in the Kitchen and the Art of Eating Well) was published in Florence in 1891. He recommends using smaller cutlets but planning up to three per person. The name* "Saltimbocca" *means "it jumps into the mouth," a sure indication of the popularity of this dish, as well as of the high regard in which it is held in Italy. It is a classic in the kitchens of Rome, quick and easy to prepare, and packed with flavor. Artusi's bestselling book was the first cookbook to document and describe many regional dishes across Italy, making it the standard work on the subject. He was a wealthy merchant and gourmet with the means to travel and sample various regional cuisines, and he had the opportunity to sample* Saltimbocca alla Romana *first-hand in Rome, at the Trattoria Le Venete on Campo Marzio, a famous trattoria in his time.*

Flatten the cutlets slightly and top each with a slice of ham. The ham should not hang over the sides. Then place a sage leaf on top of each and use a toothpick to secure both to the meat.

Heat half the butter in a skillet and sauté the cutlets for 1 minute on the sage and ham side and 2 minutes on the other side. The ham should not become dry.

Pour in the white wine, season with salt and pepper. Remove the cutlets and keep warm. Let the alcohol evaporate, add the remaining butter to the skillet, and let it reduce. Arrange the finished cutlets on plates, drizzle the sauté drippings over each, and serve immediately.

OUR TIP Crusty white bread tastes great with saltimbocca. A Verdicchio from the Marche region, which has ideally already been used to season the veal, is recommended to accompany this dish.

Guancia di Manzo brasata al Nebbiolo

Braised Veal Cheeks in Nebbiolo Wine

Serves 4

PREP TIME
30 minutes

COOK TIME
3 ½ hours

INGREDIENTS

1 large carrot

3 ½ oz. (100 g) celery root

A scant 3 oz. (80 g) shallots

2 ½ lbs. (1.2 kg) veal cheeks (pre-ordered from the butcher)

5 tbsp. mild extra virgin olive oil

1 tbsp. triple concentrated tomato paste

3 bay leaves

1 cinnamon stick

15 black peppercorns

2 cups plus 4 tsp. (500 ml) Nebbiolo wine

A generous 1 cup (250 ml) red port wine

A generous 1 cup (250 ml) veal stock

Fine sea salt

1 tsp. sugar

A scant ½ cup (90 g) butter, softened

Freshly ground pepper

This is braising at its traditional best, using vegetables, spices, and a really good red wine, Nebbiolo, the traditional grape varietal of the Piedmont region. During cooking, its aroma wafts through the home, whetting the appetite for both food and wine. One of the most frequently used muscles of beef, the well-marbled cheeks are ideal for braising, as they either get very juicy during the long cooking time or retain their original juiciness. Their texture is incomparable, and the flavor of the meat is intense. This recipe is based on brasato, the Piedmont region's famed roast, but we use a cut of meat that is purportedly not as good. Beef and veal cheeks have, however, grown in popularity in recent years and can now also be found on the menus of many good restaurants.

Trim and peel the carrot, celery root, and shallots. Cut into walnut-sized pieces. If the butcher has not already done so, remove the thick outer sinews from the veal cheeks, then pat the meat dry. Heat the olive oil in a cast-iron roasting pan on high heat and sear the meat on all sides. Remove the meat, reduce the heat, and sauté the carrot, celery root, and shallots in the drippings until golden brown. Add the tomato paste, bay leaves, cinnamon stick, and peppercorns, and sauté briefly while stirring continuously. Pour in half of the Nebbiolo, use a wooden spoon to loosen any drippings stuck to the bottom of the pan, and let it reduce. Then add the remaining Nebbiolo and let it reduce again. Add the port wine and bring to a boil. Add the veal stock, then season with salt and sugar. Now add the veal cheeks; there should be enough liquid to slightly cover them. Place the lid on the roasting pan and simmer over low heat for about 3 ½ hours.

When the cheeks are so tender that you can pick the meat off with a fork, remove them from the stock and cut into slices. Pour the stock through a fine mesh sieve and add it to a tall container. Add 3 tablespoons of the braised vegetables and the butter, then blend using an immersion blender. Season again with salt and pepper to taste.

OUR TIP It is important to serve this dish with soft white bread, polenta, or mashed potatoes to soak up all the delicious gravy. Carrots with lemon in robust olive oil and seasoned with black pepper make a great vegetable contorno here.

Tagliata di Manzo con Radicchio

Sliced Entrecôte with Braised Radicchio

Serves 4

PREP TIME
10 minutes

COOK TIME
20 minutes

INGREDIENTS

4 entrecôte steaks, 4 to 6 cm thick

2 Treviso radicchio

¼ cup (60 ml) medium extra virgin olive oil

2 sprigs rosemary

2 tbsp. butter

Fine sea salt

4 tbsp. powdered sugar

Fleur de sel salt

Tagliata *is not a traditional dish in itself, but rather a variation on the well-known* Bistecca alla fiorentina. *In Italy, it is served pink on the inside, or medium rare. If medium rare is how you like it, you can use the finger test. Connect your thumb and your index finger and press the fleshy area below your thumb. If its softness equals that of the cooked meat, the meat will be nice and pink on the inside. Tagliata only began to appear on menus in Italy as of the 1970s. It is usually served on a bed of arugula with Parmiggiano Reggiano and balsamic vinegar. But the subtle bitter taste of the braised radicchio and the sweetness of the caramelized sugar go even better with the roasted flavors of the meat. We recommend the elongated, torpedo-shaped Treviso radicchio here, as it is firm and has strong leaves. Like the steak, it can still be a little uncooked on the inside (and crisp).*

Remove the meat from the refrigerator at least 1 hour before cooking. Rinse the radicchio and cut in half lengthwise. Heat a large skillet, add a scant 3 tablespoons (40 ml) olive oil. The oil is hot enough when it forms small bubbles on a toothpick.

Place the steaks in the oil and sear for 1 minute on each side. Add the sprigs of rosemary to the skillet. Reduce the heat and add the butter, making sure it does not burn. Gently sauté the steaks for another 5 minutes per side. Remove the steaks from the skillet, wrap each one in aluminum foil, and let them rest for a few minutes.

In a different skillet, heat the remaining olive oil over medium heat. Salt the radicchio halves and rub the powdered sugar on the areas exposed when cut in half. Place the radicchio in the skillet with the cut sides down, allowing the sugar to caramelize. Turn over after about 3 minutes and brown the other side.

Remove the steaks from the aluminum foil, season with *fleur de sel*, cut into slices ¾-inch thick (2 cm), and arrange on plates. Drizzle the meat juices from the aluminum foil over the steaks. Place one radicchio half on each plate.

OUR TIP Along with fleur de sel, place a very good Aceto Balsamico Tradizionale on the table for added seasoning.

Ossobuco alla Milanese

Milanese-Style Beef Shanks

Serves 4

PREP TIME
20 minutes

COOK TIME
Approximately 4 hours

INGREDIENTS

4 slices of beef shank, approximately 1½ inches (4 cm) thick

Fine sea salt

Freshly ground pepper

¼ cup (30 g) flour

½ cup (120 ml) extra virgin olive oil

4 tbsp. butter

1 onion

1 carrot

1 stalk celery

2 cups plus 4 tsp. (500 ml) dry white wine

2 cups plus 4 tsp. (500 ml) beef stock (see p. 268)

Osso buco is a wonderful stew with classic ingredients like carrots, celery, and onions. Slices of the shank are full of fat and tendons; both ensure there will be a great deal of flavor. Their use by the cattle gives them an intense taste, but you can always trim the fat and tendons if you prefer. The marrow of the beef bones is particularly delicious and tastes wonderful on toasted bread with a little salt. In Milan, osso buco is typically served with saffron risotto. Gremolata with parsley, lemon zest, and olive oil also goes very well with the meat in this recipe. A traditional variation on this stew adds tomato passata (pureed, strained tomatoes) made using San Marzano tomatoes; it is added to the vegetables in the casserole dish and simmers with them.

Rub the sliced shanks well with salt and pepper, then roll in flour. Brown them in a large skillet in olive oil over medium heat with the lid on for about 10 minutes.

Preheat the oven to 300 °F (150 °C) using the convection setting. Place 3 tablespoons of olive oil and the butter in a casserole dish. Chop the onion, carrots, and celery and add to the dish. Cook in the oven until the vegetables are soft. Then add the wine and stock, followed by the sliced shanks. Let everything simmer in the oven for 3 to 3½ hours.

OUR TIP The meat should fall apart when it is finished cooking. When it comes to side dishes, you can't go wrong with risotto, polenta, or pasta.

staub

Bistecca di Fassona

Fassona Steak with Garlic and Rosemary Potatoes

Serves 4

PREP TIME
15 minutes

COOK TIME
45 minutes

INGREDIENTS

A generous 17 oz. (500 g) waxy potatoes

1 bulb garlic

Fine sea salt

2 pounds 3 oz. (1 kg) Bistecca di Fassona

1 sprig fresh rosemary

Freshly ground black pepper

Sea salt flakes

The focus of this recipe is on the quality of the meat: This bistecca, a T-bone steak, comes from the Piedmont region's Fassona cattle, also known as Razza Piemontese, or Piedmontese cattle. This large breed of cow has tender, lean meat that needs to be prepared with great care. In the Piedmont region, it is the preferred meat for making carne cruda, a raw meat dish. When cooked on the grill, its bone keeps the meat juicy. In Tuscany, this famous signature dish goes by the name Bistecca alla fiorentina. *Ideally, its meat comes from Chianina cattle, an even larger breed of cattle from Tuscany's Chiana Valley, which produces very large, finely marbled steaks. Ideally, when making this recipe it helps if you know a good butcher or even a farmer who offers high-quality beef and allows it to age for two weeks. This will allow you to discuss things like the cut of meat, aging, and the thickness of the steak, which should be at least a good 1 ¼ inches (3 cm).*

Heat up the barbecue and get the coals glowing. Using a vegetable brush, brush off any excess dirt and then rinse the potatoes, leaving the peel on. Cut them into large cubes. Divide the garlic bulb into cloves and clean the individual cloves, leaving the skins on. Fill a pot with cold salted water, add the potato cubes and garlic cloves, and simmer for 8 minutes.

Trim some of the fat from the room-temperature steak, finely dice the fat and melt it in a large, cold skillet, preferably a cast-iron skillet, over medium heat. Drain the potato cubes and garlic cloves. When they have finished steaming, add them to the pan with the melted steak fat and sauté for 25 minutes until golden brown. After 20 minutes, season with the fine sea salt and chopped rosemary.

Salt the steak and grill it as close to the coals as possible for 4 to 6 minutes per side. Put it on a heated plate, cover it, and let it rest for 5 minutes. Season with black pepper and sea salt flakes. Serve with the potato cubes.

OUR TIP In Italy, hosts like to offer their guests lemon wedges and a robust olive oil on the table to season their steaks. Salsa verde (see p. 263) makes a good accompaniment here, and it is easy and quick to make using fresh herbs of your choosing, such as flat-leaf parsley, basil, or mint, along with capers, garlic, lemon zest, and extra virgin olive oil.

Brasato al Barolo

Braised Beef in Barolo Wine

Serves 6 to 8

PREP TIME
30 minutes plus 1 night to marinate

COOK TIME
Approximately 3 hours

INGREDIENTS

2 large carrots

2 onions

2 to 3 stalks celery

2 bay leaves

1 cinnamon stick

3 cloves

4 juniper berries

1 tbsp. black peppercorns

A generous 3 lbs. (1½ kg) roast beef from the inner hind quarter or shoulder

1 bottle of Barolo wine

Fine sea salt

3 sprigs thyme

2 sprigs rosemary

2 sprigs sage

4 tbsp. extra virgin olive oil

Freshly ground black pepper

This is what Sunday tastes like in the Piedmont region. The aroma of roasting meat wafts through the kitchen into the rest of the home; ideally the meat is from the Razza Piemontese, the region's large cattle that produce excellent quality meat. For those not lucky enough to be cooking in Italy, we highly recommend meat from Angus, Galloway, Simmental, or Charolais cattle, which spend most of the year out in the pasture. Moreover, there is no shortage of good wine in the Piedmont region. The people there cook with it and drink it too, showing a true appreciation of Piedmont quality. This dish is rounded off with a Mediterranean flavor combination of carrots, celery, onions, and cinnamon, resulting in a taste that has great depth and makes Sunday a day to look forward to.

Rinse and coarsely chop the carrots. Peel the onions, remove the strings from the celery, and cut both into large pieces. Crush the bay leaves, cinnamon stick, cloves, juniper berries, and black peppercorns using a mortar and pestle. Place the beef roast in a large bowl with the carrots, onions, and celery, along with the crushed spices. Pour the Barolo over it, cover the bowl, and let it marinate overnight in the refrigerator.

Remove the meat and dry well. Drain the vegetables in a sieve, reserving the wine. Heat the olive oil in a roasting pan, rub the meat generously with sea salt, and brown on all sides in the roasting pan. Remove the meat, then brown the drained vegetables in the remaining oil and fat in the roasting pan. Add the fresh herbs along with the remaining marinade and return the meat to the roasting pan. Add the wine and let the roast simmer approximately 3 hours, with the lid on, but not completely covering the pan.

Remove the meat and let it rest. Remove the herbs and vegetables, then puree some of the vegetables, depending on how thick you want the sauce to be. Add the pureed vegetables to the wine sauce and bring to a boil. Season with salt and pepper to taste.

OUR TIP If there are any roast leftovers, they make an ideal filling for *Ravioli al Brasato* (see p. 106).

Polpette di nonna Lulla

Grandma Lulla's Meatballs

Serves 5 or more

PREP TIME
1 hour

COOK TIME
Approximately 15 minutes

INGREDIENTS

1½ oz. (40 g) stale white bread

½ cup plus 2 tbsp. (150 ml) milk

A scant ¾ oz. (20 g) dried porcini mushrooms

14 oz. (400 g) ground veal

14 oz. (400 g) ground pork

4 sprigs fresh marjoram or fresh basil, chopped, or 1 tbsp. dried marjoram

2 tbsp. flat-leaf parsley, chopped

1 clove garlic, chopped

1¾ oz. (50 g) Parmigiano Reggiano cheese, grated

3 eggs

Fine sea salt

Freshly ground pepper

Flour

Mild extra virgin olive oil

There are a lot of different recipes for polpette *in Italy. Grandma Lulla Viani's recipe comes from Genoa, and is made using porcini mushrooms and Liguria's much-loved marjoram or flavorful basil from the Prà district west of Genoa. The recipe uses raisins and pine nuts in Naples, mint, pecorino, and onions in Sicily, only pork with mortadella and ham in Bologna, and boiled veal with potatoes in Tuscany. So, as you see, the various polpette versions take you on a journey through the regions of Italy. Since polpette are so versatile, it is a good idea to make large quantities like in this recipe. They taste great hot or cold, coated in breadcrumbs and deep-fried to enjoy with an aperitif, or, as the most preferred variety, with pizzaiola sauce. They go wonderfully with numerous side dishes such as potatoes, pasta, or risotto, or even just bread.*

Soak the bread in the lukewarm milk and the mushrooms in lukewarm water, both for approximately 1 hour. Squeeze the bread out well and chop into small pieces. Place the bread, meat, marjoram or basil, parsley, and garlic in a bowl; combine thoroughly. Squeeze out the porcini mushrooms to remove any excess water, coarsely chop, and add to the bowl, combining well. Next, add the grated Parmesan and eggs, combining well again, preferably by hand. Season with salt and pepper to taste.

Wet your hands, take a small handful of the ground meat mixture, and shape it into a ball. Then flatten the ball a little. Coat each ball in flour and fry in plenty of hot olive oil, turning each one over several times.

OUR TIP Nonna Lulla recommends *patate arrosto* (oven-roasted potatoes baked in olive oil) and steamed vegetables as side dishes. Whenever Nonna Lulla had leftover polpette, two days later she would whip up a pizzaiola sauce like *Sugo Pomodoro* (see p. 265) using San Marzano tomatoes with Taggiasca olives and capers, seasoned with a touch of oregano, and reheat the polpette in this sauce.

Carne

Meat

At the dawn of human history came fire, and it wasn't long before a piece of meat fell into the flames, instantly captivating early humans. This fascination persists in Italy to this day, where it remains an integral part of culinary culture. Hardly surprising, given its world-famous reputation for exceptional quality and incredible recipe variety, not to mention the immense diversity of domestic and wild animals, with numerous treasured indigenous breeds.

Bovino In the land of culinary connoisseurs, *manzo*, or beef, was not held in high regard for a very long time. The animals were primarily used for agricultural labor, resulting in meat that was quite tough. However, as cattle breeding gradually became more prevalent, it gave rise to a diverse array of breeds, each with its own unique advantages. Among these are the renowned Chianina from Tuscany, known for its impressive size and porcelain-white coat; the rustic, dark-haired Sicilian Modicana; and the elegant black and white Valdostana from the Aosta Valley.

Suino *Maiale*, or pork, was already widely consumed in Roman times. As recently as a century ago, Italy had around 30 different pig breeds; today, only six are officially recognized by the breeders' association, but these are true legends in their own right. Among them are the exceptional Cinta Senese DOC from Tuscany and the *Mora Romagnola* from Emilia Romagna.

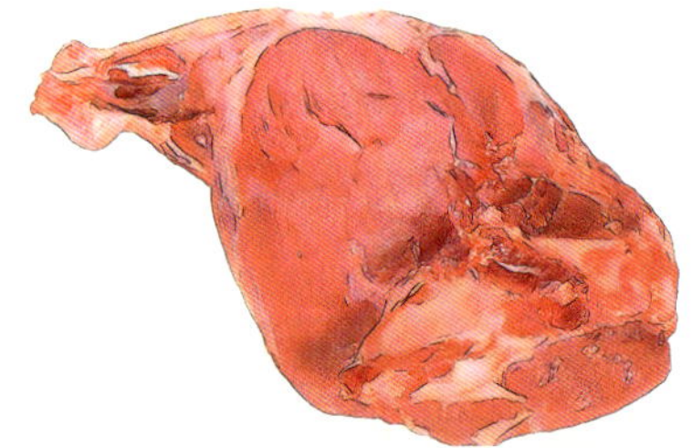

Cinghiale Wild boar, celebrated as the king of Tuscany, is extremely popular both in the region and beyond, as it deliciously combines the flavors of pork and game. However, wild boar meat is prone to spoilage, so it is often made into sausage. To temper its intense flavor, fresh wild boar meat is frequently marinated in red wine, vegetables, and herbs for an extended period before cooking.

Capra Although the goat is one of the oldest domesticated animals and Italy is home to nearly 50 different breeds, its meat is seldom served. In fact, goats are quite uncommon in Italy. If you happen to encounter it on a menu, it will likely be served directly from a wood-fired oven, tantalizingly crispy, adorned with plenty of herbs and accompanied by potatoes.

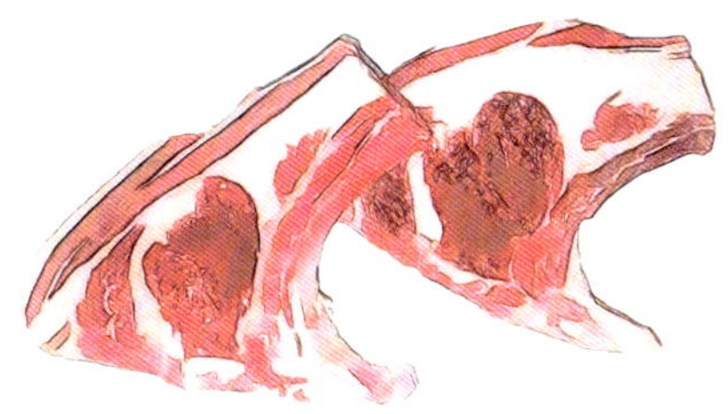

Pecora Sheep, however, are a familiar sight across the Italian landscape. The country has 17 primary breeds and countless native subspecies. But their meat is not frequently found in Italian kitchens, with one exception: *Agnello*, or lamb, which is extremely popular, and not just during Easter. On Easter Sunday, however, roast lamb is a must. In Tuscany, it is traditionally cooked on a spit with bacon and herbs. In Abruzzo, a delicious lamb treat is *arrosticini*, delectable skewers of lean and fatty meat cubes.

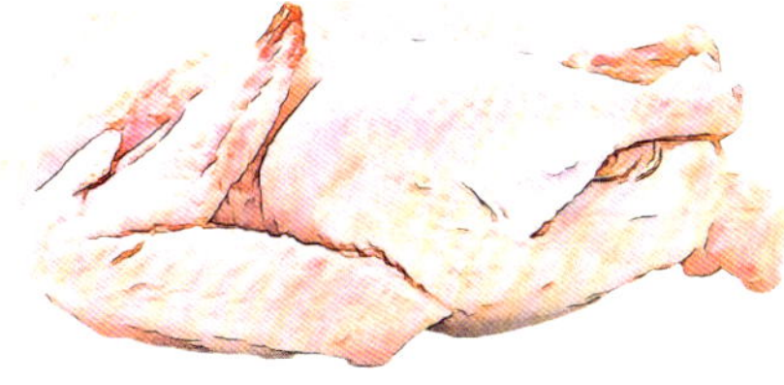

Oca Alerted by honking geese, the Romans were able to ward off a night-time attack on the Capitol, earning these birds reverence. However, this does not stop them from being enjoyed on the table when stuffed, roasted, or in a ragu. On St. Martin's Day, Northern Italians traditionally feast on *Oca Arrosta col Sedano*, goose breast with celery.

Pollo Chickens came with the Romans. Today, Italy has more chicken breeds than it does provinces, with many ancient breeds among them. The ubiquitous *pollo* graces menus across the nation. One particularly spectacular recipe is *Pollo alla Diavola*, a specialty of Tuscany and Rome. It begins with the butterflying of a whole chicken, splitting it along the spine and then flattening with it a brick. The flattened bird is then generously coated with a fiery oil and chile marinade before being pan-fried to crispy perfection on both sides, resulting in a dish that's both spicy and succulent.

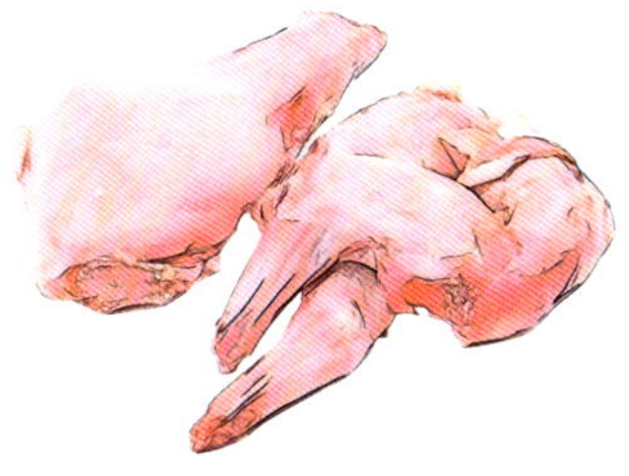

Coniglio Lean and tender rabbit meat is popular throughout Italy. When rabbits are reared for food, they fall under the category of farm-raised animals, or *animali da cortile*. When cooking rabbit, key herbs include bay leaf, sage, rosemary, fennel, and thyme, with garlic playing a crucial role in seasoning. Many recipes suggest marinating the meat in water with a splash of white wine vinegar. Typically, the meat is initially seared to reduce moisture. Tuscan cuisine features rabbit braised until it falls apart, then served with fresh pappardelle, or prepared *alla cacciatora* with tomatoes. In Liguria, the tender legs are served with pine nuts and Taggiasca olives.

Piccione In Italy, pigeons are prized as a delicacy, available at butcher shops and local street markets. They are bred and slaughtered young, while their meat is still tender and lean. Wild pigeons offer darker, more flavorful meat. Common preparations include grilling or roasting. To keep it juicy, pigeon is often wrapped in pancetta or basted with marinade during grilling. *Piccioni Farciti*, or stuffed pigeons, feature a stuffing made from the bird's liver, soaked bread, prosciutto crudo or pancetta, and herbs. Typically, one pigeon usually serves two people.

"The hardest thing to explain to people is that the fillet is not the best part of the cow."—Dario Cecchini

It is certainly a fact that Italy is home to some truly unique meat products. These specialties showcase Italy's rich culinary traditions and regional diversity:

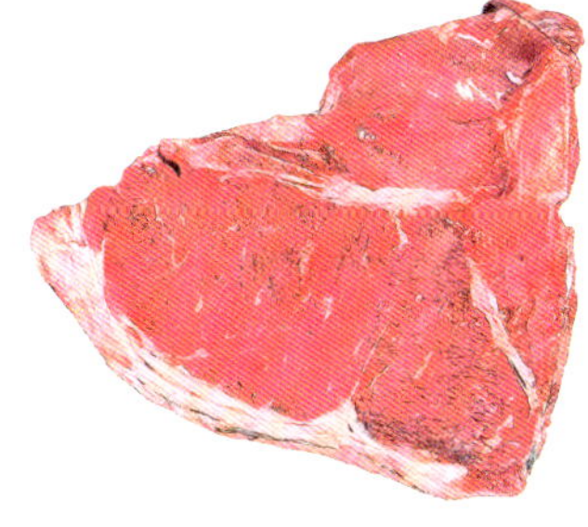

Bistecca Fiorentina di Chianina This legendary steak comes from the loin of the iconic Chianina cattle, among the world's oldest and most beautiful breeds, which once served as artistic inspiration for sculptors in ancient Rome. The meat is prized for its high protein and low cholesterol content. This substantial *bistecca* is a T-bone steak with fillet on one side and sirloin on the other, weighing as much as two pounds or more. After being briefly grilled over charcoal, it is simply seasoned with salt and freshly ground pepper before serving.

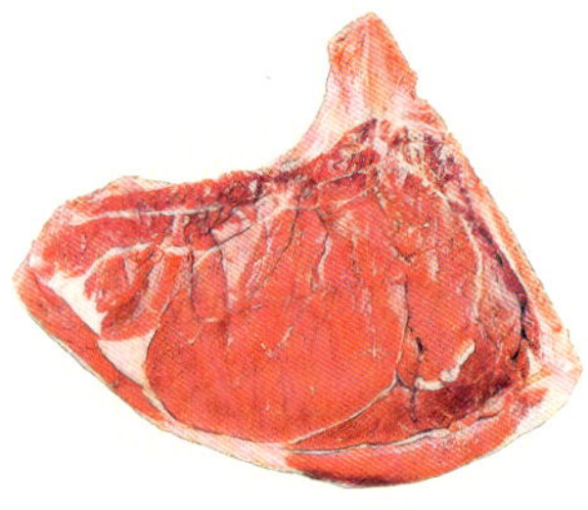

Costata di Razza Piemontese Fassona This exceptional rib eye steak comes from Fassona cattle, a historic breed native to the Piedmont region, which is raised free-range primarily in the provinces of Cuneo, Asti, and parts of Turin. The animals graze on fresh grass and herbs, eschewing industrial feed, resulting in a uniquely lean *costata* cut devoid of marbling and outer fat. Yet the meat's unparalleled tenderness and succulent flavor are sure to elicit tears of joy from beef aficionados and gourmet enthusiasts alike, ultimately making each bite an unforgettable experience.

Cotoletta alla Milanese This breaded, pan-fried veal cutlet is a true culinary classic. It is one of the most important Italian specialties and believed to be the forerunner of the Wiener schnitzel, although this has not been proven beyond a doubt. Tradition holds that it is an imitation of the gold-plated dishes popular in wealthy circles during the Middle Ages. But even without the gold, it is a true masterpiece of Italian cuisine.

Salsiccia Most regions of Italy have their own pork sausage, with all of them, of course, claiming to have the best. It is also not clear where this sausage originally came from. One story says it came from Monza, when the sixth-century Lombard queen Theudelinde shared her recipe with the citizens of the city: Fresh pork from the shoulder or belly is ground, salted, and seasoned—using fennel, garlic, pepper, paprika, and nutmeg, depending on the region, and in Abruzzo even using honey and liver. However it is seasoned, salsiccia can be grilled, sautéed, or sliced. Finely chopped, it enhances risottos, and the sausage meat can also be used to make a pasta sauce. It is also added to pizzas or sandwiches for an extra burst of flavor. From festive feasts to everyday meals, salsiccia captures the essence of Italian culinary heritage.

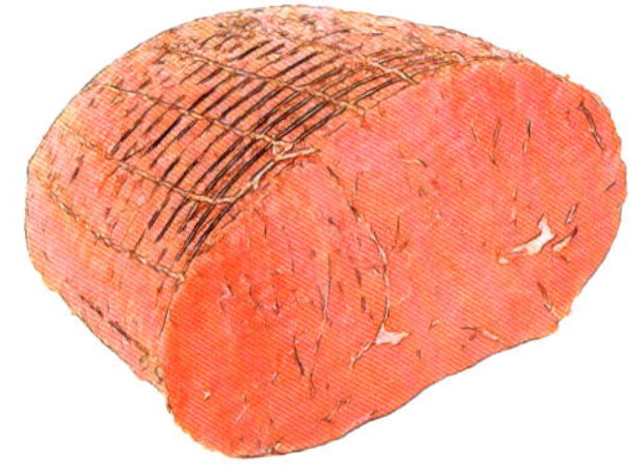

Carne Salada The Trentino region's traditional salted meat dish, originating from the area around Arco, was born out of the necessity to preserve large quantities of meat. Situated along the vital Adige Valley trade route connecting Central Europe with the Mediterranean, a savvy prince-bishop implemented regulations mandating that one fifth of the transported goods be slaughtered locally, greatly benefiting the diocese. However, as the meat could not always be consumed immediately, preservation techniques were essential. *Carne salada*, a lean cut of beef, is salted and seasoned before being stored in a container for 20–25 days, after which it is ready for consumption.

Spezzatino di Agnello con Aceto balsamico

Lamb Goulash with Balsamic Vinegar

Serves 4

PREP TIME
20 minutes plus 1 hour to marinate

COOK TIME
Approximately 2 hours

INGREDIENTS

1¾ lbs. (800 g) leg of lamb, boneless

A scant ½ cup (100 ml) balsamic vinegar, aged

1 onion

1 carrot

1 stalk celery

½ red chile pepper

1 clove garlic

2 tbsp. (30 ml) extra virgin olive oil

Fine sea salt

1 sprig rosemary

1 sprig sage

⅝ cup (150 ml) white wine

5 tbsp. canned San Marzano tomatoes, crushed

1 bay leaf

1 cinnamon stick

1 pinch ground cloves

Freshly ground pepper

Lamb dishes in Italy are usually traditional shepherd's dishes characterized by their simplicity. The recipes come from regions where sheep are farmed to produce cheese, including Tuscany, Abruzzo, the area surrounding Rome, and Sardinia. Popular Easter dishes are agnello arrosto, a roast lamb made in the oven, and Tuscany's agnello imbottonato, a lamb roasted on a spit with pancetta and herbs. Abruzzo's favorite cibo di strada, or street food, is arrosticini made from lamb shoulder and belly: Small pieces of meat on wooden skewers are grilled over charcoal and only salted afterward. The lean and fatty pieces combine to make a deliciously appealing taste and juiciness. This recipe is a little more sophisticated owing to its use of balsamic vinegar, but it combines all the traditional lamb ingredients such as bay leaf, sage, rosemary, and garlic.

Cut the lamb into cubes. Place in a wide bowl and cover with the balsamic vinegar. Let it marinate for about an hour, then remove the meat and pat dry. Reserve the balsamic vinegar for later.

Meanwhile, finely dice the onion, carrot, and celery. De-seed and finely dice the chile pepper. Peel the garlic. Heat the olive oil in a skillet, lightly sauté the garlic clove and the meat in it, season lightly with salt. Then remove the garlic and the meat, and lightly sauté the onion, carrot, and celery, along with the rosemary and sage sprigs. Return the meat to the skillet and deglaze with the white wine. Let the alcohol evaporate, then add the tomatoes to the skillet. Add the bay leaf and cinnamon stick, a pinch of ground cloves, and the reserved balsamic vinegar.

Braise the lamb goulash for around 2 hours on low heat. If it gets too thick, add a little warm water. Remove the rosemary and sage sprigs, the cinnamon stick, and the bay leaf. Season with salt and pepper to taste.

OUR TIP Serve with polenta or wide, flat pappardelle pasta.

Coniglio alla Ligure

Ligurian-Style Rabbit

Serves 4

PREP TIME
10 minutes

COOK TIME
Approximately 1 hour

INGREDIENTS

1 rabbit, cut up and oven-ready

1 sprig rosemary

6 sage leaves

2 sprigs marjoram

2 sprigs thyme

4 bay leaves

3 cloves garlic, lightly crushed

6 tbsp. extra virgin olive oil

⅝ cup (150 ml) dry white wine

Fine sea salt

Freshly ground pepper

A scant ½ cup (100 ml) chicken stock, heated, if needed (see p. 265)

3 ½ oz. (100 g) Taggiasca olives in oil, pitted

A generous 1 oz. (30 g) pine nuts

Meals made with rabbit are considered a very rustic dish in Italy. In Liguria, a region whose landscape (narrow, steep coastline; mountainous, wild hinterland) offers little space for pigs and cattle, smaller animals such as rabbits, poultry, and sheep are traditional main ingredients of a special meal such as Sunday dinner, eaten around noon. Ligurian rabbit dishes benefit from ingredients that are exclusively available in a certain quality in the region: mild olive oil, exceptionally delicious Taggiasca olives, pine nuts, and marjoram, which Ligurians are particularly fond of. If you like innards, you can add the rabbit's liver and kidneys to the roasting pan shortly before the cooking time ends and then enjoy them on crostini. Bread and baked potatoes make delicious sides here.

Carefully clean the rabbit parts, removing any excess bones and fat. Chop the rosemary, sage, marjoram, and thyme, place in a large pot along with the bay leaves, garlic, and oil, and lightly sauté.

Add the rabbit pieces and sauté. Deglaze with the white wine, then season with salt and pepper. Cover and simmer gently for 30 to 40 minutes. Keep turning the pieces of meat and add some warm chicken stock if needed. When the meat is finished cooking, add the olives and pine nuts. Continue to braise for about 10 minutes.

OUR TIP Although there are only a limited number of Ligurian wines, the white wines in particular have a very strong character. The Pigato grape varietal can be called the Riesling of Italy. These wines have Mediterranean herb aromas, along with fruit and floral notes, making them perfect for this recipe!

Polpo alla griglia e Gremolata di Pomodoro

Grilled Octopus with Tomato Gremolata

Serves 2

PREP TIME
20 minutes

COOK TIME
6 to 8 minutes

INGREDIENTS

2 medium tomatoes, firm

½ celery stalk

1 clove garlic

½ red onion

½ red chile pepper

½ bunch flat-leaf parsley

1 untreated lemon

2 tbsp. extra virgin olive oil

Fine sea salt

Freshly ground black pepper

2 octopus tentacles, pre-cooked

2 tbsp. balsamic vinegar, aged for at least 4 years

Salt crystals

Polpo, *or octopus, is a popular dish in Italy, often eaten as a salad to start a meal, simply prepared using parsley, garlic, olives, and lemon. In Liguria, it includes potatoes and Taggiasca olives. Polpo is also popular in ragus, usually with tomato sauce or, cooked in red wine, as is done in Tuscany. Its smaller relative is the* moscardino, *or musky octopus, which is served in Venice as* cicchetti, *a snack enjoyed with wine. This recipe, on the other hand, is very minimalist to make; the balsamic vinegar adds a nice touch here. The interpretation of Lombard gremolata used here goes well with the roasted flavors of the octopus tentacles. The original recipe for gremolata* *(see p. 264)* *only uses flat-leaf parsley, garlic, olive oil, and lemon zest, and is traditionally served with osso buco. But here, the tomato is given a leading role alongside the parsley, the fresh taste of celery, and some chile pepper. This Mediterranean version of gremolata goes perfectly with this summery recipe.*

Core and finely dice the tomatoes. Trim the celery and remove the strings wherever necessary. Finely dice the celery. Finely chop the garlic clove, onion, and chile pepper. Wash the parsley thoroughly and chop with a mezzaluna, or crescent cutter. Rinse the lemon in hot water, then use a zester to peel off the yellow zest in thin strips. Combine the tomatoes, celery, garlic, onion, chile pepper, parsley, and lemon in a bowl. Stir in the olive oil and season with the sea salt and pepper. Set the mixture aside to allow the flavors to infuse.

Light the barbecue and, when the coals are very hot, position the grill rack as low as possible over the coals. Grill the pre-cooked octopus tentacles for 3 to 4 minutes on each side. Plate the grilled tentacles, drizzle them with the balsamic vinegar, and season with the salt crystals and pepper. Serve with the tomato gremolata and white bread.

OUR TIP If you are using frozen octopus that has not been pre-cooked, defrost the tentacles, then put them in a pot of lukewarm water with a little vinegar. Heat slowly and simmer for at least 45 minutes, making sure it does not boil. Near the end of the cooking time, check whether the octopus is soft enough.

Pesce Spada alla griglia con Caponata di verdure

Grilled Swordfish with Sweet and Sour Vegetables

Serves 4

PREP TIME
30 minutes

COOK TIME
Approximately 50 minutes

INGREDIENTS

2 tbsp. pine nuts

2 red onions

1 stalk celery

1 grilled red bell pepper (see p. 24)

3 eggplants

4 ½ cups (1 L) vegetable oil

2 tbsp. extra virgin olive oil

4 anchovy fillets

2 cloves garlic

1 tsp. peperoncino flakes

½ cup (100 ml) vegetable stock (see p. 267)

⅓ cup (50 g) golden raisins

1¾ oz. (50 g) Taggiasca olives

¼ cup (60 ml) San Marzano tomato passata

2 tsp. Crema di Balsamico

2 tbsp. red wine vinegar

Fine sea salt & ground pepper

4 swordfish steaks, 5 to 7 oz. (150 to 200 g) each

Fresh basil

Caponata *is an ideal summer dish. Although it is a simple vegetable dish, the olive oil makes it a filling meal. It is delicious when eaten with bread or as a side dish with fish, like in this recipe with swordfish—a specialty of the big island of Sicily, where it is often enjoyed grilled. It can still be a little pink on the inside when you eat it. As we have mentioned, people in Sicily like to eat lukewarm food, as a result of the high temperatures in the summer. Eating lukewarm dishes is a surprisingly pleasant experience for non-Sicilians, and one that you will definitely want to try; caponata is no exception. Another Sicilian specialty is the combining of sweet and sour, agrodolce, which caponata pays homage to with its vinegar and raisins, and sometimes with a little sugar, too.*

Toast the pine nuts in a pan without oil. Peel and dice the onions. Finely dice the celery, peppers, and eggplants. In a pot, heat the vegetable oil and deep-fry the diced eggplant in it. Once the eggplant is soft, remove and dab with a paper towel.

Sauté the onions in the olive oil, add the finely chopped anchovy fillets and let them melt, then add the celery and peppers. Add the chopped garlic and peperoncino flakes. Add some vegetable stock and simmer for 10 to 15 minutes.

Then add the raisins, pine nuts, and Taggiasca olives, the passata, and the Crema di Balsamico, and simmer for another 10 minutes. Add more stock if needed. Once the celery is soft, add the deep-fried eggplant cubes and pour in the red wine vinegar. Season to taste with salt and pepper and simmer for another 5 minutes.

Brush both sides of the swordfish steaks with olive oil and pan-sear in a hot grill pan for 2 to 3 minutes per side. Do not let them dry out. Season with salt and pepper. Place the swordfish steaks on plates and arrange the caponata next to them. Garnish with the basil.

OUR TIP We recommend a dry, fruity red wine that does not contain a lot of tannins and has a pleasant red berry flavor, such as a Monica di Sardegna from Sardinia. Along with the basil, you can also add chopped flat-leaf parsley and mint to the caponata.

Peperonata con Polpo

Bell Pepper Vegetables with Octopus

Serves 4

PREP TIME
20 minutes

COOK TIME
4 to 5 hours

INGREDIENTS

1 bunch flat-leaf parsley

1 red onion

2 cloves garlic

1 small carrot

1 stalk celery

A generous 2 lbs. (1 kg) mixed bell peppers (red, green, and yellow)

A scant ½ cup (100 ml) mild extra virgin olive oil

7 oz. (200 g) red onion slices

A scant ½ cup (100 ml) dry red wine

1 14-oz. (400 g) can San Marzano tomatoes

Fine sea salt

Freshly ground pepper

1 tsp. oregano

1 tsp. sugar

2 bay leaves

Peperoncino oil

4 octopus tentacles, fresh or precooked

Peperonata *is a true jack-of-all-trades. This stew, which is popular throughout Italy, is delicious hot or cold. It makes a wonderful side dish for meat or fish, or like in our version, a secondo the polpo is cooked in. This recipe is a longstanding tradition in the Viani family, whose roots are in Liguria, where fresh octopus is readily available and occasionally even harpooned by the cooks themselves. You can buy the best octopus in the morning directly from a fishing boat in one of Liguria's many harbors. You can also buy precooked tentacles that are vacuum-packed or frozen. The quality of the vegetables is essential for the success of this dish. Both the peppers and any tomatoes you potentially add should be fully ripened and flavorful. When it comes to canned San Marzano tomatoes, you can be certain they were fully ripened before processing in Campania. When buying the peppers, it is advisable to look for smaller open field varieties and buy them directly from the grower at the farmer's market or at their farm store. Red onions are milder than white ones and have more of a vegetable flavor, making this choice ideal for peperonata.*

Finely chop the parsley with the stalks. Peel and finely dice the onion and garlic. Trim and peel the carrot and finely dice. Trim the celery, remove any strings, and finely dice.

De-seed the peppers and cut into cubes slightly larger than 1 × 1 inch (3 × 3 cm). Heat the olive oil in a sauté pan and sauté the soffritto (parsley, diced onion, garlic, carrot, and celery) in it for 5 minutes. Add the pepper cubes and onion slices, and brown well. If you have any fresh, fully ripened tomatoes in the kitchen, you can cut them into pieces and add them.

Deglaze with the red wine, let it reduce somewhat, then add the San Marzano tomatoes. Season with salt, pepper, oregano, sugar, bay leaves, and a few dashes of peperoncino oil. Cut the tentacles into pieces ⅜ inch (1 cm) long and add. Now let it simmer on the lowest possible heat for 4 hours. If using pre-cooked tentacles, add these after 3 hours.

OUR TIP Serve with coarse-ground polenta, which soaks up the delicious vegetable broth very well. Alternatively, if you prefer to make the finer polenta fioretto and let it cool, you can cut it into diamond-shaped pieces and fry it in olive oil. Like *Patate al Forno*, the Italian roast potato, the fried polenta will add delicious roasted flavors to the peperonata.

Pesce e Frutti di Mare

Fish and Seafood

With its 4,900 miles (7,600 kilometers) of coastline and four surrounding oceans and seas, Italy is enveloped by water and an abundance of fish. The vast array of fresh seafood on Italian menus may be daunting for some, but Italians are passionate about their fish. The ancient Romans incorporated the *Mare Nostrum*, as they called the Mediterranean, and all its inhabitants into their diet. Historically, fish was considered a food for those of modest means, but today it is a true delicacy, particularly in the form of *brodetto*. This soup-like fish stew was originally prepared by fishermen on their boats using seawater and fish too small or too damaged to be sold. Today, it is popular throughout the country. The rich variety of seafood continues to be sold fresh on the docks, with countless unique varieties available. Some of these have had a particularly enduring impact on Italian culinary culture:

Acciughe / Alici In Italy, anchovies have two names. The word *acciuga*, derived from Latin, is commonly used on the Ligurian coast, while *alice* is prevalent in Naples and Sicily. Either way, anchovies hold a permanent place in the cuisine throughout the country, used as an invisible seasoning, a welcome side dish, and a delicious main course. Anchovies are typically placed in oil or brine, and outside of Italy, they are referred to as *alici* anchovies. Immediately after being caught between March and July, these small, silvery-blue fish are salted raw and fermented before being bottled or canned in oil or brine. In any form, anchovies are a true delight—on a simple piece of buttered bread or as a seasoning to add unique flavor to countless sughi and dishes. Ideally, their presence is subtle, leaving you wondering what makes the dish taste so incredibly good. Classic recipes include *Spaghetti alla Putanesca*, bagna cauda vegetable dipping sauce, and salsa verde, a cold sauce made from raw anchovies and vinegar.

Baccalà The world would be very different without stockfish, typically made from cod. It served as the main sustenance on numerous European expeditions and conquests, crucial in supplying provisions to the vast numbers of ship crews and soldiers colonizing America,

Asia, and Africa. Stockfish is still preserved using the same process as back then, by being heavily salted and then dried on a wooden rack, hence its Italian name, *baccala*, as *baculus* is Latin for stick. Before cooking, stockfish must be soaked to remove the excess salt. In Neapolitan eateries, *baccalajuole*, some even local celebrities, handle this. For centuries, the village of Somma on Mount Vesuvius has been the import and distribution hub for cod in southern Italy. Here, "red" recipes with tomatoes are popular, whereas "white" tomato-less recipes are favored elsewhere.

Sarde Sardines can be considered the bigger siblings of anchovies, with generally fattier flesh, making them especially popular on plates, in sandwiches, or grilled. Seasonal sardines fished exclusively in late fall are regarded as the best variety due to their particularly high fat content, resulting in a richer flavor and more succulent texture.

Tonno In May, large tuna migrate from the Atlantic to the Mediterranean to spawn. They are well-fed and at the peak of their flavor at this time of year. Due to its red, firm, and fatty flesh, tuna is one of the most important edible fish varieties and a welcome addition to any menu. In Italy, it is enjoyed raw as carpaccio, fresh from the grill, on pizza, and—of course—with pasta. However, the most sought-after part is the ventresca, or the belly. This tender, flavorful cut is prized for its rich taste and smooth texture, making it a culinary delicacy.

Pesce Spada Swordfish are among the fastest fish in the sea, and they typically live in pairs. If one is caught, the other becomes an easy target as well. However, this usually only occurs during the summer when the fish travel from the far reaches of the ocean to the Italian coast to spawn. It is here, in the Strait of Messina, that fishermen await an epic duel with these majestic creatures. If the angler emerges victorious, the reward is a particularly tasty fish that can be enjoyed smoked as carpaccio, cooked, or served in pieces with pasta. The ultimate prize is the collar, considered the most delectable part.

Vongole Ancient peoples believed mussels were asexual creatures born from sea foam, a notion reflected in Roman mythology and Botticelli's famous painting of Venus emerging from the ocean on a shell, giving the culinary world's highly prized Venus clams their name. In Italian, however, *vongola* represents the entire genus of mussels. Venus clams are found along the Adriatic coast most often atop a steaming pile of spaghetti. Further south, in Apulia, *cozze*, blue mussels, take center stage, served stuffed, cooked, deep-fried, sauteed, or au gratin.

Polpo An octopus is a decidedly aristocratic dish; it has blue blood, after all. This unique adaptation allows octopuses to survive in the deep sea, where blood with a copper base transports oxygen more efficiently than blood with an iron base. The octopus flesh is also exquisite, but requires tenderizing—a process the fisherfolk sometimes undertake themselves by banging the freshly caught octopus against large rocks. Once tenderized, octopus can be served in a variety of ways, in a ragu or salad, or with pasta. In Sicily, a wine cork is commonly cooked in the pot with the octopus to further enhance its tenderness.

Aside from classic seafoods, virtually everything caught in the waters surrounding this fish-loving nation finds its way to the table, often perfectly paired with pasta. However, the methods of preparing fish are diverse: *Zuppa*, soup, is a rustic dish made with fish cut into pieces, or *da taglio*. *Brodetto* is a popular fish stew with the fish is cooked in broth. *Grigliata* is a whole fish grilled to perfection. Lastly, *Guazzetto* is a ragout of premium fish braised in high-quality wine and fresh tomatoes. The following sea creatures are particularly well-suited for these:

Branzino Sea bass, also known as *spigola*, has a very delicate flavor that is particularly enhanced when grilled or baked in the oven.

Muggine Mullets are also known as *cefalo* in the south of the country. Its firm flesh has a distinctive flavor, and it is typically prepared by being sautéed in a pan, baked in the oven, or grilled.

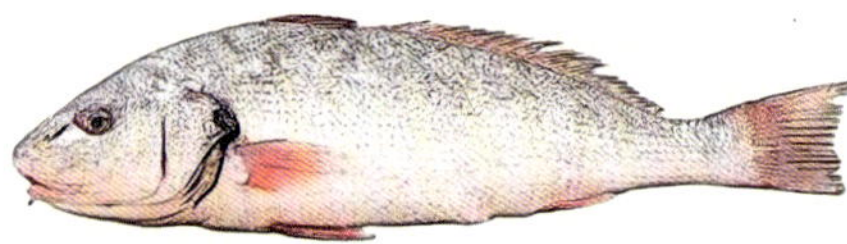

Ombrina Croakers are very rich in protein and minerals and prized for their delicate flavor. They are prepared with seawater, lemon, and white wine.

Orata The gilthead sea bream has soft flesh that tastes slightly salty and is rich in protein and vitamin B. It is often prepared in the oven or on the grill, and is a favorite in Mediterranean cuisine.

Calamari These small squid are de rigueur on Italian tables. The Romans loved them as dumplings, in ragout, or stuffed, but today they are usually grilled with fresh lemon, garlic, and a sprinkle of parsley, often served with a side of tomato sauce.

Aragosta The clawless *aragosta*, or spiny lobsters, are primarily found along the coast of Sardinia, where they are often served with the island's traditional *fregola* pasta.

Astice This Italian lobster variety with claws, has delicate meat that is usually just boiled, and is the crowning glory of menus at Ligurian and Venetian seaside eateries. *Linguine all'Astice*, linguine with lobster, is a festively served on Christmas and New Year's Eve in Italy.

Gamberi These small crustaceans are available along the entire Italian coast, with the best specimens coming from Trapani, Sicily. Shrimp meat tastes slightly sweet and firm to the bite. They are usually cooked and served with pasta or baked in the oven.

Scampi Norway lobsters are a type of lobster-like crustacean. Their meat has a slightly nutty flavor and a tender texture. Only their tails are served, for example, as a starter with lemon or fried with garlic as bruschetta. A true coastal classic.

"Time is distilled in every drop."
– Gennaro Castiello, Aquapazza Gourmet

Although the majority of fish lands on the table while fresh, sometimes it is processed, becoming a unique specialty along the way:

Colatura di Alici This fermented fish sauce from the small fishing village of Cetara near Naples, has not only conquered the entire country of Italy; it has also found its way into kitchens beyond the Alps. This amber-colored, intensely flavored anchovy sauce maintains a long tradition dating back to the ancient Romans, who called it *garum*. In accordance with the regulations, the anchovies, cleaned and heads removed, are placed in salt, and after 24 hours, they are placed in barrels and layered with ample sea salt, then slowly pressed. The resulting liquid is collected and stored in large glass bottles under the sun for the entire summer. This process yields a thick concentrate that is poured over the fish stored in the barrels in the fall, slowly seeping through the individual layers. As a result, the colatura acquires an increasingly rich flavor until it is ready, just in time for Christmas dinner. Colatura di Alici is incredibly versatile, adding a surprising depth of flavor to many dishes. A few drops added to salad dressing or vegetables enhances the taste without giving the food a fishy flavor.

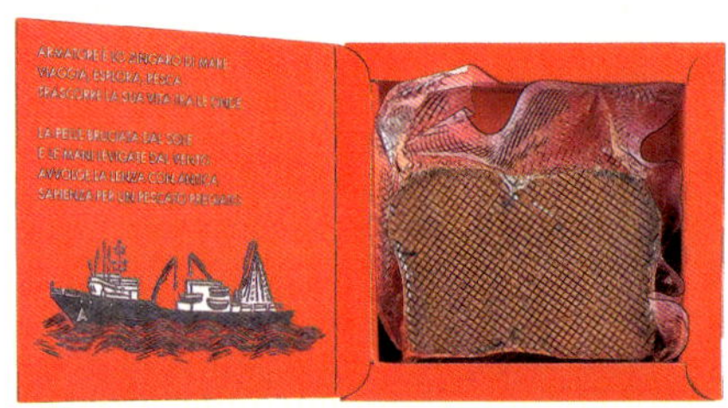

Bottarga The Sardinian caviar, is dried mullet or tuna roe. With a history of over 3,000 years, it was particularly valued by the Phoenicians as a staple for seafarers. The production process is largely unchanged: The roe sac is pressed whole, then salted and dried. Bottarga is used to season a variety of dishes, including vegetables, pasta, risotto, or simply sliced thinly and enjoyed on bread.

ZODIAC
ZODIAC

Frittata della Nonna

Grandma's Frittata with Chard

Serves 4

PREP TIME
30 minutes

COOK TIME
30 minutes

INGREDIENTS

2 pounds 3 oz. (1 kg) chard

Fine sea salt

1 large onion

1 bunch flat-leaf parsley

2 to 3 cloves garlic

Extra virgin olive oil

1½ stale kaiser rolls

A scant ½ cup (100 ml) milk

6 to 8 eggs

1 tsp. dried marjoram,
or 1 handful fresh

Freshly ground pepper

5¼ oz (150 g) Parmigiano
Reggiano DOP cheese

Unlike the French with their omelette, Italians do not fold their frittata. An Italian frittata is robust, thick, and packed with delicious ingredients. It also serves as a perfectly juicy filling for a roll, ideal for picnics and various other casual occasions such as a simple midweek lunch or a late Sunday breakfast. One frittata recipe has remained a favorite in the Viani family across at least four generations: frittata with chard, seasoned with marjoram. Vegetables and herbs are common ingredients in Ligurian cuisine, in pesto sauces, in stuffed pasta, or in sauces that accompany a range of dishes. This is the original recipe from Remo Viani's nonna, who passed it on to her son Antonio, who passed it on to his son, with great-granddaughter Anna now making the frittata as well. So today we will be making our frittata just like it was made on the Ligurian coast many decades ago!

Clean and trim the chard leaves; separate them from the stalks. In a pot of salted water, cook the stems for 15 minutes, adding the leaves for the last 5 minutes. Then rinse with cold water and drain well. Thoroughly squeeze out any excess moisture from the leaves. Finely chop the leaves and stems and set aside. Finely chop the onion, parsley, and garlic, then sauté in some olive oil. Soak the bread roll in the milk, squeeze out any excess milk, then chop into small pieces.

Crack the eggs into a large bowl and season with marjoram, salt, and pepper.

Add the sautéed parsley, onion, and garlic, the chopped bread rolls, and the chard to the bowl; combine thoroughly until the mixture is uniform. Grate the Parmesan and add it with freshly ground pepper to the mixture.

Add olive oil to a high-sided frying pan (we recommend a pan with an 11-inch diameter (28 cm)). Heat the oil over medium heat and pour in the egg mixture. Cook for around 15 minutes, until the surface is set. Make sure it does not get too hot. Cook it slowly without letting it burn. To flip the frittata, place a round board on top of the pan, quickly turn it over, and let the frittata slide back into the pan. Let it cook slowly on this side for about 15 minutes.

OUR TIP This frittata goes well with a tomato salad with Taggiasca olives packed in olive oil and some white bread. The frittata gets even more flavorful when left to stand in the refrigerator overnight.

Parmigiana di Melanzane

Eggplant Casserole

Serves 6 to 8

PREP TIME
1½ hours

BAKE TIME
25 minutes

INGREDIENTS

4 eggplants, approximately 2 lbs. (900 g) total

Fine sea salt

4 cloves garlic

A scant ½ cup (100 ml) extra virgin olive oil

2 14-oz. (800 g) cans San Marzano peeled tomatoes

Freshly ground pepper

1 pinch peperoncino flakes

1 pinch sugar

14 oz. (400 g) mozzarella di buffala or fior di latte mozzarella cheese

5 sprigs fresh basil

1 sprig fresh mint

7 oz. (200 g) Parmigiano Reggiano DOP cheese, finely grated

The word Parmigiana evokes visions of Parma and Parmesan cheese, of northern Italy. But when you eat this casserole, you are immediately transported to Sicily or Naples. The eggplants, tomatoes, and mozzarella make sure of this. This dish is such a tasty comfort food that it has found a home in numerous regions in Italy. In Apulia, people add hard-boiled eggs or mortadella and ham to it. The original recipe here, without meat and eggs, captures the essence of summer. The eggplant makes it so wonderfully full-bodied that you don't even realize it is a vegetarian dish. Therein lies the beauty of the Italian cuisine we adore: cucina povera, the cuisine of thoseon a strict budget who could seldom afford meat, resulting in so many surprisingly simple yet intensely flavorful recipes using vegetables, herbs, and legumes. Parmigiana is not quite as modest as those dishes, but certainly makes for a very satisfying dining experience.

Rinse and trim the eggplants; cut into slices approximately ⅜ inch (1 cm) thick. Salt on both sides and let sit for 10 minutes to draw the excess moisture out. Place the slices on paper towels to dry and wipe off the salt. You can also skip this step if you are short on time.

Peel and finely chop the garlic, then sauté in a small pot in 2 tablespoons of olive oil. Add the tomatoes, crushing them with a wooden spoon. Season with salt, pepper, peperoncino flakes, and sugar, then bring to a boil and let reduce uncovered over medium heat for approximately 20 minutes.

In the meantime, roast the eggplant slices in batches on both sides in a large, non-stick grill pan without oil. As you continue to roast each batch of eggplant slices, sauté the roasted slices in a separate grill pan in olive oil. They should be soft, have a nice grilled pattern on them, and have absorbed some of the oil. Preheat the oven to 360 °F (180 °C) using convection. Oil a casserole dish with olive oil. Thinly slice or cube the mozzarella. Tear the basil and mint leaves into pieces. Pour some tomato sauce into the dish, place a layer of eggplant slices on top, add some basil, mint, Parmesan, and mozzarella, then another layer of tomato sauce; repeat. Finish with tomato sauce and sprinkle with plenty of Parmesan cheese. Bake in the preheated oven for around 25 minutes.

OUR TIP In Italy, this casserole is often eaten lukewarm or even cold, making it easier to cut; plus it doesn't separate into its various layers. Be sure to serve with bread—the sauce absolutely begs for dipping.

Verdure d'autunno

Fall Vegetables

As temperatures drop, the light changes, and the landscape's colors put on a dazzling display, Italian cooks continue to create dishes using the freshest seasonal vegetables. Several of the most popular varieties reach their peak during autumn. While they may be less plentiful compared to spring or summer produce, these fall vegetables are heartier and equally essential to authentic Italian cuisine. Having absorbed the summer's abundant sunshine, they provide the perfect ingredients for meals that nourish both body and soul, ensuring that even as the weather cools, the flavors remain delightfully vibrant.

As Gaius Valerius Catullus once said, "the pot chooses its vegetables."

These vegetables are particularly popular in pots and on plates in the fall:

Fagiolini Autumn brings a cornucopia of bean varieties cherished by Italians, especially in Tuscany, to the market. Some are fresh, others newly dried from recent harvests. These legumes, like lentils, have long been a crucial protein source for rural communities. The moniker *Mangiafagoli* or "Bean Eater," immortalized in Annibale Carracci's famous painting of the same name, is sometimes playfully used for Tuscans, especially in Florence. One popular way to cook white beans like cannellini or *fagioli di Sorana* is *fiasco*. Sautéed with olive oil, sage, and garlic, they make a popular side dish for *Bistecca alla Fiorentina*. Another well-liked side dish, *Fagioli all'Uccelletto*, features beans stewed with tomato puree and sage.

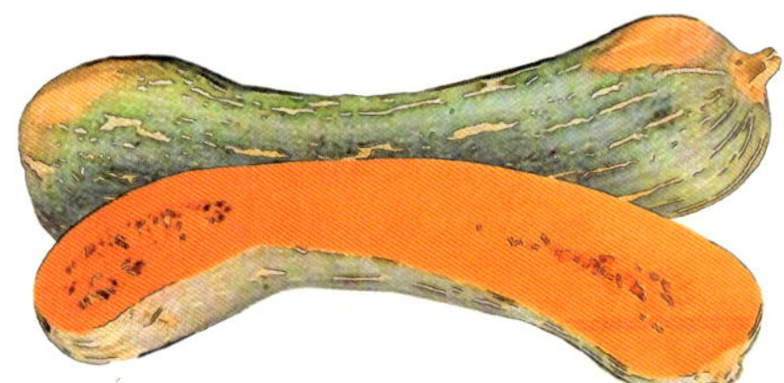

Zucca With 850 different varieties, pumpkins come in a wide array of sizes, shapes, colors, and flavors. Only around 200 of these are suitable for consumption, while the remaining varieties are visually appealing, but unpalatable, potentially containing toxic, bitter-tasting compounds. Edible pumpkins are rich in beta-carotene, which the body converts into vitamin A, essential for healthy eyesight, a robust immune system, and responsible for the characteristic orange of many pumpkin varieties. Thanks to their firm flesh and a delicate hint of honey, edible pumpkins lend themselves to both sweet and savory dishes, popularly used in numerous authentic Italian recipes, baked with sugar, served in a sweet and sour dish in Sicily, or in hearty soups, gnocchi, quiches, and flans. Pumpkin also pairs wonderfully with pasta.

Spinaci Spinach, available year-round, boasts firmer leaves and a more robust flavor during the autumn months. It is a true hero in the kitchen, not only for its ability to give color to other foods, but also for its wealth of essential minerals that make it so healthy. While the legendary high iron content is more myth than reality, spinach does contain ecdysteroids, which can lead to increased strength, albeit not to the levels portrayed by Popeye. Spinach pairs beautifully with cheese, eggs, bacon, and fish, and can be enjoyed both raw and cooked. However, it's important to note that it shrinks to a mere 1/8 of its original size when cooked, making it advisable to plan for significantly larger quantities when making frittatas, risottos, and ricotta-filled ravioli. Fortunately, this is something most cooks are more than happy to do. In northern Italy, spinach is particularly prized as a filling for pasta like ravioli and lasagna, and in savory pies called *Torta salate*. In Emilia Romagna, spinach is also one of the ingredients in *erbazzone*, a pastry stuffed solely with green vegetables. Spinach also lends its vibrant hue to pasta, such as lasagna sheets.

Indivia Belga Belgian endive owes its discovery—and its name—to chance. Legend has it that around 1870, Belgian farmers stored the chicory roots grown as a substitute for coffee in the greenhouse after harvesting. During the winter months, pale oval leaves grew from the roots in the absence of light, boasting a remarkably delicate flavor. Fully grown, these leaves offer a delightful crispness and a bittersweet taste, making them a perfect addition to salads featuring bacon, capers, and citrus fruits. This crisp lettuce variety also frequently finds its way into cooked dishes, paired with chicory and guanciale in risottos, or velvety vegetable soups.

Finocchio Crunchy and firm to the bite, succulent, and boasting a sweet, anise-scented flavor, fennel is a multifaceted vegetable. Beyond its culinary applications, it is a medicinal plant known for aiding digestion. But it can also be braised, breaded, sautéed, or cooked in risottos. It harmonizes perfectly with olive oil and citrus fruits (and also has twice their vitamin C content). In Italian cuisine, fennel is both vegetable and spice, with its seeds, leaves, and bulb finding use in numerous authentic dishes. Its influence even permeates the language, as *infinocchiare* means "to cloud, to deceive," stemming from fennel's ability to mask the taste and smell of less-than-fresh food. In the past, restaurateurs capitalized on this, serving crunchy fennel alongside subpar wine and stale dishes. At least the fennel was good and healthy.

Zuppa Etrusca This soup contains an authentic medley of various types of beans, peas, and red lentils, a stew that is the epitome of traditional peasant cuisine. While you can, of course, customize the combination of ingredients, this recipe ensures uniform cooking of all legumes. True to Italian custom, it begins with a soffritto base. Legumes are then added and topped up with vegetable stock. Fresh tomato chunks provide a zesty finish. Grated Parmesan or Pecorino and toasted bread complete this satisfying dish. For an even more vegetable-rich variation, try Tuscan *Ribollita*, a classic Italian favorite.

Pesto Finochietto Selvatico Sicily's landscape is dotted with wild fennel, its sweet aroma permeating the air under the Mediterranean sun. This freshly picked culinary staple garnishes salads and seafood, while whole fish are often stuffed with it. It is often preserved as a pesto, blended with capers, tomatoes, pine nuts, garlic, parsley, and occasionally raisins. This versatile condiment makes wonderful summer pasta dishes, goes well with grilled fish, meat, and vegetables, and adds zest to marinades and salad dressings.

Verdure d'inverno

Winter Vegetables

Stillness permeates the air. Beneath the earth's surface, nature quietly gathers its strength for the warmer days ahead. However, some vegetables defy the cold temperatures and develop particularly strong flavors. In the comfort of warm kitchens, these vegetables add a multitude of authentic dishes to Italy's vibrant cuisine. Hearty soups, slowly simmered stews, and braised creations brimming with vegetables fill homes with an enticing aroma that holds the promise of delicious meals to come. Winter may be a quiet season, but it is by no means a time of culinary deprivation.

"To get the best results, you must talk to your vegetables."—King Charles III.

Some say it is the mild climate that allows Italy to harvest an abundance of the finest vegetables even in winter. But there are also hardy vegetable varieties able to withstand frost. Here are the best of those:

Carciofi Zeus fell in love with the nymph Cynara, but she spurned his advances. In a fit of anger, he transformed her into an artichoke. This truly divine vegetable has been popular in Italy with the rich and famous since ancient times; today, the country remains the world's foremost producer and consumer. Artichokes come in an incredible variety of shapes, textures, and flavors, ranging from fleshy or tender to bitter or sweet, all offering an exceptionally exquisite culinary experience. Notable varieties include the Spinoso di Sardegna DOC from Sardinia, a rather thorny variety that is best served baked with mint and ricotta or served alongside lamb, or the Carciofo Tema del Sulcis DOC, another thorny Sardinian variety that absolutely must be grilled, and lastly, the Carciofo Romanesco de Lazio IGT from Lazio, a round artichoke ideally suited for the numerous Roman dishes featuring this ingredient. Indeed, Rome is not only the capital of the *Bel Paese*, or beautiful country, but is also the undisputed capital of the artichoke.

Cavolfiore The cauliflower's fresh flavor and attractive appearance make it a favorite in authentic Italian cuisine. Its popularity is unsurprising, as Italy offers an array of colorful varieties, ranging from pale green and rich yellow to vibrant purple. It is often cooked as the main dish, such as in tarts, quiches, or crostata. Whether cooked, deep-fried, or marinated, cauliflower cuts a fine figure in any dish. The Cavolfiore di Torbole variety from Lake Garda is especially prized for its earthy, genuine flavor that pairs perfectly with robust, savory dishes.

Patate Potatoes are both poisonous and extremely nutritious. Their skin contains a lot of solanine, a toxin the plant produces to defend itself against predators, so potatoes should always be cooked and peeled before consumption. Their cultivation dates back 8,000 years in the South American Andes, brought to Europe by Spanish conquistadors. Initially, Europeans admired this night-shade plant for its attractive flowers, growing as a decorative plant. It wasn't until the 18th century that potatoes found their way into cooking pots, eventually becoming a staple across the continent. While potatoes are often relegated to the role of side dish abroad, in Italy, they frequently take center stage, such as in the popular dish of gnocchi. The best potato varieties for gnocchi are the floury ones, as they have a higher starch content from exposure to more sunlight than their waxy counterparts. However, this makes them no less delicious.

Carote These root vegetables are incredibly nutritious, boasting high levels of carotene, vitamin C, potassium, and iron, which play a crucial role in building resistance against various illnesses. Moreover, carrots are remarkably versatile in the kitchen. In Italian cuisine, people love to eat them raw or cooked, often paired with cheese, cream, celery, and herbs, whereby their slightly sweet flavor comes through best when they are cooked in butter. Carrots are an indispensable ingredient in minestrone, they are also an essential part of sofritto, and are the perfect accompaniment for bagna cauda.

Broccoli For a long time, the only place broccoli, hailing from Asia Minor, could be found in Europe was in Italian kitchens. Then Caterina de' Medici introduced this magnificent vegetable to France and the rest of Europe. Today, Italy remains a primary broccoli producer and undoubtedly one of its main consumers as well. Broccoli is a popular side dish there, bringing both abundant nutrients and delightful flavor to the table, especially when made with cheese, anchovies, and pine nuts. It can be enjoyed sautéed as a side dish, transformed into a pesto, or cooked al dente and tossed with pasta.

Cime di Rapa Broccoli rabe, also known as rapini and Italian broccoli in the US, goes by the name *friarielli* in Campania, a term derived from the classic Neapolitan dish whose name is in turn derived from the Neapolitan word *frijere*, or frying. While broccoli rabe remains a lesser-known vegetable, it enjoys immense popularity throughout southern Italy. Its intense, bitter, and delightful flavor provides a perfect contrast to grilled meat or hearty pasta dishes.

Barbabietole Underrated elsewhere, red beets are highly revered in Italy. Not only because high folic acid content puts them among the healthiest vegetables, but also because their subtle flavor adds a truly unique dimension to many dishes. Their flavor is earthy, yet very mild, and further enhanced through cooking. Thoroughly cooking beets can be a time-consuming process, though, so pre-cooked options are often available for purchase. Beets pair perfectly with gorgonzola cheese, but they also taste great on their own: roasted, diced, or in a salad with a generous amount of oil. In the past, beets were used as a source of dye, and while this still happens today, it is usually unintentional. As such, avoid wearing white when making this vibrant vegetable.

Porri While toxic to animals, leeks are incredibly beneficial for humans, with a high folic acid content. In ancient Egypt, they were credited with helping workers build the pyramids. In Italy, they are often used to enhance other vegetables in broths, stews, and casseroles. But these dishes don't fully showcase the nuanced flavor of leeks. They really come into their own in risottos, quiches, and gratins, with tomatoes, cheese, and cream.

GELATÈ
G
GELATERIA
CAFFETTERIA
APERITIVI
PIATTI FREDDI
CREPES
LOTTO

Zabaione

Creamy Egg Foam with Marsala

Serves 4

PREP TIME
3 minutes

COOK TIME
20 minutes

INGREDIENTS

4 egg yolks

½ cup (100 g) sugar

A scant ½ cup (100 ml) dry Marsala wine

You can of course enjoy zabaglione all by itself, but it can also be deliciously combined with panettone, amaretti or ladyfingers, either the Savoiardi version or the Sardinian variety. Zabaglione practically begs you to dip something in it. Marsala wine is the most obvious choice of alcohol here, but other sweet wines are used in some regions. In Piedmont, for example, it is made with Moscato d'Asti, and sometimes a sweet, red sparkling wine such as Brachetto d'Acqui, which is a good recommendation for other occasions as well. With its egg yolk and sugar, this dessert is not just a feel-good recipe that provides a nice finish to a meal; it has also proven its worth for those tough moments when you just need a boost. In Italy, it is made alla nonna, *or Italian grandmother-style, in the winter or for breakfast before a busy day, with or without alcohol.*

Place the egg yolks and sugar in a metal bowl and mix briefly using a hand mixer. Place the metal bowl in a hot water bath that is simmering, not boiling, for 10 minutes, then whisk the mixture until creamy. Pour in the Marsala and whisk for another 10 minutes to form a light, frothy cream. The cream should be stable, and the sugar should be completely dissolved.

OUR TIP If you love this dessert, you might want to find out more about Marsala wines. Not only are they available in different qualities, there are also dry, semi-dry, and sweet Marsala wines. Marsala is wonderful to sweeten zabaglione and add variety to its taste, but you may also discover you enjoy a dry version as an aperitif or a sweet dessert wine paired with pastries to end your meal, for example.

Tiramisù

Tiramisu

Serves 6 to 8

PREP TIME
20 minutes

REFRIGERATION TIME
At least 5 hours

INGREDIENTS

4 fresh eggs

Salt

⅓ cup (80 g) sugar

2 ¼ cups (500 g) mascarpone

⅞ cup (200 ml) cold espresso

4 tablespoons sweet Marsala wine

Approximately 30 (300 g) Savoiardi ladyfingers

2 tablespoons unsweetened cocoa powder

Since 2017, the city of Treviso, nestled in the Veneto region, marks March 21st as Tiramisù Day, celebrating the dessert believed to have first been created there. This testifies to the popularity of this dessert, whose complex harmony captivates the taste buds: The slightly bitter flavors of the espresso and the dark cocoa powder meet the creamy milkiness of the mascarpone and the delicate sweetness of the lady-fingers (called Savoiardi in Italian, they trace their origins back to the court of the Duchy of Savoy). Sweet Marsala wine adds a little jolt of excitement; some prefer to use Amaretto as an alternative. And the creaminess combined with spongy ladyfingers make its consistency irresistible. Tiramisu is available at most Italian restaurants. It tastes even better when it is homemade using the best ingredients, such as genuine Savoiardi *ladyfingers; freshly brewed, strong espresso; sweet Marsala wine; and artisanal mascarpone, just like in our recipe here. Then, despite the richness of its ingredients, it truly earns its name: Tiramisù, which means "lift me up" or "pick me up."*

Separate the egg yolks and whites and gently transfer them to two separate bowls. Beat the egg whites with a pinch of salt until stiff. Whisk the egg yolks with the sugar. Stir the mascarpone into the egg yolk mixture, making sure it is combined well, then fold in the stiff egg whites.

Combine the espresso and the Marsala wine. Arrange the lady-fingers next to one another in an 11 × 17 × 2 inch (25 × 25 × 5 cm) casserole dish, covering the entire bottom. Drizzle with the coffee-Marsala mixture, but do so sparingly so they don't get too soft. Spread half of the mascarpone-egg cream on top. Cover with the next layer of ladyfingers and carefully drizzle with the coffee-Marsala mixture again. Finish with a cream layer. Then cover the tiramisu and refrigerate it for at least 5 hours to allow the flavors to develop. Sift the cocoa powder over the cream layer right before serving.

OUR TIP A glass of dessert wine pairs well with this. Enjoy a sweet Marsala with at least 10 % vol. or a Vin Santo.

Bunet

Piedmont-Style Caramel Pudding

Serves 6 to 8

PREP TIME
30 minutes

COOK TIME
1 hour, plus 30 minutes to cool

INGREDIENTS

3 oz. (85 g) Amarettini di Saronno (dry almond cookies), plus a few for decoration if desired

4 eggs

A scant 1 cup (170 g) sugar

2 cups + 4 teaspoons (500 ml) milk, lukewarm

A scant 3½ tbsp. (50 ml) rum

1¾ oz. (50 g) cocoa powder

Bunet *is the Piedmont region's oldest known dessert. Historical records from the 14th century reference this* dolce, *or dessert, being served in aristocratic households in the Langhe region. Its name is believed to have come from a hat whose shape was similar to that of the copper pot used to make bunet at the time. Its taste is reminiscent of a chocolaty caramel pudding and was originally flavored with fernet, a traditional herbal bitter from the same region. Rum has since replaced it, making for a more elegant version. Piedmont is known for its refined dolci and its coffee house culture, especially in its capital city of Turin. Cocoa powder and Piedmont hazelnuts often form the bases for these desserts. Specialties include* Tartufi Dolci, *Gianduia hazelnut pralines, the minimalist hazelnut cake* Torta di Nocciola, *and* baci di dama, *a crumbly hazelnut sandwich cookie filled with chocolate cream, best enjoyed with an espresso. We highly recommend visiting the local coffee houses, and bunet is a wonderful introduction to the sweet treats of the Piedmont region.*

Preheat the oven to 210 °F (100 °C) using the convection setting.

Blend the *amarettini* in a blender until they become a very fine flour-like powder; alternatively, use a rolling pin to finely crush them in a plastic bag. Beat the eggs with a scant ½ cup (90 g) of the sugar until frothy. Add the amarettini powder, lukewarm milk, rum, and cocoa powder, and mix well.

Heat the remaining sugar in a small pan with 3 tablespoons of water until it melts into a light-colored caramel. It should have a syrupy consistency. Pour the caramel into an ovenproof loaf pan (10 × 4 inches/ 25 × 10 cm) or small molds. Pour the egg mixture on top of the caramel, and place the loaf pan or molds in a deep ovenproof container. Add lukewarm water until it is two thirds of the way up the side of the pan or molds. Cover the container with aluminum foil, and place in the lower third of the preheated oven for 1 hour. The water bath poaches the pudding. Insert a wooden skewer to test the consistency. If there is still a lot of pudding clinging to the stick and it is moist, let the pudding bake a little longer.

Let the molds or loaf pan cool completely for at least 30 minutes, then turn the pudding out onto a platter, or, if you used molds, onto individual plates. Decorate with amarettini if desired.

OUR TIP Orange liqueur goes very well with this chocolaty pudding. You can also heat up orange fillets in the liqueur to serve with the bunet.

Cioccolato

Chocolate

We have the Holy See to thank for this divine indulgence. In the late 16th century, a pope found the taste of chocolate so disgusting that he did not hesitate to permit its consumption as a drink while fasting. This was the catalyst for chocolate's triumphant advance throughout Europe and in Turin's traditional pastry shops.

The Spaniards introduced chocolate to Europe when they brought it from the New World, where the Aztecs had already been drinking it. That drink, however, made from cocoa beans and water, had nothing in common with today's deliciously sweet cocoa. It was bitter and spicy—as the name suggests, chocolate comes from the Aztec word *xocóatl*, a combination of *xócoc* (bitter) and *atl* (water). It was only after honey and cane sugar were added that it became a drink suitable for European palates—and its popularity exploded. Even Casanova himself preferred cocoa to champagne as an aphrodisiac.

Before the first chocolate bars appeared on the market in 1847, chocolate was still sold in pharmacies as a pick-me-up. There is no evidence that chocolate could be physically addictive or habit-forming. At least not officially.

If you are both a chocolate lover and a pet lover, it is crucial that you store all chocolate out of reach of your pets, as chocolate is toxic for them. This is because, like caffeine, the theobromine in chocolate has a stimulating effect, which is literally too much for canine and feline nervous systems.

The chocolate production process is quite demanding:

Cocoa beans grow in West Africa and Central and South America. There, they are harvested, dried, and fermented for ten days, then roasted and ground, heated, and rolled a number of times. The dry mass is then combined with cocoa butter, sugar and, in some cases, milk powder, then heated again and scraped. This is the only way to give it its typical, delicate melt-in-your-mouth consistency and wonderfully mild flavor. However, this conching process can take up to 72 hours for good chocolates. The subsequent tempering, which involves gradual cooling, must also be carried out with great care to ensure the proper crystallization occurs and the resulting chocolate melts in your mouth as desired.

And this is something all three types of chocolate do, no matter how different they are from one another. Dark chocolate is bitter and crunchy, with lots of cocoa but not as much cocoa butter and sugar, and no milk whatsoever. Milk chocolate, on the other hand, is softer and sweeter thanks to the added milk. And white chocolate is particularly creamy, consisting only of cocoa butter. A good rule of thumb is, the shorter the list of ingredients, the better the quality of the chocolate.

When chocolate experiences fluctuations from cold to warm temperatures, whitish streaks may form on its surface. This is not mold; it is cocoa butter escaping—the chocolate is still edible, but it may not taste quite as smooth and full-bodied. To avoid this, chocolate should be stored in a cool, dark place, ideally at a constant temperature of 54–64°F (12–18°C), and not in the refrigerator. Even the Pope says so.

"Nine out of ten people like chocolate; the tenth is lying."—John Tullius

Besides the major industrial companies, there are a few traditional chocolate makers in Italy who have created true originals, and they remain committed to quality.

Venchi This Turin chocolatier and former royal court supplier is famous not only for its exquisite chocolates and ice cream, but also for its nougatine, which has remained unchanged since its creation in 1905, and it is simply fantastic.

Caffarel One of Turin's oldest chocolatiers, Caffarel created an iconic product synonymous with the Piedmont region. *Gianduiotti*, small chocolates reminiscent of the shape of the hat of famous Carnevale character *Gianduia*, melt in your mouth like no other.

Bonajuto A newspaper article and TV appearance by Sicilian master chocolatier Franco Rita brought Modica chocolate both fame and popularity. Signore Rita steadfastly adheres to the authentic traditional recipe in making his company's delectable offerings.

Amedei This Tuscan chocolate manufacturer is highly exclusive. Everything is done here in-house one hundred percent bean-to-bar, from purchasing the cocoa beans directly from the farmer to roasting, refining, processing, and packaging. The extremely rare *Amedei Porcelana* is the best proof of Amadei's incredible quality.

Antica Torroneria Piemontese The Sebaste family launched its *Tartufi dolci* at its manufactory just outside Alba. Alongside *gianduia*, this hazelnut and chocolate truffle chocolate is the most famous sweet treat from the Piedmont region. And the most irresistible too.

"I wouldn't even consider changing a thing."
—Pierpaolo Ruta

Chocolate is happiness you can eat. And you can find it in many different forms in Italy:

Tartufi dolci These sweet truffles from Piedmont are made exclusively from local hazelnuts and the finest of chocolate. And they always go well before a meal, after a meal, with an espresso, with a glass of wine, or really anytime at all.

Gianduia Exorbitantly high cocoa prices prompted the *cioccolatieri* of Piedmont to roast hazelnuts and utilize their cocoa notes. The result is an incomparable melt-in-the-mouth texture that unfolds its velvety goodness in your mouth. The small version, the ingot-shaped *Gianduiotti*, has become a symbol of Italian unity.

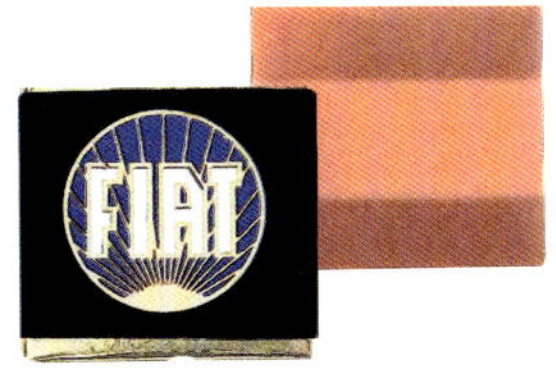

Cremino The sophisticated Fiat Cremino is a legend among Italian boxed chocolates. Developed in 1911 by Aldo Majani to advertise the newly launched Fiat Tipo 4 automobile, it boasts four decadent hazelnut and almond layers. And its immense popularity has not waned to this day.

Cioccolato di Modica IGP This chocolate from Modica, Sicily uses a traditional recipe, manually ground at low temperatures instead of conching. It contains only cocoa, butter, and sugar, giving it a grainy, rough texture with tiny air bubbles and an intense coffee flavor.

Cioccolato calda Once the favored beverage of Louis XIV, hot chocolate has since become a beloved indulgence among Italians. The color of the cup plays a crucial role; research has shown that hot chocolate tastes best when drunk from an orange cup, followed by a cream-colored cup. In contrast, it was found to be the least tasty in a white cup or a red one. The hallmark of true Italian hot chocolate is its rich, dessert-like consistency. This is particularly true in Sicily, where Arabs introduced the decadent cocoa-sugar pairing. In Italy's northern chocolate capital of Turin, cafés serve a unique hot beverage called *bicerin*; a luxurious concoction combining hot chocolate, steamed milk, and espresso. Its creation dates back to the 18th century at Café al Bicerin, where you can still order it today.

Torta della Nonna

Nonna's Cake

Makes one 11-inch (28 cm) round pan

PREP TIME
30 minutes plus 45 minutes standing time

BAKE TIME
45 minutes

INGREDIENTS

4 cups (480 g) flour, plus flour to dust the pan

Fine sea salt

⅞ cup (200 g) butter, plus softened butter to grease the pan

5 eggs + 1 egg yolk

2 cups (385 g) sugar

1 organic orange

3 cups plus 2 tbsp. (750 ml) milk

1 vanilla bean

4 scant tbsp. (30 g) corn starch

2 tbsp. pine nuts

Powdered sugar

OUR TIP Lemon zest can be used in place of the orange zest and peel, giving the *torta* a refreshing touch.

Torta della Nonna is a simple Tuscan recipe for success. The delicate shortcrust pastry and delightful cream filling are not too sweet, perfect to treat yourself to with a cup of coffee when your meal has come to an end. The pastry top and base of this cake provide a delicious framework for the creamy pudding layer, making it definitely worth biting into. Torta are commonly found on the dessert menus of cafés and trattorias in Italy. Despite their usually modest appearance, you will want to treat yourself to them again and again. Family torta recipes enjoy a special status, each with their own individual touches, perfect for hosts to showcase their talents to family and guests alike.

Place 3 ⅓ cups (450 g) of the flour, a pinch of salt, and the butter in a food processor or mixer, mix it until it feels like damp sand. Place it on a work surface and make a well in the center. Zest three fourths of the orange, leaving one fourth of the peel intact. Place 2 eggs, ⅔ cup plus 2 ½ tsp. (160 g) of the sugar, and the orange zest in the well. Use a fork to combine the eggs, sugar, zest, and flour, then knead into a dough. Wrap the dough tightly in plastic wrap; refrigerate for 45 minutes.

In the meantime, heat the milk in a pot, peel off the remaining ¼ orange peel in one piece, and add to the milk. Let it briefly infuse; set the pot aside. Scrape out vanilla bean seeds; add to the pot.

Place 3 eggs, 1 egg yolk, and the remaining sugar in a bowl. Stir until creamy. Sift in the remaining flour and the cornstarch and combine. Remove the orange peel from the milk. Add a dash of the milk to the cream and stir. Then add the cream mixture to the milk in the pot and gently heat, stirring constantly until it has a pudding-like consistency. Set the pot aside and cover with plastic wrap.

Remove the dough from the refrigerator, cut off a third, and set aside for the top. Roll out the remaining dough into a round shape sized to fit an 11-inch (28 cm) round pan, plus an additional 1 ½ inches (4 cm) for the rim. Preheat the oven to 355 °F (180 °C) on top and bottom heat. Grease the pan with softened butter; finely dust with flour. Place the dough inside and pull it up to cover the sides. Dock the base by pricking holes with a fork. Spread the cream on the base, roll out the dough for the top, and place on top. Carefully prick holes in the lid with a fork as well.

Sprinkle the pine nuts over the top and bake for 45 minutes. Let cool, then sprinkle with powdered sugar.

Torta di Nocciola

Hazelnut Cake

Makes one 11-inch (28 cm) springform pan

PREP TIME
10 minutes

BAKE TIME
30 minutes

INGREDIENTS

6 eggs

1½ cups (300 g) sugar

4½ cups (500 g) roasted hazelnut flour from the Piedmont region

5¼ oz. (150 g) Piedmont hazelnuts, roasted and chopped

The IGP Piedmont hazelnut is truly the queen of hazelnuts. As of a few years ago, its official name was Tonda e Gentile, *the round, gentle one. It still retains these characteristics, but a legal dispute over the name prompted a re-branding that lacks the original's poetic flair. The marvelous curves of this Piedmont specialty, which doesn't have the usual pointy end, make it ideal for roasting. The taste of these hazelnuts, especially when roasted, is uniquely flavorful and distinct; they are crunchy when you bite them, without having a woody consistency. They grow in the Langhe subregion of Piedmont, where low-growing hazelnut trees and grapevines intersperse to create a beautiful landscape. The condensed form of this torta recipe brings out the special flavor of these nuts so very well and so purely that it really can't be topped. With each bite, the fluffiness and airiness of this cake allow the flavor and deep, velvety nuttiness to unfurl on your palate.*

Preheat the oven to 395 °F (200 °C) using top and bottom heat.

Whisk the eggs with the sugar. Combine the hazelnut flour with the chopped hazelnuts, gently fold into the egg mixture, and work it in to a smooth batter.

Pour the batter into the springform pan and bake in the preheated oven for about 30 minutes.

OUR TIP A pinch of fine sea salt is good for any cake, and this torta is no exception. It brings out the wonderful flavor of the hazelnuts even more.

Noci

Nuts

The Queen of Sheba declared nuts to be exclusively a royal food and barred the common people from eating them. Or so the legend goes.

In fact, nowadays nuts are a superfood for everyone. They can help you lose weight, reduce the risk of heart attacks, lift your mood, and improve your ability to concentrate. Above all, however, they elevate original Italian cuisine to an unparalleled level.

Stone Age people already prized nuts, but they have only been systematically cultivated since the ancient world, and it is mainly thanks to the Romans that they enjoy such popularity throughout Europe.

Nuts have always been assigned great importance—as a symbol of fertility. Walnuts played an important role in Roman wedding customs. Hazelnut branches were considered a symbol of peace, and are still in use today as divining rods. Almonds and pistachios in particular were highly valued as snacks by ancient travelers. These nuts proved their worth as provisions on the lengthy treks along the ancient Silk Road between China and the Mediterranean because of their high nutritional value and long storage life.

Well-dried nuts lend themselves very well to storage. Without their natural protection, their shells, it is best to store them in a dark, dry place. Once they look oily, or smell or even taste rancid, it means they have been stored a little too long.

Fresh chestnuts, on the other hand, do not last very long. They lose their flavor and become tough after just a few days. But that didn't happen to the peasant peoples in the mountain regions long ago. For a lack of alternatives, chestnuts were their main staple until the late 19th century, and were consumed quickly.

By then, however, the Queen of Sheba was already ancient history.

"God gives the nuts, but he does not crack them."—Johann Wolfgang von Goethe

There are many different nuts. The following varieties are particularly popular in authentic Italian cuisine:

Nocciole The hazelnut is often scoffed at elsewhere for its lack of sophistication, and no wonder: The mass-produced variety from Turkey ends up in most ready-made baked goods and industrial spreads. In Italy, on the other hand, the hazelnut is revered. Alongside many other growing regions, the Piedmont region stands out in particular. There, connoisseurs consider the local Nocciola tonda gentile delle Langhe IGP to be the best in the world, as it has a superior texture and particularly velvety flavors, which are further intensified by roasting—just as if it were covered in a fine layer of premium chocolate. But Sicily is also home to the ultimate culinary delight, Nocciola tonda dei Nebrodi IGP, which offers an unrivalled balanced flavor and a rich aroma with a particularly intense aftertaste.This exceptional hazelnut variety is celebrated in local cuisine for its unique, unparalleled quality.

Noci While California is the main source of walnuts for most of the world's kitchens, Italians particularly cherish those grown in Campania. Only there does the most widespread, treasured variety grow, the particularly digestible Noce di Sorrento. Along with its delicate crunch and refined taste, this variety also contains less oil, making it particularly long-lasting and very healthy.

Mandorle Italian almonds mainly come from Apulia and Sicily, but they are prized everywhere. Tuono, with its balanced flavor, is certainly the best-known variety. Pizzuta d'Avola from Sicily is more intense, almost wild; it has a particularly thick skin that preserves the oils and flavors found in the kernel particularly well. But the elegant Mandorla di Torritto from Apulia is also very special, with its wonderful softness and surprisingly delicious buttery notes, making them a true gourmet delight.

Pistacchi Not all pistachios are the same. There is a world of difference between the cardboardy specimens grown abroad and those grown in Italy. The Pistacchio Bronte DOP is certainly the best. This "green gold" from the small town of Bronte at the foot of Mount Etna grows approximately 1,300 to 2,950 feet above sea level without fertilization or irrigation. The volcanic soil produces strong flavors, unparalleled juiciness, and unique sweetness.

Pinoli Pine trees (*Pinus Pinea*) are found almost everywhere in Italy—hardly anything exudes more Mediterranean flair than these trees. But pine nuts are a rarity, since a tree only starts producing them after around 15 years of life, and yields a maximum of a little over two pounds (1 kg) of pine nuts per season. And because they are also difficult to harvest, pine nuts are considered one of the most expensive dried foods on the market. Unfortunately, there are also plenty of inferior products available. Pine nuts without a declared origin tend to be tasteless. You can easily recognize the good ones by their elegant and slender shape—and their rich taste.

Castagne The sweet chestnut tree is also called *albero del pane*, or "bread tree," in Italian. Due to their high carbohydrate content of 75%, chestnuts have been eaten by humankind for centuries. They were long disparaged as "the food of the poor," yet they give countless dishes that special touch. Italy has the largest acreage of chestnut groves in Europe—and the expertise to match when it comes to the quality of its nuts. There are countless chestnut varieties here and many of them also carry a DOP or IGP seal, which are only bestowed on outstanding varieties. Chestnuts are particularly popular throughout Italy—and quite rightly so—as *Caldarroste*, scored and roasted over an open fire for 20 minutes.

"Only three out of ten kilograms of roasted nuts possess the quality required to be sold as whole nuts."—José Noé

For Italians, nuts are not just a tasty snack or a pretty decoration; they are a source of identity, deeply rooted in tradition and culture. They symbolize family gatherings, local festivals, and cherished recipes passed down through generations.

Crema di pistacchio The rich, creamy texture of this Sicilian specialty stems from the nut's high fat content of 45%. A perfect blend combines pureed and finely chopped pistachios, but it must be stirred before each use to ensure consistency. Adding a pinch of salt is a must to enhance its nutty flavor profile. This versatile spread goes well with cornetti and panettone, and even adds a luxurious touch to pasta all'uovo.

Crema Gianduia If you enjoyed eating hazelnut spread as a child, you will love this mature take on the beloved classic using prized Piedmont IGT hazelnuts. This luxurious cream blends hazelnut paste, cocoa, and cane sugar, with a dash of bourbon vanilla. Available in light and dark varieties, it is equally delightful straight from the jar or with a cornetto. Hazelnut cream is also the perfect choice to give desserts, cakes, and pastries that something extra. During the Christmas season, it transforms traditional panettone or *pandoro* into indulgent holiday delicacies.

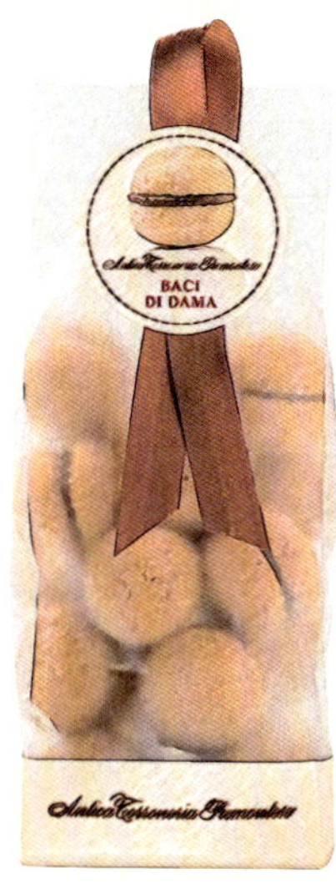

Pasticceria You can't have quality baked goods without quality nuts. The Italian originals amarettini and *cantuccini* (both with almonds), the "ugly but tasty" *brutti ma buoni* (made from hazelnuts), the sweet "ladies' kisses" baci di dama (also made from hazelnuts), and countless more are the stuff of legend.

Torrone This Italian nougat, made from honey, sugar, egg white, and almonds, is a favorite Christmas treat in Italy. *Torrone* is a very regional product, which is why there is such an incredible variety of fruit and spices. But Torrone di Cremona IGT with vanilla and cinnamon and Torrone di Benevento IGT with almonds or hazelnuts are particularly exceptional versions.

Torta The pride of the Piedmont region (one of many) is *Torta Nocciole*, a traditional hazelnut cake, made, of course, exclusively with original Nocciole Tonda gentile delle Langhe IGP hazelnuts.

Gelato Pistachio and *nocciola* are the measure of all things. Italians use these two varieties to determine the quality of a gelateria. If they are able to satisfy their high standards and refined palates, the remaining gelato varieties can't be bad.

Pesto The permitted variations of the traditional pesto recipe the Ligurians have given their blessing to include one with pistachios and one with hazelnuts.

Strudel di Mele

South Tyrolean Apple Strudel

Serves 4 to 6

PREP TIME
30 minutes plus 30 minutes standing time

BAKE TIME
1 hour

INGREDIENTS

FOR THE DOUGH
2 ½ cups (300 g) flour

A scant ½ cup (50 g) powdered sugar

1 pinch fine sea salt

⅔ cup (150 g) butter, softened

1 egg

¼ cup (60 ml) whole milk

FOR THE FILLING
⅓ cup (50 g) raisins

3 tbsp. brown rum

3 sweet, tart apples

A generous ¼ cup (60 g) butter

A scant 1¾ oz. (45 g) brown sugar

A scant 1¼ oz. (35 g) pine nuts

3 tbsp. Piedmont hazelnuts IGP, chopped

Zest from 1 organic lemon

2 tbsp. melted butter for brushing

FOR DECORATING
20 pistachios

2 tbsp. powdered sugar

In contrast to Viennese apple strudel, the South Tyrolean version is made with shortcrust dough. Perhaps it is a little more rustic, but it is also more inviting in terms of what you can enjoy it with, aside from the usual vanilla sauce, ice cream, and coffee: A glass of Moscato d'Asti, the sweet bubbly from Piedmont, or a Lagrein Rosato from South Tyrol, for example, go well with this version. Zabaglione with red currant or raspberry sauce is also a delicious choice. South Tyrolean cuisine takes its cues from the surrounding Alps, which include the Dolomites. Its proximity to Austria and the Ottoman influence have also had a lasting impact on the cuisine. This apple strudel is proof of this: Its recipe is said to have been inspired by baklava, a thin phyllo pastry similar to puff pastry that is filled with nuts, pistachios, and honey, still a popular Turkish food today.

Combine the flour and the powdered sugar. Add the salt and softened butter, knead briefly. Then add the egg and knead well. Finally, add the milk and knead everything to form a smooth dough. Shape the dough into a ball, wrap in plastic wrap, and refrigerate for about 30 minutes.

Drizzle the raisins with the rum and let them soak in it for a while. Peel the apples and cut into quarters, cut out the core, then cut the quarters into slices just under ¼ inch (½ cm) thick. In a skillet, melt the butter over low heat, then add the apple slices. Sprinkle with the brown sugar and let it caramelize. Add the raisins and pine nuts to the pan and simmer for about 7 minutes. Finally, add the chopped hazelnuts and lemon zest and let cool.

Preheat the oven to 425 °F (220 °C) using the convection setting. Remove the dough from the refrigerator and place it on baking paper. Use a rolling pin to roll it out into a rectangular shape as thinly as possible, about ⅛ inch (3 mm) thick. Cover the shortcrust pastry with the filling, then roll it up. Place on a baking tray with the baking paper, brush with the melted butter, and bake for around 1 hour.

Toast the pistachios in a skillet. Sift the powdered sugar over the finished strudel and sprinkle the pistachios on top.

OUR TIP When choosing an apple variety, it is a good idea to stick to the regionally available sweet, tart apples. It might be best to ask about this at a fruit stand at the farmer's market.

Ciambellone all'arancia

Bundt Cake with Oranges

Makes one savarin mold / Bundt cake pan

PREP TIME
15 minutes

BAKE TIME
Approximately 40 minutes plus standing time

INGREDIENTS

A generous ¾ cup (200 g) sugar

4 eggs, room temperature

1 to 2 tsp. vanilla extract

3 untreated oranges

½ cup plus 2 tbsp. (150 ml) extra virgin olive oil

3⅓ cups (400 g) flour

3 ⅛ tsp. cream of tartar and 1 ¼ tsp. baking soda

Powdered sugar

They say Italy has as many kinds of regional cuisine as it does church steeples, but this holds even more true when it comes to the wide variety of recipes for ciambellone, a simple and delicious Bundt cake. You only need a few ingredients to make this fluffy, flavorful cake, and it doesn't take long to make, but by adding a pinch of finesse you can give it your own personal touch. It is ideal for the way Italians like to eat breakfast: Sweet, but not too sweet, light and easygoing, enjoyed with a cup of coffee—what more could you need? Olive oil is the fat traditionally preferred here. We recommend a mild oil from Liguria or Umbria, for example. To make the cake particularly moist, some recipes use ricotta cheese or whole milk yogurt. Citrus fruits, added to the cake complete with juice and zest, make the cake juicy too—like here in our recipe with its untreated and ripe Sicilian oranges. If you let the cake stand overnight to give the flavors time to infuse, your patience will be rewarded the next morning: You'll encounter its delicious smell first before sinking your teeth into an orange grove turned cake.

In a bowl, add the sugar and room-temperature eggs and mix them at high speed using a hand mixer. Then add the vanilla and mix it in. Use a zester to grate the orange peel, then juice the oranges. Gradually add the olive oil to the batter while continuously mixing at high speed. Add the orange juice and zest and continue mixing until the batter is creamy and fluffy. Slowly sift the flour and cream of tartar-baking soda combination into the batter and continue mixing until the batter is smooth.

Grease your Bundt cake pan or savarin mold well, preferably using olive oil. Preheat the oven to 335–355 °F (170–180 °C) if using convection, or 370 °F (190 °C) if using top and bottom heat. Bake the *ciambellone* in the middle of the oven for approximately 40 to 45 minutes, until the surface is golden brown and the cake is done on the inside. To be on the safe side, use a wooden skewer to check: If it is dry when you pull it out, the cake is done.

Remove from the oven and let stand for several hours, preferably overnight. Sprinkle with powdered sugar before serving if you like.

OUR TIP Ciambellone is not only tasty at breakfast, it also serves as a nice dessert after other meals. Moscato d'Asti, a sparkling dessert wine from Piedmont, or a sweet wine like a Dulcis from Umbria pair well with this delicious treat.

Panna Cotta con Marmellata di arancia e Menta

Panna Cotta with Orange Marmalade and Mint

Serves 4

PREP TIME
30 minutes

REFRIGERATION TIME
At least 3 to 4 hours

INGREDIENTS

6 sheets of gelatin

1 vanilla bean

2 ½ cups + 4 tsp. (620 ml) cream

⅓ cup (75 g) sugar

4 to 6 tbsp. Sicilian orange marmalade (see p. 269)

A small handful of mint leaves

Panna cotta, the classic dessert from the Piedmont region, has made its way into the world of international cuisine. It is really no surprise, as this "cooked cream" boasts a milky-sweet taste and creamy texture. It is usually served with berries that are both fruity and tart, creating a delightful contrast. Our version uses bittersweet orange marmalade, turning the panna cotta into an exciting work of art. Legend has it this dessert first appeared under its current name on the menu of a restaurant in the Piedmont city of Cuneo in the 1960s. However, it seems likely that the recipe, with its convincing simplicity, is much, much older than that: Panna cotta was probably made by farmer's wives who wanted to use up extra milk and cream. The cooking technique used to make it may also date back to the French influence in Piedmont, originating from the region's time under the House of Savoy's rule. Traditional Piedmontese cuisine includes a savory version of panna cotta to this day: vegetable flans cooked in ramekins and inverted onto plates.

Soak the gelatin in cold water. Cut the vanilla bean lengthwise and use a sharp knife to scrape out the seeds and pulp. In a pot, bring the cream to a boil together with the vanilla bean, seeds, and pulp. Remove the pot from the heat and slowly add the sugar, stirring continuously until it has dissolved completely. Remove the vanilla bean. Squeeze any excess water from the gelatin, then add the gelatin to the hot cream while stirring; continue to stir until it dissolves.

Pour the mixture through a sieve into four small dessert dishes and let it cool to room temperature. Then refrigerate it for 3 to 4 hours, or, even better, overnight.

Either invert the panna cotta onto small plates or serve it in glasses. Using a spoon, spread orange marmalade on top of each panna cotta portion to a thickness of just about ½ inch (approximately 1 cm). Slice the mint leaves into thin ribbons and sprinkle them over the marmalade.

OUR TIP Panna cotta is particularly rich when made with cream containing 35 % fat.

Crostata classica

Shortcrust Tart with Apricot Jam

Makes one round 10-inch (25 cm) tart

PREP TIME
20 minutes plus at least 3 hours standing time

BAKE TIME
40 minutes

INGREDIENTS

A generous ¾ cup (190 g) cold butter, plus butter for the pan

A generous 2 ¾ cups (375 g) Italian flour type 00, plus flour for the pan

Fine sea salt

1 ¼ cups (150 g) powdered sugar, plus powdered sugar for dusting

3 egg yolks

1 jar of apricot jam

This crostata *is a family recipe that you can easily bake while doing other kitchen activities. The classic version is made with apricot jam, also a popular item at breakfast in cornetti, the Italian croissants. Crostata is eaten as a dessert, but also enjoyed for breakfast, fulfilling the Italian desire for crumbly pastries in the morning. In the Lazio, Marche, and Trentino regions, sour cherry jam is often used in place of apricot jam; one special version even uses ricotta and various dried fruits. The wonderful thing about a crostata is that it is a great way to offer your preserved summer fruits a starring role. Butter also plays a major part, of course. When dining out, you are more likely to find crostata in trattorias, often served with a scoop of ice cream.*

Cut the cold butter into pieces. Using a food processor or by hand, knead the butter with the flour and a pinch of salt until it becomes a smooth dough. In a bowl, pour the powdered sugar and create a well in the center. Place the egg yolks in the well and use a fork to stir gently. Combine and knead the two mixtures. Shape the dough into a ball, wrap in plastic wrap, and refrigerate for around 3 hours.

Preheat the oven to 340 °F (170 °C) using top and bottom heat; grease the tart form with butter and dust with flour. Roll out the dough on a cool surface, such as marble or stainless steel, to a thickness of just under ¼ inch (½ cm). Remember to frequently lift the dough off the surface somewhat to prevent it from sticking. Place the rolled-out pastry in the tart pan, press down the edges, use a fork to evenly prick holes in it, and cut off the dough hanging over the lip. Knead these scraps of dough together, roll out to a length of 10 inches (25 cm), and cut into strips around ¾ inch (2 cm) wide.

Spread the apricot jam on the tart base and arrange the dough strips on top to create a lattice pattern. Bake in the preheated oven for around 40 minutes. Then sprinkle with a little powdered sugar.

OUR TIP This uncomplicated, sturdy crostata is ideal for a picnic, best enjoyed with a semi-dry Moscato d'Asti.

ZWILLING
ZWILLING

Frutta

Fruit

Authentic Italian cuisine is known for its use of fresh, high-quality ingredients. This is particularly true of fruit—while fruit is enjoyed plain with cheese and dessert as the fourth course of a classic Italian meal, it is frequently an important component in the preceding courses as well.

This is not merely a matter of enhancing flavors; fruit also offers a nutritional boon, as it contains many essential nutrients such as vitamins, minerals, fiber, and phytochemicals. Picked at peak ripeness and processed quickly, sweet fruits are generally the healthiest, since they develop more of these important nutrients as they become sweeter.

Italy is truly blessed in this respect. The north of the country is effectively the orchard of Europe, with grapes, apples, apricots, cherries, and much more growing here. Further south, you find figs, peaches, persimmons, and prickly pears alongside the country's many citrus fruits. All of these fruits are used to produce a whole range of uniquely Italian products, such as the famed *Mostard* and the mouth-watering *Marmellate*.

Although these are certainly not the worst way to preserve fruit, it is best enjoyed fresh, within a day or two of harvesting. If you have no other option, you can put berries and other fruit in the refrigerator—apples, however, should be stored at room temperature or in a cool cellar. This helps keep away those pesky fruit flies, which multiply all the faster in warmer weather. The most effective way to avoid them, however, is to eat the tasty fruit very quickly.

"Fruit tastes most delicious just when its season is ending."—Seneca

Italy has much to offer when it comes to the following fruits:

Mela This classic fruit is a veritable vitamin explosion. Not without reason do Italians (and others) say *Una mela al giorno toglie il medico di torno*, or "An apple a day keeps the doctor away." This seems to have been common practice as early as the Stone Age, and hardly any other fruit has had so much significance for humankind. As a symbol of love, fertility, beauty, and hope, apples have played an important role in cultural history. For culinary purposes, apples are an essential ingredient for making sweet baked goods like cakes, tarts, and strudels, while also playing a vital role in savory Italian dishes. Fortunately, thanks to their long shelf life, they are available practically all year round. The only thing to bear in mind is that apples release ethylene, a substance that causes other fruit and vegetables to ripen faster than desired, so they should be stored separately. Most Italian apples come from South Tyrol, a region that has ideal conditions and supplies almost half of all of Europe's organic apples.

Albicocca Its captivating aroma and flavorful sweetness make this fruit so irresistible. Apricots were already adored and grown in Roman times. Today, probably the best apricots still come from Vesuvius, whose soil is particularly suitable for cultivating them and produces around 70 different varieties. Most of them are sold at the local markets, while the rest are used to make wonderful marmellata. Another Italian original is made from the bitter pits of this fruit: amaretto.

Fragole In Italy too, these berries, which are actually nuts in botanical terms, are loved for their beautiful red color, intense aroma, and wonderful sweetness—especially wild strawberries. In ancient times, Roman poets sang their praises, but then they almost fell into obscurity, replaced by larger and higher-yielding varieties from abroad. Almost. Sicilian wild strawberries from Ribera are a true delicacy. They grow at the foot of lemon, orange, and peach trees, and should be eaten within two days of picking. Their sweet, aromatic flavor is a testament to the fertile Sicilian soil. They taste best with a homemade panna cotta, as they not only give the dessert a beautiful color, they also add a slight acidity and freshness that complements perfectly its sweet cream, elevating the flavor profile.

Fico South of the Alps, this sweet, juicy fruit epitomizes summer unlike any other fruit. As one of the world's oldest cultivated plants, figs are very popular throughout the Mediterranean; in Italy mainly in Apulia, Calabria, Sicily, and Campania, where they are enjoyed with cheese or a fresh salad, pasta, or risotto. In Tuscany, you can also find them in *Torta di Fichi*, a sinfully delicious treat made with figs, almonds, cinnamon, and honey. Dried figs are particularly popular in the winter and during the Christmas season as a no-fuss snack or to garnish pastries and cakes. Dried figs di Cosenza (DOP) from Calabria are especially appealing. The famous Bianchi del Cilento (DOP) variety from Campania complements anything and everything. And anytime.

Caco This fruit with its strong character is often overlooked outside Italy, but considered very special there. Originating in China some 2,000 years ago, this "food of the gods," as the translation of its botanical name (*diospyros kaki*) reads, should only be eaten fully ripe, when its skin is almost bursting, otherwise its astringent tannins will cause your mouth to pucker. But when ripe, a taste akin to dark chocolate unfolds. And it's very healthy to boot. Just cut it in half and eat it by the spoonful as a snack.

Fico d'India Prickly pears are called "Indian figs" in Italy because Italian explorers of the late 15th century discovered them in the West Indies and brought them back upon their return. Today, the fruit of the prickly pear cactus is not only an iconic element of the southern Italian landscape; it is also a genuine culinary treasure. In Sicily, where it is primarily grown, people enjoy prickly pears for breakfast in a fruit salad, as an appetizer in a savory salad, with cheese after a meal, or in between meals as granita, ideally using the varieties Fico d'India dell'Etna (DOP) or Fico d'India di San Cono (DOP).

Ciliegie Summer just isn't summer without the fresh, juicy crunch and bright red color of cherries. Yet these little fruits have only been found in Europe since Roman times. Roman general and gourmet Lucius Lucullus brought the dark red fruit to Italy from the Black Sea port of Kerasus in 74 BC, with the port giving the fruit its name. Since then, the Amarena cherry, an ancient Italian variety of sour cherry, has grown here.

And been consumed pure and unadulterated, crushed on a slice of bread as an afternoon snack. Cherries are also excellent as a syrup served with ricotta or gorgonzola, or on ice cream, cakes, or Apulian cookies. The special variety Brusche di Modena (DOC), however, is best enjoyed as a jam.

Mirtilli Myrtle branches are recognized as a symbol of virginity, vitality, and having many healthy children—the Greeks and Romans even adorned their virgin brides with a myrtle wreath. This plant also has culinary uses. In Sardinia, it serves as the basis for *Mirto rosso*, a sweet liqueur made from its berries. *Mirto bianco*, which uses the leaves and flowers of the myrtle, is rather dry. What's more, the name "mortadella" is derived from the original recipe for this cold cut, because it was seasoned with myrtle berries before pepper became popular in Europe. Today, these berries are mainly used in traditional Roman cuisine much like juniper berries, but with a deliciously fruity flavor.Additionally, myrtle's fragrant leaves are used for flavoring meats, stews, and even baked goods.

Pesca Originally a Chinese fruit, Alexander the Great brought the peach tree from Persia, and all of Italy is still grateful to him. There are an infinite number of purely local and equally popular varieties there. Sicilian peaches are famous for their sweet, juicy taste, especially the rare and extremely flavorful Tabacchieria dell'Etna variety, known by the name tobacco tin because of its shape. Peaches are popular in fruit salad, or *macedonia di frutta*, in ice cream, and pureed in the iconic Bellini cocktail. A signature drink at the famed Harry's Bar in Venice for decades, The Bellini is white peach puree topped off with dry prosecco. Peaches are often cooked to enjoy for desserts, like *Pesche al Vino Rosso*, where they are poached in red wine. Then the wine is reduced and the peaches steep in the syrup for hours, intensifying their flavor. These wine-infused peaches pair exquisitely with ice cream, panna cotta, and mascarpone cream.

Uva People have been making wine from grapes throughout history, presumably as early as ancient Egyptian times. Today, around 85 percent of grapes are pressed into wine, only 10 percent are eaten fresh as table grapes, and 5 percent are dried into raisins. Grapes are also delicious unfermented. Table grape varieties contain less acid, have a thinner skin, and are usually seedless, and they contain important nutrients such as antioxidants. Dark grapes usually taste sweeter and have more flavor, while light-colored grapes tend to be tarter. Either way, grapes pair perfectly with ricotta and mascarpone. And, of course, with cheese like Taleggio, the creamy, red, milky-tasting cheese from the Lombard region, as well as sheep's-milk and goat's-milk cheeses.

"It all started with the black book our Nonna Palmira used to jot down recipes in, and her Mostarda d'Uva.*"*—Roberto Santopietro

Unfortunately, fruit does not keep for very long in its pure form. But fortunately, the Italians have developed ways to make it last a little longer:

Mostarda di Frutta Italians have been making mostarda since 1621. At that time, mostarda was mainly enjoyed during the Christmas holidays. Nowadays, there are countless variations in northern Italy, with whole pears and quinces being used in Mantua, while candied fruit takes the stage in Voghera. In Cremona, on the other hand, figs, apricots, and peaches are commonly used. And all of them create a wonderfully fruity taste on your plate, especially when served with meat dishes or enjoyed with a cheese platter.

Marmellate / Confettura On warm toast, with cheese, in yoghurt, quark, or cake, or even spooned straight into your mouth, Italian marmellata are always delightfully fresh and fruity. And an essential part of a simple but (always) sweet breakfast.

Cioccolata Italians may not actually have invented the perfect combination of fruity freshness and bittersweet chocolate, but they certainly have perfected it. If you don't believe this, try the hand-scooped bars from Calabrian manufacturer Dolci Pensieri with lemon, mandarin orange, or strawberry, or the Modica chocolates from Bonajuto, which undergo cold processing, and are made with bergamot, orange, or ginger.

Formaggio
Cheese

Referring to France, Charles de Gaulle famously asked, “How can you govern a country which has 246 varieties of cheese?” Well, Italy has more than 400 varieties to offer. And they are all wonderfully authentic creations.

Few things are as much a part of Italy’s culinary culture as cheese. Every region has its own unique specialties, whether they are made from the milk of cows, buffalos, goats, or sheep. This kind of diversity is rarely found anywhere else. And the same goes for the flavors: from creamy and smooth to tangy and spicy to salty—in Italy, there is the perfect cheese for every occasion.

This tradition goes back to antiquity. The Romans already produced various types of *caesus*. During the Middle Ages and the Renaissance, Italian cheese production experienced a particular upswing, when monks refined the processes and varieties and called them *formaticum*, “the formed,” from which the Italian term for cheese, *formaggio*, takes its name.

Traditionally, nearly all cheese varieties, with the exception of cream cheese, are produced using animal rennet, which facilitates the curdling of milk, is tasteless, and enables extended aging periods. In some cases, cheese can acquire significant value—in Italy, over 300,000 wheels of Parmesan, worth more than €200 million, are securely stored in specialized bank vaults.

In traditional Italian dining, cheese is served as the final course because it effectively “closes” the stomach. The fatty acids present in cheese stimulate the production of digestive hormones, causing food to remain in the stomach for a longer time and resulting in a noticeably prolonged sense of satiety. To return to Monsieur de Gaulle’s question, perhaps those who are content and satisfied may even be more amenable to being governed.

“Cheese is milk’s leap toward immortality.”
—Clifton Fadiman

Italy is home to some of the world’s most timeless cheeses. Renowned globally for their exceptional flavor and quality, they have earned a distinguished place in international culinary culture as authentic masterpieces:

Ricotta Ricotta, which translates to “cooked again,” derives its name from the unique production process that involves reheating and stirring the whey left over from the making of other cheeses. This separates the liquid from the ricotta solids, which can then be skimmed off and savored immediately. If it doesn’t end up in your mouth right away, ricotta also serves as a delectable filling for fresh pasta, sweet cannoli, or delicious cakes.

Mozzarella This renowned stretched-curd cheese, or *pasta filata* (literally “spun paste”), undergoes kneading, stirring, and pulling in hot salt water until it becomes soft, pliable, and ready to be shaped into balls. Legend says the monks of the San Lorenzo ad Septimum Abbey in Aversa would offer participants in the annual procession a small piece of the cheese, or *mozzetta*, with a bit of bread. One thing is certain, the more flavorful, authentic Mozzarella di Bufala Campana DOP must be made solely from buffalo milk, with the entire production process taking place in Campania. The extra effort is well worth it, as this cheese is the crowning glory atop a caprese salad or Margherita pizza.

Gorgonzola The world's most famous blue cheese, originally called Stracchino di Gorgonzola ("the tired one from Gorgonzola"), has a legendary origin story. It is said that a distracted dairyman who was supposed to be milking the cows was kept busy by a maid's visit until morning, then, in his exhausted state, mixed fresh morning milk with curdled milk from the previous evening. The result was a new type of cheese, which was named "the tired one" in reference to his lost night of sleep. Made with milk from two milkings, the cheese is injected with *penicillium roqueforti* blue mold, giving it its strong flavor and striking blue marbling. Gorgonzola comes in two varieties: the significantly milder *gorgonzola dolce*, aged up to 80 days, and the particularly strong *gorgonzola piccante*, aged up to 270 days. It is extremely popular as a bread spread, is ideal with pasta and risotto, and pairs very well with fresh fruit, mostarda, and even dark chocolate.

Taleggio With a history spanning over a millennium, Taleggio, one of the oldest soft cheeses, is still crafted by hand today. It was first made in the caves of Val Taleggio near Bergamo in the Lombardy region. The cheese's indescribable creaminess is said to have inspired Giacomo Casanova to write an encyclopedia of cheese varieties, though, presumably preoccupied with other pursuits, he never completed his work. During the aging process, the cheese is rinsed with salty seawater once a week, resulting in its slightly reddish rind with its characteristic mold spots. Taleggio adds a certain elegance not only to a cheese platter, but also to risotto and polenta dishes.

Pecorino Rather than a single variety, there exists a vast array of salty sheep milk cheeses, with each region of Italy boasting its own unique version, many of which have a rich history. One of the most renowned is Pecorino Romano, which has been produced in the mountains of Lazio since ancient times, although today the name is more indicative of a production method. The common thread among these cheeses is that they are made exclusively from sheep's milk and are the preferred grated cheese for pasta dishes south of Emilia Romagna. Aged for periods ranging from 3 to 12 months, the younger, fresher cheeses are relatively soft and mild in flavor, while the older cheeses develop a firmer texture and a tangier, sharper taste, making them the perfect choice for dishes like pasta *Cacio e Pepe* or carbonara.

Parmigiano This hard cheese, or *grana*, has a distinctive grainy texture and a long history, having been produced in nearly the same basic form for at least eight centuries. While many cheeses are referred to as Parmesan, only the eponymous Parmigiano Reggiano, protected by the DOP designation, is the true original. It hails exclusively from Parma and Reggio nell'Emilia, where traditional cow breeds are fed a diet consisting solely of grass, hay, and a specific type of legume. Like with fine wine, the terroir plays a crucial role for Parmesan, as does the aging process, which allows the cheese to increase its flavor over time. The youngest Parmigiano Reggiano must be aged for a minimum of 12 months, but 24 to 30 months is the norm. In contrast, specimens aged for 72 months are exceptionally rare. These aged treasures are far too exquisite to be simply grated over pasta or risotto; instead, they should be savored on their own, accompanied by a carefully selected wine.

"I only add as much to my cheeses as is necessary. Local herbs, wood ash, larch needles, and red smear cultures enhance the flavor of the milk without overpowering it."
—Michael Steiner

Alongside the well-known classic cheeses, there are so many more Italian originals in DOP quality just waiting to be discovered, each with its own unique flavor:

Asiago DOP This cheese from the Veneto region ranges from young and mild to aged with spicy, robust notes.

Bettelmatt This intense, semi-firm summer cheese from the Piedmont region tastes of flowers and herbs, with a hint of bitterness.

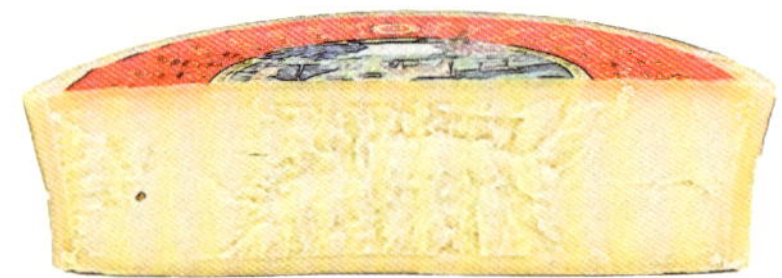

Bitto DOP This hard cheese from the Lombardy region has a flavorful, buttery taste with a hint of fruitiness.

Bra tenero DOP The milky flavor of this semi-firm cheese from the Piedmont region is complemented by a subtle hint of acidic yogurt.

Burrata Its creamy, soft, almost liquid center of cheese and cream gives the impression that this Apulian *pasta filata* cheese could burst open at any moment.

Caciocavallo Younger cheeses are often used as a topping for baked dishes, while aged versions are grated over pasta and risotto. Caciocavallo is almost always made from cow's milk. For the aging, two cheeses are tied together and slung over a beam. Its distinctive shape resembles saddlebags, inspiring its name, which literally means "cheese on horseback."

Caprino This cream cheese made from the milk of both cows and goats is produced in the Piedmont region and typically available in slices or bars.

Castelmagno DOP This hard cheese blends cow's, sheep's, and goat's milk. Aged up to five months in Piedmont's natural caves, it develops a tangier flavor over time.

Fontina This semi-hard cheese from the high mountains of the Aosta Valley has a mild and delicate flavor at first, but as it ages it develops somewhat woody notes.

Grana Padano DOP This hard cheese may come from the Lombardy region, but it is found throughout the Po Valley, making its production area much larger than that of Parmigiano Reggiano. In addition, the animals' diet may include silage alongside grass and hay. Its aging process is also briefer than the typical Parmigiano, resulting in a cheese with a pleasantly milky and subtle flavor.

Mascarpone This cream cheese originally comes from the Lombard city of Lodi, but is now produced throughout Italy, owing its popularity to its wonderfully creamy texture.

Montasio DOP This semi-firm cheese from Friuli has subtle alpine flavors when young but develops strong umami notes when aged.

Mozzarella fior di latte Fior di latte, or "milk blossom," can be considered the little pasta filata sister of buffalo mozzarella. Crafted solely from cow's milk, it offers a more subtle flavor profile. However, the absence of a protected status for this cheese results in huge differences in quality.

Murazzano DOP This delicate soft cheese made with a high percentage of sheep's milk has a slightly grassy finish and is still made by hand in the Piedmont region. *Murazzano* has subtle notes of cream and butter and tastes delicious with fruit such as apples.

Paglietta This soft cheese from the Piedmont city of Cuneo has a slightly piquant flavor, but it literally melts in your mouth, leaving behind a full, tangy taste.

Parmigiano Reggiano Vacche Rosse DOP In Reggio nell'Emilia in particular, the original Vacche Rosse, or red cows, are being rediscovered. These cows produce a distinctive milk that is used to make a hard cheese with a very special melting quality.

Pecorino Romano DOP Despite its name, this sheep's-milk cheese with its unmistakable flavor of Mediterranean herbs is almost exclusively produced in Sardinia.

Pecorino Sardo DOP While it is still white and mildly flavored when young, this Sardinian sheep's-milk cheese develops strong Mediterranean notes as it ages. In Sardinia, it is eaten with pine nuts and *pane carasau* flatbread.

Pecorino Siciliano DOP This hard cheese made from Sicilian sheep milk with aromatic herbs remains quite mild even as it ages.

Pecorino Toscano DOP This Tuscan sheep's-milk cheese is initially rather soft and mild, but over time it develops its typically intense and slightly tangy flavor.

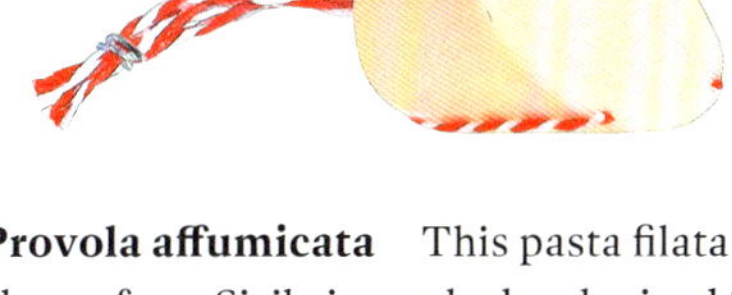

Provola affumicata This pasta filata cheese from Sicily is smoked and prized for its mild, rounded flavor.

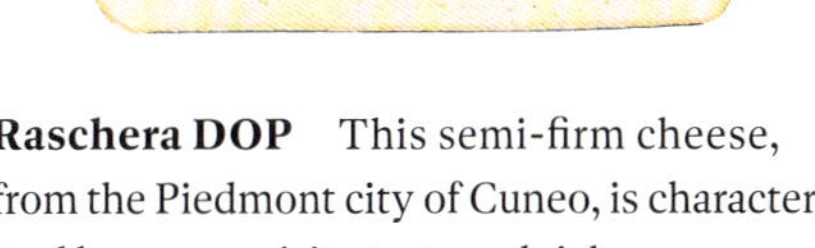

Raschera DOP This semi-firm cheese, from the Piedmont city of Cuneo, is characterized by an exquisite taste and rich aromas.

Robiola di Roccoverano DOP This soft goat's-milk cheese from the Piedmont region has a very unique flavor thanks to its floral and grassy notes.

Robiola due latti Made from a combination of cow's and sheep's milk, this soft cheese is produced by hand in the Piedmont region and is valued for its extremely delicate flavor.

Scamorza This southern Italian pasta filata cheese is hung in brine to mature, giving it its typical pear shape and dark yellow rind. It is often subsequently smoked.

Stracchino There are a number of different varieties of this soft cheese from the Lombardy region. What they all have in common is their unmistakably creamy flavor, making them one of the most popular spreads in Italy.

Toma Piemontese DOP This semi-firm cheese from the Piedmont region melts delicately in your mouth, leaving behind a wonderfully buttery flavor.

Olive e Olio

Olives and Oil

It was the olive tree that brought prosperity to the entire Mediterranean region.

With it came a cultural, economic, and culinary boom. Every part of the tree has value. Its wood is coveted by furniture makers, its leaves are used as tea to treat a variety of ailments, and its fruits are used to make liquid gold, or they are baked, cooked, or enjoyed on their own.

This has been the case since the early history of humankind. The first archaeological finds of olive pits are over 9,000 years old; the first olive oils were pressed around 6,000 years ago. This tree has always been held in the highest regard. Its branches were made into the victory wreath used to crown the winners of the Olympic Games. The Romans had their citizens pay taxes paid in olive oil—after they had introduced olive trees throughout their area of influence. And olive trees are the reason Athens bears its name. Legend has it that Poseidon and Athena fought for supremacy over Attica. Poseidon caused a spring to gush forth in Athens, while Athena grew the first olive tree on the Acropolis. The Athenians decided the olive tree was more useful and chose Athena to be the goddess of their city.

And how right they were! The oil derived from the fruit of the olive tree forms the basis for traditional Italian cuisine, and even taken literally—the word "oil" comes from *olea*, the Latin word for olive.

In general, we have the Italians to thank for the fact that olives have continued to be cultivated and olive oil produced even after the collapse of the Roman Empire. There are over 1,500 different olive varieties worldwide, but Italy has the most diverse range of varieties: More than 43 DOP and four IGP varieties are grown here.

As different as the olive varieties are, so too are the flavors of the oils they produce. They can, however, be roughly categorized, mainly geographically:

In northern Italy, the oils tend to be rather mild, with a delicate fruity character—in Liguria, the Taggiasca variety is almost exclusively cultivated for this purpose. The farther south you go, the more robust the olive oils become. The stronger oils dominate in Tuscany and Umbria, while in Sicily they are downright excitingly pungent and bitter. Puglia is an exception; Italy's largest olive-growing region offers the full range of intensity levels.

A distinction is also made between the olive varieties used to produce oil and those that end up on our plates. In fact, only a few varieties are suitable for use in both. One of these is the famed Taggiasca olive from Liguria. At first glance, it looks completely unremarkable; these olives are quite small and come in different sizes and colors, from light green to dark purple. Benedictine monks brought them to the Ligurian town of Taggia from Île Saint-Honorat, the French island off the coast of Cannes, in the 11th century and cultivated them to perfection there. Today's fruit is indescribably flavorful with a particularly mild and round taste; it has hardly any bitter substances, but a high oil content. And that is precisely why it is so popular, both as an oil and as a fruit.

"I stick to my Mediterranean diet: fresh products and olive oil."—Andrea Pirlo

The fruit itself is green when it is unripe, but it turns black or purple as it ripens. And it is not edible when raw, straight from the tree—it will only lose its bitterness after repeated marinating in brine, which flushes out the bitter substances.

This is why around 90 percent of olives are pressed into oil. And the quality varies greatly. As we say in Liguria, *"E pane nu sun urive, e urive nu sun öriu e l'öriu u nu l'è sodi,"* which translates as "The olive blossoms are not olives yet, the olives are not oil yet, and oil only becomes money if it is of good quality."

The big question here is, how do you recognize good quality?

First of all, the price—good olive oil is very expensive to produce and its price won't be cheap.

You can also recognize it by the fact that it has a nice fruitiness and bitter notes, and it scratches your throat.

Good oil is also always *extra vergine*, or extra virgin. This means that only perfectly unblemished olives are cold-pressed mechanically and naturally, without heat and oxygen damaging the oil. So the oil remains absolutely flawless.

Most importantly, however, the quality depends on the olive variety, the soil, the climate, and the work done by people and machines. Greece, for example, has great trees with good fruit, but sadly it also has outdated processing technologies. This is why, contrary to popular belief, good oils are rarely found in Greece, although the variety of olive itself is actually more important than its country of origin.

Blends, or mixtures of several varieties, are more balanced and complex than the single varietal monocultivar oils. However, the original, rather racy flavor of the latter is absolutely captivating.

The general rule is, the earlier the olives are harvested, the more bitter and pungent the oils become. The olives are still green and intensely flavorful. If the olives are left on the tree longer, the oils generally become milder. And the yield increases, but the quality decreases. Every olive oil miller is faced with a decision: quality or quantity?

You can also recognize good oils by the fact that the exact harvest period is indicated on the bottle—in contrast to organic seals, which do not list this information, but are organically impeccable anyway.

The very best way to recognize a good olive oil is that you enjoy its taste. It should also have a DOP seal, ensuring its quality. A genuine DOP seal guarantees that the oil is produced under strict regulations.

"I know my olive trees—and I know what they are up to."—Franco Roi

Olives are not only an indispensable ingredient in authentic Italian cuisine in the form of oil, they have other uses too:

Olive in salamoia The salted olives soak in brine in a barrel for a year before they are bottled in the brine. This process removes the bitter substances, making them soft and preserving them for a long time to come, unless, of course, they are destined for quick consumption on focaccia.

Olive sott'olio Olives marinated in oil are perfect for enjoying with an aperitif. They are also soaked in brine, but then they are marinated in good-quality olive oil. This rounds off their intense flavor a little better. And preserves them.

Oli aromatizzati Flavored olive oils add a very special kick to any unique dish. The olives are crushed and pressed directly with basil, oranges, lemons, peperoncino, or rosemary. Each one imparts a distinct, rich flavor you can truly savor and enjoy.

Crema di olive Olive spreads add their very own zesty touch. The olives are pitted and processed into a fine paste or cream with a dash of extra virgin olive oil. And then they're off to bedeck your crostini.

Aceto

Vinegar

Italians know that "*L'aceto donato è più dolce del miele*"—a gift of vinegar is sweeter than honey. And vinegar is so much more than just fermented wine. Anyone who has ever tasted the original Aceto Balsamico Tradizionale is sure to agree. But other, less exclusive vinegars are also an indispensable element of Italian cuisine. The most important thing is to always use a good product.

In theory, vinegar can be made from any fruit, vegetable, or grain containing sugar that can be converted into alcohol. Almost all ancient civilizations did just that: the Egyptians, Persians, Romans, Greeks, and Babylonians all made and enjoyed vinegar. Usually made from fermented fruit juices, wine, or beer, it was diluted with water and enjoyed as a refreshing drink. Roman legionaries carried this concoction in their canteens, as it was only with *posca*, as it was called, that drinking water was actually drinkable.

The process of making vinegar was likely discovered by accident, as wine left exposed to the air will eventually turn into vinegar on its own. However, the reason behind this process was still unknown until the 19th century, when Louis Pasteur identified the tiny organisms responsible: bacteria. The surface of the original substance forms a bacterial film when it comes into contact with air. The vinegar sinks to the bottom and the alcohol rises to the surface, layer by layer. The raw vinegar is then stored in barrels that still contain a little of the original vinegar. The vinegars then age for several months—or decades, in the case of Aceto Balsamico Tradizionale.

When the vinegar is ready, it can be diluted and enjoyed as a beverage, used to dress salads, to pickle vegetables or fruit, to marinate dishes, or add the finishing touch to a dish. It also makes a thoughtful gift.

"It takes four men to dress a salad: a wise man for the salt, a madman for the pepper, a miser for the vinegar, and a spendthrift for the oil."—Francois Coppée

In Italy, vinegars are not only used as salad dressing; they are considered a seasoning that can transform the simplest of dishes into a feast, if their quality is good:

Aceto Balsamico For a long time, this richly flavored, dark vinegar crafted from grape must, remained a privilege enjoyed by only a select few. Today, however, even discount stores stock a product labeled "Aceto Balsamico," although these mass-produced versions bear little resemblance to the authentic masterpiece.

Even the original version comes in various grades: Aceto Balsamico Tradizionale di Modena DOC and di Reggio Emilia DOC are the most premium vinegars. They undergo rigorous quality control and must be produced entirely within the towns of Modena and Reggio nell'Emilia, from grape to bottling, following a time-honored and rather tedious process:

The journey to becoming Aceto Balsamico begins immediately after harvest, with the must of the Trebbiano grape (Modena) or the Lambrusco grape (Reggio Emilia) slowly simmered in copper kettles before being sealed in airtight glass demijohns. The must settled through the winter, and is transferred to wooden barrels in the spring. Air is introduced through a small opening, initiating the alcohol fermentation process that gradually transforms it into acetic acid. As the years pass, the aging vinegar is moved to progressively smaller barrels made from various types of wood. These barrels are stored in the *acetaia* directly beneath the roof and exposed to natural temperature fluctuations to help the liquid slowly evaporate, intensifying the taste. The vinegar is periodically topped up with the remains from the previous barrel until it is finally removed from the smallest barrel after 12, 18 or 25 years of aging.

Aceto Balsamico di Modena IGT, while not quite as exclusive, still maintains its authenticity. Here, a small amount of wine vinegar may be added to the grape must, and the duration of its aging is also left unspecified. Nevertheless, this category still boasts some very good quality products.

In stark contrast, the balsamic vinegar found in supermarkets is often little more than a blend of common wine vinegar and thickened grape must, with caramel coloring frequently used to achieve its brown hue.

You can easily recognize the original Aceto Balsamico Tradizionale di Modena by its inky black color. It tastes pleasantly pervasive and intensely flavorful, and when swirled in a glass, it leaves a syrupy coating on the inside of the glass.

A few dashes over fresh strawberries, Parmesan cheese, or ice cream elevate these simple pleasures to true gourmet delights.

Condimento bianco This "white seasoning" is a blend of white wine vinegar and grape must concentrate and retains its pale hue because it is concentrated at a lower temperature. While only the finest of these are allowed to bear the name *aceto condimento*, or vinegar seasoning, they are not technically classified as vinegars because their acidity levels fall below 6 %. They are frequently used to enhance the flavors of fish and shellfish, seafood, vegetable salads, and fruit.

Aceto di vino As with wine, the quality of wine vinegar is determined by the quality of its source, and the differences in the end product can be substantial. Italy undoubtedly has a home advantage in this regard, as the finest vinegars are made exclusively from local grapes, with no other ingredients. After fermentation, these vinegars are aged in barrels for an extended period, giving the final product pleasant barrique notes. Italian red and white wine vinegars boast delicate, fruity nuances and a fresh, mild acidity. They are the go-to ingredients for a wide range of culinary applications, including canning, pickling, preserving, seasoning, and creating delectable antipasti dishes.

Vinegar is primarily a standard staple in Italian cuisine, but some foods containing vinegar have evolved into authentic specialties in their own right:

Crema di Balsamico This thick, almost honey-like balsamic cream has a much sweeter and fruitier flavor profile compared to balsamic vinegar, which is exactly what makes it so appealing. It is made from Aceto Balsamico di Modena IGP with a high percentage of concentrated grape must. Used sparingly, it is delicious with fruit salad or individual fruits, vanilla ice cream, and cakes made with fruit. Balsamic cream also brings complexity to dark meat gravies that can handle a subtle sweetness and a hint of acidity.

Cipolle Borettane A must on any well-crafted antipasti plate, these flat little onions are ideally pickled in balsamic vinegar, becoming delightfully soft with a delicious sweet-and-sour flavor that perfectly complements a range of foods, including salami, ham, cold meats, tuna, and anchovies.

Erbe e Spezie

Herbs and Spices

Small and inconspicuous, they grow right underfoot. And yet herbs are exactly what transform a clump of rice, a flatbread, a pasta dish, or a casserole into something authentically Italian. Basil, oregano, sage, parsley, and the like are what make the *Cucina Italiana* so remarkably fresh and flavorful. And in addition to these, there are so many more herbs and spices that add the finishing touches to dishes in Italy.

Their secret lies in the essential oils found in the herbs. However, their potency and content vary based on the variety of herb and the timing of the harvest. Plants reach their peak flavor just before blooming or as they begin to bloom, since it takes a great deal of energy for the plant to produce its blossoms. This energy is no longer available to produce essential oils, so they lose flavor and their effect is also lessened.

Beyond their culinary prowess, many herbs also possess healing properties. Mint helps with headaches, oregano with coughs, basil with digestive ailments, sage with inflammation, and thyme with stomach troubles—there's an herb for every kind of ailment. Even Charlemagne recognized their virtues, and he left extra pages for herbs in his meticulous *Capitulare de villis*, a decree guiding the management of his royal estates, ensuring these botanical treasures were properly cultivated.

Unfortunately, herbs themselves are quite fragile. They do not keep particularly well—unless dried, of course—they are best eaten fresh, in other words, when added to the dish after it has finished cooking. Only sage, thyme, rosemary, and oregano can be cooked with the other ingredients; the rest will quickly lose flavor and nutrients.

But as a fresh finish on an authentic Italian dish, they look even more delicious.

"Herbs are the friend of the physician and the pride of cooks."—Charlemagne

These herbs and spices in particular are the pride and joy of Italian cuisine:

Basilico Basil is one of the cornerstones of Italian cuisine and the king of herbs. Its name is derived from the ancient Greek *basileus*, which means "king," perhaps because of its use in the mummification of Egyptian pharaohs. Basil is believed to have originated in India, where its consumption was forbidden (except in Ayurvedic medicine), but it was a faithful sidekick of Genoa's captains on their voyages. They never wanted to be without their *Pesto alla Genovese*, even while traveling. The only basil approved for use in pesto is the basil specifically from Genoa with its Protected Designation of Origin, Genovese basil DOC, with a long-lasting flavor that is finer and less minty than that of other varieties. Neapolitan basil, the well-known and most common basil variety, has menthol notes and is ideal for use in an *Insalata Caprese* or a *Pizza Napoletana*. Intensive, fresh Tuscan basil, on the other hand, is the best choice for *Panzanella*. Its rich flavor enhances this traditional Tuscan bread salad.

Ortica Subtly acidic, flavorful, and highly valued—young nettle shoots in particular are rich in minerals, vitamins (about twice as much vitamin C as oranges), and protein. No wonder they have always been used in simple homemade fare. You can avoid the unpleasant burning sensation caused by the nettle hairs by wrapping the leaves in a cloth and wringing them thoroughly, or by rolling them vigorously with a rolling pin, or boiling them. They taste best with ricotta or in fillings for pasta, tarts, or Easter bread.

Capperi The whole plant is a wonderful gift. The closed, unripe flower buds, which are harvested by hand in spring, are not edible in their raw state. But when they are soaked for a day and then pickled in brine and vinegar, they develop a spicy, tangy flavor. As this flavor quickly dissipates, capers are only added after cooking. Once they are added, however, they transform tuna, for example, into a masterpiece. Caper berries are the plant's fruit, *cucunci*, which are usually marinated in vinegar and are an essential part of any antipasti platter. The caper leaves lend a particularly exquisite flavor to dishes. Their delicate yet characteristic taste is perfect for enhancing salads or *Pizza Tonno*. Italy's entire harvest comes from the small islands around Sicily, with Salina and Pantelleria producing the best. Pantelleria capers (IGP) almost became extinct, but thankfully only almost, as the volcanic soil here is too perfect for them not to grow. From salads to pasta dishes, capers are a versatile ingredient that can elevate any dish. So next time you're looking for a unique flavor to add to your cooking, reach for a jar of capers.

Aglio No recipe in Italy is complete without garlic. Not only the legendary *Spaghetti Aglio e Olio*, but also countless other traditional dishes are inconceivable without garlic. Many people love the flavor, but not the smell. It comes from the sulfur metabolites, which are actually poisonous to animals. But there is an herb to counteract this; chewing parsley helps here. And you can easily eliminate the smell from your hands with a little salt and lemon juice.

Garlic from Emilia Romagna—more specifically from the Ferrara region, where Voghiera garlic DOC grows—is the best choice for adding to your pot. Or perhaps Vessalico garlic, an old, almost forgotten variety from a small Ligurian village with a particularly refined flavor, which is twisted into long braids. Finally, there is Nubia red garlic from Sicily, always a winner in the kitchen with its crunchy bite, potent aroma, and strong flavor. We also highly recommend black garlic. Fermentation gives it a soft consistency and a sweet taste reminiscent of stewed plums, licorice, and balsamic vinegar. With its own unique flavor, garlic is a versatile ingredient that can be used in a wide variety of dishes.

Alloro The nymph Daphne transformed herself into a laurel tree to evade the romantic pursuit of the immortal Apollo. This gave laurel a sacred status in ancient Rome, and a laurel wreath is still viewed today as a symbol of glory, victory, and peace. In the kitchen, its leaves lend their distinctive flavor to an array of dishes, elevating soups, stews, meat dishes, and fish—and bestowing honor upon those who use it.

Menta Mint is a familiar flavor in tea, drinks, and ice cream. A peek into the cooking pots of Lazio shows what else its fresh, pungent taste goes well with—here you can find it with vegetables such as zucchini and eggplant, with ricotta in ravioli, as a pesto with pasta, and, of course, with beans and lamb. Not only is it delicious, it is also extremely beneficial. Mint helps relieve stomach pain, headaches, and sore muscles. And helps inspire imagination in the kitchen.

Origano Its name says it all: "splendor of the mountain," from the ancient Greek *oros*, or "mountain," and *ganos*, or "splendor." This rather inconspicuous mountain herb ignites a veritable explosion on the palate. Perfect with tomatoes, oregano is also great with meat, eggs, and any kind of pastry. It is also thought to ward off evil spirits when burned as incense. Its close relative, marjoram, is a little milder and sweeter. Its verdant sprigs adorned brides and grooms in ancient times, and it was thought to help with speech disorders during the Middle Ages. Today it supplies flavor for stews, frittatas, and all kinds of meats.

Peperoncino These fruity, spicy pods from South America arrived in Calabria in the 16th century, and initially dubbed Pepe d'India, peppers from India. They quickly gained popularity in southern Italy as a preservative, a role still evident in the recipes for nduja and salame spianata. Mainly cultivated in Calabria and Basilicata, their hot flavor spices up dishes such as *Aglio, Olio, e Peperoncino* and *Spaghetti all'Arrabiata*. These chiles are also pressed with olives, with the resulting spicy oil used to flavor pizza, pasta, and risotto, and in Sicily, it even finds its way into chocolate, offering a spicy twist.

Prezzemolo While the curly variety is mainly used north of the Alps, in Italy people prefer the much more flavorful flat-leaf parsley variety. Raw, or only briefly heated, it is used in mushroom dishes or soups in northern Italy, while it dresses up fish and seafood in southern Italy. Above all, however, parsley is absolutely essential for gremolata, the magic ingredient of authentic Italian cuisine. This herb adds a bright, fresh flavor that elevates any dish; from simple pasta sauces to complex meat braises.

Rosmarino Rosemary, the "dew of the sea," was not only used for cooking in the past, it was also part of numerous cultural ceremonies. Its fragrance is indeed beguiling. The thin, needle-shaped leaves develop their flavor particularly well in grilling and cooking. Rosemary is an integral part of numerous hearty dishes with meat, fish, eggplant, and zucchini, and a proper focaccia would not dare be seen without it.

Zafferano This precious spice (and pigment) is extracted from the stigmas of the crocus flower. Saffron is harvested entirely by hand in an extremely arduous process, as it only blooms once a year for a few weeks in the fall. This scarcity has rendered saffron the most expensive of spices since ancient times. Its intense golden yellow color mainly comes from the crocin it contains, while its aromatic fragrance is rather delicate, which is why saffron should not be cooked very long. However, it is a must in authentic Milanese risotto. The best saffron comes from Aquila DOC, where it is only harvested by hand at dawn between mid-October and November 1st, or from Sardinia (DOC), where it has the highest crocin content. Both make an excellent investment, and are sure to add a touch of luxury to any dish.

Salvia The healing powers of sage are reflected in its name, which comes from the Latin *salvare*, meaning "to heal." This is precisely why the Romans considered sage sacred. Today, this herb is ubiquitous. It is boiled, fried, and baked, it accompanies meat, gnocchi, stuffed pasta, and many other rather heavier dishes. After all, sage aids in digestion, and its earthy, slightly peppery flavor makes it a culinary chameleon.

Timo Thyme with its silvery-green leaves is not only popular among physicians; chefs love it too. Its distinctive flavor complements meat and fish dishes, as well as casseroles, pasta, and risottos. The entire plant contains essential oils that provide its taste and effect, but only the leaves can be used for seasoning. The stem of the thyme sprig contains numerous bitter substances that can ruin many an authentic dish.

Italy's herbs not only add the finishing touch to refined dishes, they are also essential ingredients in many basic recipes of the following pages ...

Pesto alla Genovese

Basil Pesto

To make truly authentic pesto, ideally you would live in Liguria and buy the Protected Designation of Origin (DOP) basil at the market in Prà, a district in the west of Genoa. Its leaves are particularly rich in essential oils and possess a subtle sweetness. The mild olive oil from Taggiasca olives, also a regional specialty, goes perfectly with the fruity basil. Along with the customary pine nuts, our favorite pesto recipe from Liguria also contains walnuts, a special variation that gives it even more character. The name "pesto" is derived from the verb pestare, which means "to grind." You can probably still find a large mortar and pestle in every Ligurian household today, which is put to use to make the pesto paste. Pesto not only tastes good with pasta, but it is also used as a cold seasoning sauce for vegetables, fish, meat, sausage, and cheese. A dollop of pesto on a bowl of minestrone gives the soup a true Ligurian touch. Pesto is also delicious on bruschetta or pizza.

Serves 4

PREP TIME
20 minutes plus 10 minutes the following day

INGREDIENTS

1¾ oz. (50 g) small basil leaves

A generous 1 oz. (30 g) Grana Padano DOP riserva cheese, aged approximately 20 months

A generous ¼ oz. (10 g) pine nuts

A scant ¼ oz. (6 g) walnuts, shelled

¾ tsp. (4 g) fine sea salt

½ clove garlic

¼ cup (60 ml) mild extra virgin olive oil

Rinse the basil leaves and spin dry in a salad spinner. Lay out paper towels and spread the basil on them to dry overnight, which creates a more intense flavor.

The next day, grate the cheese semi-coarsely and set aside. Combine and crush the basil, pine nuts, walnuts, salt, and garlic using a mortar and pestle, adding a third of the olive oil (4 tsp. / 20 ml) without allowing it to become soupy. Stir in the remaining olive oil, then carefully fold in the cheese.

OUR TIP If you use a food processor instead of a mortar and pestle to blend the pesto ingredients, make sure they don't heat up too much to prevent the flavors of the essential oils from evaporating. The pesto will keep for several days in the refrigerator if you put it in a jar and add a layer of olive oil on top.

Pesto piccante

Red Bell Pepper Pesto

Serves 4

PREP TIME
30 minutes

INGREDIENTS

½ red bell pepper

20 g semi-dried tomatoes in olive oil

½ red chile pepper, de-seeded

A scant ¾ oz. (20 g) almonds, roasted

3 tbsp. extra virgin olive oil

1 stalk basil

1 pinch smoked paprika powder

Fine sea salt & freshly gounded pepper

To make the pesto piccante, place the bell pepper half in a preheated oven at 395 °F (200 °C) until the skin starts to blister. Remove and cover with a damp cloth. When it has cooled, remove the peel and coarsely chop the pepper. Add the chopped pepper to a blender along with the semi-dried tomatoes, chile pepper, almonds, basil leaves, and olive oil, and blend to form a paste. Season to taste with smoked paprika powder, and salt and pepper if needed.

Salsa verde

Green Sauce

Serves 4 to 6

PREP TIME
10 minutes

INGREDIENTS

2 small bunches flat-leaf parsley

2 cloves garlic

4 anchovy fillets in oil

Fine sea salt

1 ¼ cups (300 ml) medium to robust extra virgin olive oil

If you want the freshness and hearty taste of herbs, there is also a creamy salsa verde from Lombardy. Lots of parsley and anchovy fillets are used for the base of this sauce, then bound with good-quality olive oil. It is traditionally served with boiled meat, bollito misto, *but it is also quite tasty with grilled meat, fish, or vegetables. You can add chopped almonds to it as well.*

Wash and dry the parsley, pluck the leaves from the stalks. Coarsely chop the leaves and put them in a blender. Peel the garlic cloves and dab the excess oil from the anchovy fillets. Add the garlic cloves, the anchovy fillets, and a pinch of salt to the parsley in the blender. Start blending carefully, while slowly and continuously pouring in a thin stream of olive oil. You can make the consistency as you please: Either blend it just long enough for the salsa to still retain some texture, or blend it longer to make it creamy.

Bagnet Russ

Red Sauce

Serves 4

PREP TIME
20 minutes

COOK TIME
50 minutes

INGREDIENTS

½ red bell pepper

1 red chile pepper

½ onion

½ celery stalk

1 bunch basil

½ bunch flat-leaf parsley

1 clove garlic

5 tbsp. medium extra virgin olive oil

1 anchovy fillet in oil

1 14-oz. (400 g) can San Marzano tomatoes

1 pinch sugar

1 tsp. red wine vinegar

Fine sea salt

Freshly ground pepper

Bagnet Russ, *a cooked red sauce from the Piedmont region, has a spicy tomato taste. It packs a special punch thanks to the fresh chile peppers, plus a fruity taste thanks to the red bell pepper and plenty of tomatoes. A dash of balsamic vinegar gives it a sweet kick. These three originals are also good bases for making your own creations.*

Remove the skin and seeds from the bell pepper and the chile pepper. Finely chop the bell pepper, chile pepper, onion, and celery. Chop the herbs separately; set aside. Peel the garlic clove. In a pot, heat 3 tablespoons of the olive oil and brown the garlic clove in it. Remove the garlic clove, add the anchovy fillet to the pot and let it disintegrate. Add the vegetables and sauté. Pour in the tomatoes and crush them with a wooden spoon. Add the pinch of sugar. Let everything simmer uncovered over low heat for approximately 40 minutes. Add the herbs and allow the flavors to infuse for another 10 minutes. Blend the sauce with an immersion blender until smooth. Then allow to cool.

Season to taste with the remaining olive oil, vinegar, salt, and pepper.

Gremolata

Gremolata

Serves 8

PREP TIME
15 minutes

INGREDIENTS

2 organic lemons

1 bunch flat-leaf parsley

2 cloves garlic

Fine sea salt & freshly ground pepper

3 tbsp. extra virgin olive oil (optional)

Gremolata is not a sauce, but rather an enchanting combination of flavors that perfectly embodies the Italian appreciation of freshness. Gremolata is spread on meat or fish fresh from the grill, making it even more of a summery delight. You can add diced tomatoes to taste.

Rinse the lemons in hot water and use a zester to peel off the zest in thin strips that are not too long. Wash the parsley and finely chop the leaves. Peel and finely dice the garlic. Combine everything and season with salt and pepper.

Sughetto

Tomato Sauce with Olives, Capers, and Basil

Serves 3 to 4

PREP TIME
5 minutes

COOK TIME
30 minutes

INGREDIENTS

4 cloves garlic

4 tsp. (20 ml) medium extra virgin olive oil

2 tsp. dried oregano

2 tbsp. capers pickled in sea salt, rinsed

3 tbsp. Taggiasca olives from Liguria, pitted

A generous 19 ½ oz. (550 g) spaccatella (halved datterini tomatoes in their own juice)

2 tbsp. tomato paste

1 handful basil leaves

1 14-oz. (400 g) can peeled San Marzano tomatoes,

Fine sea salt

Freshly ground pepper

A scant 18 oz. (500 g) pasta of your choosing, such as spaghetti, penne, bucatini, or strozzapreti

Parmigiano Reggiano DOP cheese

In Italian households, tomato sugo, or sauce, is often cooked ahead of time for the entire week, making it possible to quickly whip up the requisite pasta dish before the main course, the secondo, often served at lunchtime. The sauce absorbs the flavors well while it is in the refrigerator, and it can also be varied if desired. The chunkier the sauces are, the larger the pasta shape can be—larger pasta types include paccheri and conchiglie. Typical herbs for this sauce are oregano and basil, like those used for a pizzaiola sauce.

Peel and thinly slice the garlic. In a sauté pan, heat the olive oil and lightly brown the garlic slices in it. Add the oregano, capers, and olives and simmer gently until all the ingredients are hot. Drain the jar of *spaccatella* and add the tomatoes to the pan. Stir, allowing the tomatoes to heat up. Stir in the tomato paste and add most of the basil leaves to the sauce, reserving a few for the end. Allow the mixture to reduce somewhat, then add the San Marzano tomatoes, stir, and continue to reduce for about 20 minutes.

Meanwhile, cook the pasta, then drain, reserving some of the cooking water. If the sauce is too thick, add some of the cooking water to achieve the desired consistency. Season with salt and pepper to taste. Add the pasta to the pan and fold into the sauce. Garnish each plate with grated Parmesan and the remaining basil leaves before serving.

OUR TIP Instead of *spaccatella* from a jar, you can use about 25 fresh cherry tomatoes. Sauté them together with the other ingredients after browning the garlic. A pinch of sugar balances the acidity of the tomatoes and tastes good in the sauce; it also allows you to use less salt.

Soffritto

Flavorful Vegetable Sauce Base

Yields 1¼ cups (300 ml)

PREP TIME
20 minutes

COOK TIME
Approximately 50 minutes

INGREDIENTS

7 oz. (200 g) onions

5¼ oz. (150 g) carrots

3½ oz. (100 g) celery stalks

A generous ⅓ cup (80 ml) mild extra virgin olive oil

Soffritto is used as a flavorful base for many sughi. The best known is Ragù alla Bolognese, whose deep flavor comes from a harmonious blend of onions, carrots, and celery. Soffritto is also a secret weapon for making quick tomato sauces, giving them a nuanced flavor, or as a perfect accompaniment to vegetable dishes and risottos that don't require extensive cooking. It could even be likened to the Italian equivalent of a natural stock cube. Making soffritto in large batches is very worthwhile given its multitude of possible uses. This recipe is the basic version, but you also can add garlic to it depending on your taste and its intended use. Herbs should only be added and left to infuse shortly before the cooking time comes to an end. If thyme and rosemary are used, they can be removed when the soffritto is done cooking, as the olive oil binds their essential oils.

Peel and finely dice the onion. Peel the carrots and finely chop them in a vegetable chopper, taking care that the pieces are equally sized. After removing any strings from the stalks, cut the celery into small pieces. Then use the food chopper to finely chop the celery, making sure the pieces are the same size as the carrots.

In a large, non-stick skillet, slowly heat the olive oil over low heat. Add the onions to the pan and sauté. As soon as they become translucent, reduce the heat to prevent them from browning. Add the diced carrots and celery; stir well. If the oil has been completely absorbed, add a little more. The vegetables should only cook very gently, so keep an eye on the temperature. Stir every 5 minutes to allow the water to cook off.

After about 45 minutes, the vegetables will change color and caramelize. At this point, it is important to remain at the stove, stirring continuously and adjusting the temperature where necessary. When the soffritto is lightly browned and fragrant, remove the pan from the heat and allow the mixture to cool.

OUR TIP You can store the soffritto in a sterilized screw-top jar in the fridge, adding a film of olive oil on top before closing it. You can also freeze it, in portions in an ice cube tray, for instance.

Brodo di Pollo

Chicken Stock

Makes approximately 9 ½ cups (2.4 L)

PREP TIME
20 minutes

COOK TIME
Approximately 2 hours

INGREDIENTS

2 carrots

1 stalk celery

1 onion

5 sprigs flat-leaf parsley

1 sprig thyme

1 chicken, 2 to 3 lbs. (1 to 1.5 kg), without giblets

Coarse and fine sea salt

Stocks form the backbone of cuisine: They give sughi, risottos, braised sauces, and vegetable creations a depth of flavor that water cannot provide. Broths are pure umami, which enhances the flavor and harmony of a dish. They are also a welcome addition to the menu as a broth containing good-quality noodles, such as tortellini or Agnolotti del Plin (meat-filled pasta), small pasta shapes such as ditalini and casarecce, or broken angel hair spaghetti spezzati. In Italy, chicken stock is often used for risottos with vegetables and mushrooms, such as Risi e Bisi (see p. 140). Vegetable stock also harmonizes well with springtime risotto and pasta recipes that use artichokes, asparagus, spring herbs, and tender young spinach. Beef stock lends flavor to meat stews, but it can also add a bit of volume to vegetables and salads with a strong character, which are popular in Italy (including radicchio and cabbages like broccoli rabe). Nicely portioned stock in the freezer, whether you use small containers or just pour it in ice cube trays, is worth its weight in gold.

Peel the carrots; cut into thirds. Cut the celery stalk and peeled onion in half. Add the carrots, celery, onion, parsley, and thyme to a pot with a generous 4 quarts (4 L) cold water and bring to a boil. Cut the chicken in half and add both halves to the pot. Add 1 teaspoon of coarse sea salt. Reduce the heat; simmer for about 2 hours.

Remove the chicken and, when it has cooled slightly, pick the meat off the bones for use elsewhere. Remove the pot from the stove, strain through a fine sieve, and season to taste with fine sea salt. Depending on your preference, remove some fat from the surface (not too much!). Use the stock immediately or let it cool and then freeze it in portions for adding to sauces and risottos.

Brodo Vegetale

Vegetable Stock

Makes approximately 12 ½ cups (3 L)

PREP TIME
20 minutes

COOK TIME
Approximately 3 hours

INGREDIENTS

A good 2 lbs. (1 kg) vegetables, including carrots, celery stalks, onions, fennel, ...

A scant 2 ¼ oz. (60 g) Parmigiano Reggiano DOP cheese rind

Coarse and fine sea salt

Add finely chopped vegetables and herbs, including leftovers like parsley stalks, cauliflower leaves, tomatoes, onion skins, and the like to a pot of 6 quarts (6 L) of cold water along with the Parmesan rinds; season with 1 teaspoon of coarse salt. Bring to a boil, then simmer over low heat for about 3 hours until the liquid is reduced by half. Strain through a fine sieve and season to taste with fine sea salt.

Brodo di Carne

Beef Stock

Makes approximately 9 ½ cups (2.4 L)

PREP TIME
20 minutes

COOK TIME
3 hours

INGREDIENTS

1 carrot

1 stalk celery

1 onion

2 cloves

2 small tomatoes

1 sprig flat-leaf parsley

1 basil leaf, fresh

1 eye round steak, beef

A generous 2 lbs. (1 kg) beef brisket

Coarse and fine sea salt

Peel and coarsely chop the carrots. Cut the celery stalk in half. Cut the onion in half and stick the cloves firmly into the onion halves. Rinse the parsley, basil, and the two meats. Fill a large pot with 4 quarts (4 L) of cold water. Add the vegetables, herbs, and eye round steak, and slowly bring to a boil. Once it is boiling, add the beef brisket along with a teaspoon of coarse salt. Reduce the heat and let the stock simmer for around 3 hours, until the meat is completely soft and almost falling apart. Then remove the meat from the stock and place it on a plate. Strain the stock through a fine sieve and season to taste with fine sea salt if desired. Remove the meat from the bone and, if it still has some flavor, use immediately.

Crema Gianduia

Chocolate and Hazelnut Cream

Makes 2 jars, approximately 7 oz. (200 g) each

PREP TIME
10 minutes

COOK TIME
15 minutes

INGREDIENTS

8 ¾ oz. (250 g) dark chocolate

7 ¾ oz. (220 g) Piedmont hazelnut paste

This chocolate-hazelnut spread for adults demands the use of premium ingredients, as there are only two: The hazelnut paste should be made of roasted Piedmont hazelnuts. They have the most delectable, deeply intense flavor. Piedmont chocolate is world famous for its quality, as is Tuscan chocolate. The hazelnut-chocolate combination was created in Piedmont in the 1800s when cocoa taxes were high, so a clever chocolate maker replaced some cocoa with ground hazelnuts, creating gianduia chocolate, now a celebrated specialty of the region.

Sterilize two jars and set aside. Coarsely chop the chocolate and gently melt it in a small pot. Once the chocolate is liquefied, bring the mixture to 100 °F (40 °C), checking the temperature with a kitchen thermometer. Once the temperature is stable, gently stir in the hazelnut paste until the mixture is completely blended. Then quickly cool it down to 68 to 72 °F (20 to 22 °C) degrees, in a pan of cold water, for example. Pour the cream into the jars and seal them.

OUR TIP This cream is not only delicious on a piece of brioche or a croissant, but it is also scrumptious when eaten on a slice of panettone.

Marmellata di arance

Sicilian Orange Marmalade

Makes 6 jars, approximately 7 fluid oz. (212 ml) each

PREP TIME
30 minutes plus 1 night to soak and 1 night to set

COOK TIME
Approximately 1½ hours

INGREDIENTS

A generous 2½ lbs. (1.25 kg) untreated Sicilian oranges

4½ cups (1 L) water

2 cups (400 g) sugar

You don't have to be English to love how this marmalade tastes! Sicilians love it too, because their island is where the flavorful oranges grow, the ones Goethe surely had in mind when he visited the land where lemons blossom. Orange marmalade not only makes a great spread on toast with salted butter, but it is also delicious in sauces, dressings, and desserts. It must be made using nothing but the best ingredients, such as ripe oranges from Sicily and especially their peels. Orange marmalade makes a wonderful glaze for a roast duck or chicken, adds pizazz to a sauce for roast beef or liver, lends a particularly fruity note to bitter lettuces like radicchio or chicory, and gives desserts made with mascarpone cheese a delightful freshness and acidity. Be sure to buy ripe oranges in season so you have a year-round supply of flavor.

Rinse the oranges in hot water. Peel and de-seed half of them, finely dice the fruit flesh. Leave the remaining oranges unpeeled, de-seed and finely dice them as well. Soak everything together in the water overnight.

The next day, add the sugar to the oranges in the water and boil over medium heat for approx. 1½ hours. Stir regularly. When it reaches a viscous consistency, pour the jam into sterilized jars, seal with lids, and stand the jars upside down, leaving them that way overnight.

OUR TIP The choice of oranges is, of course, crucial here. They should be ripe, flavorful, and have untreated peels. We recommend navelina oranges, Sorrento oranges, and Tarocco blood oranges. Blood oranges, bitter oranges, and bergamot oranges can also be combined for a more complex flavor.

Remo Viani has been passionate about Italian food and specialties since he was young. Working with his father, the founder of the Italian delicatessen wholesaler of the same name, he emphasized, in the company's communications, the origin, production, and handling of products. After many visits to local producers and manufacturers, he took over his father's company in 1995 and successfully continued the family tradition of trading in selected and original food specialties from Italy. In 1998, Remo Viani and his colleagues founded the first German Olive Oil Panel. The aim: to determine that virgin olive oils meet the necessary minimum quality requirements and to evaluate differences in taste quality on the basis of harmony and sensory balance.

Acknowledgments

Remo Viani would like to thank the Viani team, his friend Alex, his family and everyone else who supported him in this project and without whom this book would not have been possible.

Originale

Recipes and Essentials
of Italian Cooking

Remo Viani

This book was conceived, edited, and designed by *gestalten.*

Edited by *Robert Klanten*
Contributing editor: *Remo Viani*

Introduction by *gestalten*

Texts and recipes by *Sabine Knappe* and *Alex Rehm*
Recipes created by *Martin Borchardt*

Translation from German to English by *Robin Limmeroth*, copyedited by *Karen Leube*, for booklab GmbH, Munich

Food and cover photography by *Katharina Herz*

Mood photography by *Chris Abatzis*

Mood illustrations by *Oriana Fenwick* c/o kombinatrotweiss.de (pp. 30 top, 32 top, 40, 54 top, 78, 110, 130, 142, 152, 164, 188 top, 204 top, 212 top, 214 top, 224, 230, 242 top, 248 top, 252, 256, 258)

Other illustrations by *gestalten*

Editorial Management by *Lars Pietzschmann*

Design and layout by *Melanie Ullrich*

Photo Editors: *Zoe Paterniani* and *Madeline Dudley-Yates*

Typeface: Dejanire by *Ramiro Espinoza*

Printed by *appl druck GmbH*, Wemding
Made in Germany

Published by gestalten, Berlin 2024
ISBN 978-3-96704-150-7

For more information, and to order books, please visit www.gestalten.com

Bibliographic information published by the Deutsche Nationalbibliothek. The Deutsche Nationalbibliothek lists this publication in the Deutsche Nationalbibliografie; detailed bibliographic data is available online at www.dnb.de

This book was printed on paper certified according to the standards of the FSC®.